THE NEW EVOLUTIONARY
SOCIAL SCIENCE

THE NEW EVOLUTIONARY SOCIAL SCIENCE

Human Nature, Social Behavior, and Social Change

Edited by

Heinz-Jürgen Niedenzu
Tamás Meleghy
Peter Meyer

Paradigm Publishers
Boulder • London

Copyright © 2008 Paradigm Publishers

Published in the United States by Paradigm Publishers, 2845 Wilderness Place, Boulder, CO 80301 USA.

Paradigm Publishers is the trade name of Birkenkamp & Company, LLC, Dean Birkenkamp, President and Publisher.

Library of Congress Cataloging-in-Publication Data
The new evolutionary social science : human nature, social behavior, and social change / edited by Heinz-Jürgen Niedenzu, Tamás Meleghy, Peter Meyer.
    p. cm. — (Studies in comparative social science)
Includes bibliographical references and index.
ISBN 978-1-59451-396-1 (hardcover : alk. paper)
ISBN 978-1-59451-397-8 (paperback : alk. paper)
1. Social evolution. 2. Human evolution. 3. Social Darwinism. I. Niedenzu, Heinz-Jürgen. II. Meleghy, Tamas, 1941– III. Meyer, Peter, 1941–
HM626.N49 2008
303.4—dc22

                                                                    2008026396

Printed and bound in the United States of America on acid free paper that meets the standards of the American National Standard for Permanence of Paper for Printed Library Materials.

Designed by Straight Creek Bookmakers.

14 13 12 11   2 3 4 5

CONTENTS

ACKNOWLEDGMENTS

We would like to express our gratitude to all the institutions and individuals enabling us to accomplish the conference on which this volume is based. In particular our thanks go to the Federal Ministry of Education, Science, and Culture of the Republic of Austria; to the Federal State of Vorarlberg, Austria; to the Rector of Innsbruck University; to the Dean of the Innsbruck School of Political Science and Sociology; to the Head of the Department of Sociology at Innsbruck University; to the Austrian Research Association; to the Studia Bookshop; and to Bettina Posch, who supported us during the meeting. Moreover, our thanks go to Stephen Sanderson and Paradigm Publishers for agreeing to publish this volume, and last but not least to Ellen Palli, who took care of the final preparation of the manuscript.

Tamás Meleghy, Innsbruck
Peter Meyer, Augsburg
Heinz-Jürgen Niedenzu, Innsbruck

Part I
PRELUDE

INTRODUCTION

The New Evolutionary Social Science

Tamás Meleghy
Peter Meyer
Heinz-Jürgen Niedenzu

From its very beginning, sociology was concerned with problems of social change and the formation of different types of society. Many early sociologists, most prominently Herbert Spencer, took biology seriously by comparing societies to organisms. The subfield of sociology then known as *social statics* was concerned to describe how the parts of societies were interrelated in the same manner that they were in biological organisms. The other major subfield of sociology at the time, *social dynamics*, made a different kind of comparison, in this case between the long-term development of societies and ontogenetic development. This, of course, was the tradition of sociological organicism (Martindale 1960). In these early years it was also common for sociologists to take biology seriously in another way, which was in terms of conceptions of human nature. Social scientists in different fields, sociologists included, took the then new Darwinian evolutionism seriously; they thought there was such a thing as human nature, and that it played an important role in shaping social behavior and social structure. The early-twentieth-century sociologist Edward Westermarck, for example, wrote multivolumed works on human marriage practices and morality that revealed the very strong influence of Darwinian natural selectionist thinking.

However, due to disciplinary institutionalization and differentiation, most of twentieth-century sociology was characterized by a growing discord between sociology and biology. Emile Durkheim equated the "social" with moral sentiments, such as social norms and institutions, whereas Max Weber conceived of sociology as a science specializing in *verstehen*, or the understanding of human action from the subjective point of view of the actor. From the point of departure of these classical sociologists, the discipline turned sharply away from biology,

3

largely ignoring biological factors in favor of entirely social explanations. And what was true in the classical period is equally true today. In German sociology, the two leading sociological theorists have been Niklas Luhmann and Jürgen Habermas. Even though Luhmann pleaded for an evolutionary account of social behavior, he chose Stephen Jay Gould's approach (Gould and Lewontin 1997) instead of referring to mainstream evolutionary biology. Habermas envisages still another version of evolutionary thinking, one referring to a universal, quasi-teleological developmental logic (Antweiler 1985). In France the leading contemporary sociological theorist was, of course, Pierre Bourdieu, who explicitly made the point in one of his last interviews that the distinctiveness of sociology as a discipline was its rejection of all naturalistic explanations in favor of social explanations. One of his last books, *La domination masculine* (1998), had as its main theme the notion that gender is a social construct that attempts to naturalize itself, i.e., to make us think that the differences between the sexes are natural differences. And in Britain, the leading sociological theoretician, Anthony Giddens, has rarely made reference to anything biological. In his introductory textbook, for example, his exceedingly brief treatment of sociobiology regards it as an entirely speculative endeavor.

For an extended period of time, the adequacy of sociological approaches to the "social" remained unchallenged. More recently, however, sociology has been confronted with various forms of biological explanation. More and more, the approaches known as *sociobiology* and *evolutionary psychology* have had a significant influence in sociology's sister disciplines of psychology and anthropology, and are even being referred to in public discourse. These and related approaches are part of a Second Darwinian Revolution that was initiated by such biologists as William Hamilton (1964), Robert Trivers (1971), Richard Dawkins (1976, 1986), and Edward O. Wilson (1975, 1998). Hamilton introduced the notion of *kin selected altruism*, which has paved the way for a radically new understanding of individuality in social life (Maynard Smith and Szathmary 1995, 259). Along the same lines, Richard Dawkins (1976) introduced the metaphor of the *selfish gene*. These evolutionary biologists were unwilling to maintain any clear-cut separation between animal species and the human species with regard to different behavioral modes and capacities for problem solving, and therefore they insisted upon an enlarged understanding of the human social and cultural spheres. Unlike sociologists, sociobiologists and evolutionary psychologists turned to studies of the ultimate causes of behaviors in animals and in the human species. Sociobiologists were, for example, able to account for the different strategies males and females employ in both animals and humans. As pointed out by Sarah Blaffer Hrdy (2000, 40), women seem "to belong to a kind of species men know the least of." Unlike evolutionary biologists, sociologists did not bother to look into sex- or gender-specific interests in human reproduction, focusing instead on gender-typical roles in the human species.

Even though most sociologists have paid very little attention to these new approaches, they have gained increasing influence in recent years, whereas traditional sociology's impact seems to be dwindling. But the lack of interest in evolutionary theory is not characteristic of all sociologists. As sociologists interested in evolutionary theory, several years ago Tamás Meleghy and Heinz-Jürgen Niedenzu organized a workshop, "Social Evolution: The Theory of Evolution and the Social Sciences," at the Institute of Sociology, University of Innsbruck, Austria, in 2001. Contributors from various European countries convened in Innsbruck for intensive discussions of this topic. Following this meeting an edited volume was published (Meleghy and Niedenzu 2001), which was well received by specialists in the field (Pohlmann 2004; Antweiler 2005) and was soon out of print.

The present volume is the result of a second meeting held in June 2006, which was again organized at the University of Innsbruck by Meleghy and Niedenzu, this time in cooperation with Peter Meyer of the University of Augsburg in Germany. Unlike the previous meeting, this one focused largely on a specific book, Stephen K. Sanderson's *The Evolution of Human Sociality*, a work in which the author has attempted to integrate sociobiology into sociological theory through the creation of a new synthetic paradigm known as *Darwinian conflict theory*. The conference brought together sociologists and other social scientists from Europe, the United States, and Australia, who took advantage of the occasion for lively discussions with Stephen Sanderson, explaining, criticizing, defending, and applying various aspects of his theoretical approach.

Sanderson's book was chosen as the main focus of the conference because we felt it made several very important contributions that few other sociologists were making. For example:

- It links modern sociology to recent evolutionary theorizing in the social sciences.
- It critically evaluates the major theoretical approaches in contemporary sociology and attempts to draw on what is most useful in them.
- It distinguishes between different levels and modes of explanation.
- It provides by far the most extensive review ever undertaken by a sociologist of contemporary empirical research informed by sociobiological, evolutionary psychological, and related evolutionary perspectives.
- It brilliantly demonstrates the regularities among diverse societies, while at the same time not neglecting the less common or even unique features of some societies. This demonstration is for us the *raison d'être* of sociology.
- For sociologists, it is the most complete appraisal ever made of evolutionary biology's understanding of human nature, social organization, and social change.

Sanderson's work maps out the most well-developed version to date of a major new type of sociology, *evolutionary sociology* (Maryanski 1998). We view the following as the most important of evolutionary sociology's concerns:

- Disclosing the genetic, neurobiological, and other aspects of human nature and the basic dimensions of the human motivational structure. To accomplish this, evolutionary sociology must draw on theories and research findings in sociobiology, ethology, evolutionary psychology, behavioral ecology, and other evolutionarily oriented social science fields
- Clarifying whether the typical motivations that evolved during humankind's long period in its ancestral environment are manifest not only in the surviving forms of these ancestral societies, but in modern societies as well
- Understanding the various types of linkages among biological, psychological, and sociocultural phenomena
- Clarifying the relationship between ultimate and proximate explanations
- Understanding the long-term evolution of human societies and the extent to which this evolution is a Darwinian process. How well do the Darwinian concepts of "variation," "selection," "retention," etc., apply to social evolution? How is social evolution constrained by human nature?
- Reexamining the history of the relationship between evolutionary biology and sociology and the other social sciences and the reasons why these social science disciplines spurned biology for so long.

All of the contributors to the present volume address one or more of these concerns. The contributions fall into several distinct categories. In Chapter 1 Sanderson provides a brief overview of the history of sociology's reception of evolutionary theory, which also includes a summary of his Darwinian conflict theory. Part II then consists of ten critical assessments of Darwinian conflict theory. The most positive assessments are those of Michael Schmid, Rosemary Hopcroft, and Christoph Antweiler. Schmid (Chapter 2) is very sympathetic to Sanderson's theoretical project but raises numerous questions about it. For example, he contends that Sanderson's attempt to ground his arguments in a type of conflict theory seems to have nothing to do with his materialist historical analyses. In addition, since Darwinian conflict theory does not make use of concepts like "variation," "selection," and "retention," Schmid wonders in what sense it is truly evolutionary. Hopcroft (Chapter 4) believes that Sanderson's general approach is perhaps the best sociology currently has to offer. Perhaps her most significant criticism of Sanderson is that he focuses heavily on anthropological and historical evidence and rather neglects sociological evidence on modern industrial societies. She points out that, although very little current sociological research is guided by evolutionary ideas, much of it turns out to be surprisingly consistent with those ideas. Antweiler (Chapter 5), while in agreement with most of Sanderson's main arguments, contends that he does not devote enough attention to human universals and that his list of universals is incomplete.

The chapters by Nico Wilterdink, Khaled Hakami, Peter Meyer, Heinz-Jürgen Niedenzu, Tamás Meleghy, Johan van der Dennen, and Christopher Hallpike are more critical. Wilterdink (Chapter 3) claims that Sanderson is a metaphysical materialist who takes insufficient account of the role of culture in behavior. Wilterdink seeks to illustrate his point through an analysis of human sexual and reproductive behavior. Hakami (Chapter 6), who has been significantly influenced by the cultural materialism of Marvin Harris, is highly resistant to Sanderson's attempt to synthesize that perspective with sociobiology. Meyer (Chapter 7), although undoubtedly accepting of many of Sanderson's arguments, is critical of him for being perhaps too materialist in his theoretical outlook and, more specifically, for explaining human cooperation as entirely the outcome of self-interested individual strategies. The predisposition to cooperate, Meyer insists, is an integral part of the human evolutionary heritage. Niedenzu (Chapter 8) focuses on Sanderson's three different modes of materialist explanation – biomaterialist, ecomaterialist, and polimaterialist – and is critical of what he sees as Sanderson's tendency to relegate ecomaterialist and polimaterialist explanations to a derivative role. Ecomaterialist and polimaterialist explanations, Niedenzu contends, deserve equal billing alongside biomaterialist explanations in the full scope of sociological explanation. Meleghy (Chapter 9) believes that Sanderson is much too harsh in his criticisms of Lévi-Straussian structuralism and seeks to show that it can, in fact, be combined with Darwinian conflict theory. Van der Dennen (Chapter 10) deals specifically with Sanderson's treatment of warfare. He is highly skeptical of Sanderson's favored biomaterialist and ecomaterialist explanations of war, holding that they result from a "vulgar materialism." Van der Dennen argues that war is far too complex a phenomenon to be explained by only one or two types of theories. In this regard he contends that there are several important types of war that are quite different, types that Sanderson fails to distinguish. Hallpike (Chapter 11) contends that Darwinian conflict theory is inadequate to the task of explaining the development of modern science. Sanderson's theory, Hallpike submits, fails because it is based on a flawed set of assumptions derived from the social ideology of modern capitalism, that of "atomistic competitive individualism." Sanderson's model of science also assumes that science develops linearly, whereas it actually develops in a more dialectical and uneven manner.

Part III is devoted to sociological applications of evolutionary theory that refer to Darwinian conflict theory either indirectly or not at all. J. P. Roos (Chapter 12) compares the thinking of two classical sociological giants, Edward Westermarck and Emile Durkheim. Westermarck was a sociologist who was deeply influenced by Darwinian natural selectionist thinking, whereas Durkheim, of course, was the consummate antireductionist who insisted that sociological explanations had to be based on social facts. Even though Westermarck declined into virtual invisibility and Durkheim is still regarded as a key member of the founding sociological triumvirate, Roos contends that the contest between Durkheim and Westermarck was an uneven match: On all the central questions that they both considered, it was Westermarck who has turned out to be right.

Anna Rotkirch (Chapter 13) discusses a newly recognized phenomenon known as "baby fever," which is essentially an intense desire to have a child. She considers several related evolutionary explanations of this phenomenon. Like Roos, she invokes Westermarck, one of the first sociologists to discuss this phenomenon, although using different concepts and terminology. Frank Salter's contribution (Chapter 14) attempts to show that sociological explanations of individual achievement and social mobility have for the most part been resolutely environmentalist explanations. These explanations are inadequate, he argues, because they are markedly incomplete. Salter makes a case for the role of genetics, but he is not a genetic determinist. Rather, he contends that genes and environment interact in shaping individual patterns of achievement and mobility. Salter identifies his theory as an explicitly Darwinian conflict theory.

W. G. Runciman (Chapter 15) provides yet another installment in his natural selectionist theory of social evolution. He marks off two major stages in the development of human sociality. The first was the emergence of human culture itself, whereas the second, which Runciman refers to as the shift from culture to society, was the much more recent (10,000-12,000 BP) development of a form of social life based on roles and institutions. Peter Hejl's contribution (Chapter 16), though highly appreciative of Sanderson's work, faults him for ignoring the crucial role of communication. According to Hejl, Sanderson simply takes human communication for granted. He fails to theorize it and to include various forms of it into his theoretical framework as an important determinant of social relations. Hejl then draws on his own work to illustrate different modes of communication and their theoretical importance.

In Part IV, Chapter 17, Sanderson replies to his critics and offers his own assessments of the applications made in Part III.

As noted above, Darwinian evolutionary theory has made substantial inroads into the fields of psychology and anthropology, but its influence in sociology has thus far been much more limited. By using Sanderson's *The Evolution of Human Sociality* as a foundation for critically assessing the contribution evolutionary theory can make to contemporary sociology, we hope that this volume will help to stimulate greater interest in neo-Darwinian ideas among sociologists.

1

THE IMPACT OF DARWINISM ON SOCIOLOGY

An Historical and Critical Overview

Stephen K. Sanderson

INTRODUCTION

What has been the relationship between the social sciences, sociology in particular, and Darwin's theory of evolution by natural selection? In a famous statement, Darwin said that the theory of natural selection would "lead psychology to be based on a new foundation." In the late nineteenth and early twentieth centuries, some social scientists followed Darwin's lead. In his book *In Search of Human Nature: The Decline and Revival of Darwinism in American Social Thought*, the historian Carl Degler (1991) shows that at this early point in the development of the social sciences Darwinism was highly regarded by social scientists, and biology was considered a major underpinning of human behavior (cf. Gillette 2007).

In sociology, the lead was clearly taken in the most emphatic way by Edward Westermarck, a Finnish sociologist who became a major figure in both Finnish and British sociology. In the second volume of his three-volume *The History of Human Marriage*, Westermarck (1922b) developed the hypothesis on the origin of incest avoidance and exogamy for which he is today most famous, the "familiarity breeds indifference" theory. Westermarck argued that children brought up in close physical contact with each other in the early years of life would acquire a mutual sexual aversion, an emotion that had evolved by natural selection because of its ability to prevent the damaging genetic consequences of close inbreeding. Although Westermarck's theory has been much maligned, it was revived in the 1970s and considerable data now support it (Shepher 1983;

McCabe 1983; Wolf 1995; Wolf and Durham 2004; Turner and Maryanski 2005).

Westermarck was also keenly interested in the source of moral concepts and judgments, and their evolution, which was the subject of his *The Origin and Development of the Moral Ideas* (1906, 1908). Once again we find Darwinian natural selectionist reasoning at work. Westermarck argued that moral concepts are generalizations or objectifications of the moral emotions of indignation or approval, which have evolved by natural selection because they promote the interests of the individuals who feel them.

Westermarck established a reputation as a leading sociologist of his day, but one of his chief opponents was the formidable Émile Durkheim (see Roos, Chapter 12 this volume). As all sociologists know, it was Durkheim's ideas that prevailed, and Westermarck's reputation declined in the 1920s and 1930s to the point where he was no longer taken seriously as a scholar (Sanderson 2007a). The tide in sociology turned entirely toward an environmentalist or cultural determinist position and biology was pushed aside. It was not until the 1970s that Darwinian ideas would come to be revived and once again pursued by sociologists.

EARLY CONTEMPORARY WORK, 1970-1990

Some social scientists were beginning to take the biological foundations of human behavior seriously before Edward O. Wilson wrote his famous book launching sociobiology in the mid-1970s (Wilson 1975). At the beginning of the 1970s, Lionel Tiger and Robin Fox (1971), two anthropologists, wrote *The Imperial Animal*, and four years later Pierre van den Berghe (1975), a well-known sociologist, wrote *Man in Society: A Biosocial View*. These were what might be termed "protosociobiological" works. Tiger and Fox argued that humans come equipped with a *biogrammar*, or a basic set of biological templates that predispose their behavior along certain lines. Van den Berghe made the same point, referring to the human biological predispositions as *Anlagen*. The predispositions suggested by these authors overlap extensively, and they can be combined into a single list:

1. aggression
2. hierarchy
3. male dominance
4. mother-infant bonding
5. territoriality
6. incest avoidance.

Once sociobiology came to be established by Wilson, Martin Daly and Margo Wilson (1978, 1988), John Tooby and Leda Cosmides (1989; Cosmides and Tooby 1989), and others, van den Berghe readily adopted it and used it as a guiding explanatory framework for a great deal of work. Like Westermarck, van den Berghe has been much concerned with incest avoidance, and accepts Westermarck's theory as the basic explanation.

Several years after publishing *Man in Society*, van den Berghe (1981) wrote *The Ethnic Phenomenon*, a book in which he argued that ethnicity was a primordial human attachment that was rooted in kin selection. Indeed, ethnicity is an extension of kinship, and ethnic groups may thus be viewed as exceptionally large extended kin groups. However, van den Berghe also argued that ethnicity had an important social dimension, and he identified several main forms of ethnic conflict and the reasons why one type rather than another prevails at a given place and time.

With his student Joseph Whitmeyer, van den Berghe has studied the relationship between social status and reproductive success in industrial societies (van den Berghe and Whitmeyer 1990). Using the concepts of *r* and *K* selection, van den Berghe and Whitmeyer have suggested that three different reproductive strategies can be found in industrial societies. The stable working class and the middle and upper-middle classes tend to follow an extreme *K* strategy. Here people limit themselves to two or three children in whom they invest heavily. There is a quality-quantity tradeoff in favor of quality. Parental investment involves high-intensity care and the investment of economic and educational resources in order to equip offspring for success in a highly competitive environment. A second strategy is employed by the upper classes, whose members can have both quantity and quality. This is a less extreme *K* strategy. Finally, the lower classes, especially stigmatized racial and ethnic minorities, adopt a more *r* strategy. In this case fertility is higher and parental investment is lower; quantity is preferred over quality as a reproductive strategy.

Joseph Lopreato was another sociologist to accept Darwinian thinking from an early point. In his book *Human Nature and Biocultural Evolution*, Lopreato (1984) identified a set of four human biological predispositions:

1. *Predispositions of self-enhancement,* which involve the search for individual advantage through the pursuit of status and wealth (which may include the urge to victimize others).
2. *Predispositions of sociality,* which involve reciprocity, but also dominance and deference, and the needs for conformity and social approval.
3. *Predispositions of variation,* which include the need to avoid incest and to form family and ethnic groups.
4. *Predispositions of selection,* which include the denial of death, the susceptibility to charisma, and the need for ritual. Here we find the biological roots of religion.

To his credit, Lopreato situates these various predispositions, or at least most of them, within the context of the reigning sociobiological paradigm, the main principle of which he calls the *maximization principle*: People act so as to maximize the representation of their genes in future generations. However, Lopreato gives this a neat twist, reformulating it in terms of what he calls the *modified maximization principle*: Humans tend to behave so as to maximize their inclusive fitness, but this predisposition can be at least partially neutralized by the quest for creature comforts, by self-denying or ascetic tendencies often stimulated by sacred beliefs and practices, and by motivations that once produced fitness maximizing behaviors but that no longer do so in modern environments, such as sexual activity between individuals using some method of contraception.

Lee Ellis has written several articles lamenting the extremely limited use of biosocial thinking in sociology (Ellis 1977; 1996), but he has also done a good deal of empirical research. For example, in an article written with Ashley Ames (Ellis and Ames 1987), Ellis reviewed biologically oriented research on homosexuality and argued that sexual orientation in humans, as in all mammals, is primarily determined by the degree to which the nervous system is exposed to testosterone and other sex hormones during the period in which neurological organization is taking place in the developing fetus. Homosexuality develops when, during the critical developmental period, the fetus's brain receives an excess of the hormone(s) of the opposite sex. Ellis (1995) has also conducted an exhaustive review of research on the relationship between dominance and reproductive success in a wide range of animal species. For males in particular, the vast majority of studies report a positive relationship between dominance and reproductive success. He has also written on stratification and crime from a biosocial perspective (Ellis 1993; Ellis and Hoffman 1990)

In the early 1970s, Steven Goldberg wrote a book with the very politically incorrect title *The Inevitability of Patriarchy* (1973), which he revised in the early 1990s and with a new title, also very politically incorrect, *Why Men Rule* (Goldberg 1993). Goldberg is primarily concerned with explaining why men everywhere monopolize the political leadership and high-status positions of their societies. He concentrates on hormone differences between the sexes, pointing out that adult males have testosterone levels about ten times as high as those of adult females. Testosterone is known to be closely linked to aggression and to dominance and competitive behaviors. Women are at a natural disadvantage in the competition for positions of leadership and high status.

The president of the American Sociological Association in 1983 was Alice Rossi, who took the very bold and courageous step of making her presidential address an exercise in the application of biosocial thinking to gender. Rossi (1984) argued that a pattern of social behavior can be suspected of having a biological basis if two or more of the following criteria are met:

1.   There are consistent correlations between a behavior and a physiological sex attribute (body structure, sex chromosome type, hormonal type).
2.   The pattern is found in infants and young children prior to the occurrence of major socialization influences, or the pattern emerges with the onset of puberty.

3. The pattern is stable across cultures.
4. Similar behavior patterns are found across species, especially the higher primates.

Using these criteria, Rossi concluded that there are important biological dimensions to gender differences. She has summarized evidence showing that compared to males females show greater sensitivity to touch, sound, and odor; have greater fine motor coordination and finger dexterity; pick up nuances of voice and music more readily; are more sensitive to context; and are more attracted to human faces. These traits are precisely ones that would contribute heavily to the successful rearing of a small infant. Rossi notes that, because of long infant and child dependency, prolonged infant care through intense attachment of the mother and the infant is critical to human survival, and that in hunter-gatherer societies there is extremely close contact between mother and infant and infants are often nursed for as long as five years. Under such conditions, it is almost inconceivable that the female of the species would not have been selected for strong nurturant tendencies.

LATER CONTEMPORARY WORK, 1990-2008

An important study of how both biological predispositions and socialization contribute to gender differences has been carried out by the sociologist J. Richard Udry (2000). Udry studied a sample of pregnant women from whom blood samples were taken between 1960 and 1969. Samples were collected for every trimester and then frozen for 30 years. In 1990 and 1991 Udry and his research team interviewed many of the daughters born to these women between 1960 and 1963. The respondents completed a variety of questionnaires and checklists designed to determine their degrees of femininity or masculinity and their sex role socialization experiences. Udry then looked at the relationship between these sex role orientations and the levels of various sex hormones in the mothers' blood samples when their daughters were *in utero*. He found that prenatal levels of sex hormone binding globulin (SHBG) had a strong effect on the daughters' levels of femininity or masculinity when they were adults. Women who had low prenatal SHBG levels were significantly more masculine in their orientations and behavior than women with high SHBG levels. However, this was true only for SHBG levels during the second trimester of pregnancy; SHBG levels during the first and third trimesters were unrelated to masculinity-femininity. This is an extremely important finding, because it is only during the second trimester that fetal neurological organization is taking place; this is the time when the brain is being "sexed."

Udry found that socialization also played a role in determining levels of masculinity and femininity, but that socialization experiences interacted in an important way with prenatal hormone levels. Women who had low prenatal exposure to androgens were fairly responsive to their parents' socialization efforts;

feminizing socialization efforts made them even more feminine, and, presumably, masculinizing socialization efforts could turn their behavior in a more masculine direction. By contrast, women who had high prenatal androgen levels, and thus who tended to be more masculine right from the start when they were young girls, were almost completely resistant to their parents' efforts to encourage feminine behavior.

Jonathan Turner and Alexandra Maryanski are recent converts to a biosocial perspective in sociology. Turner (2000) wrote a book on the sociology of emotions in which he argued that the standard sociological perspective – that emotions are simply social constructions – was much too extreme and that emotions have a deep neurobiological substrate. Most recently Turner and Maryanski (2005) have produced a comprehensive work on the incest taboo that makes a good deal of use of primatological data. They argue that out of a primitive "horde" nuclear family patterns began to emerge around the time of *Homo erectus*, and the bonds between family members grew stronger. At the same time, old transfer patterns at sexual maturity declined and people remained in their nuclear families longer. Fathers and daughters, brothers and sisters, and mothers and sons became increasingly attached and, as they did, the potential for incestuous behavior loomed larger. This was especially the case for fathers and daughters, because, in Turner and Maryanski's view, there was no "hard wiring" in this dyad against incest (no strong "Westermarck effect"). Turner and Maryanski accept the existence of a Westermarck effect for brothers and sisters (and possibly a more limited effect for fathers and daughters), but argue that mother-son incest avoidance was especially hard wired, being a carryover from our hominoid ancestry. A culturally imposed taboo was thus needed to prevent sexual relations between fathers and daughters, and sometimes between brothers and sisters, in order both to maintain solidarity within the family and to avoid the costs of inbreeding depression. The incest taboo was therefore not the exclusive result of either biological or cultural evolution, but rather resulted from the *coevolution* of cultural and biological forces (for a more detailed summary, see Sanderson 2005).

SOCIOBIOLOGY PROPER

The sociobiology proper that was born in 1975 was rooted in an explicit theory known as the *theory of inclusive fitness* or *kin selection*, which is a specific dimension of neo-Darwinian evolutionary biology. The basic principle, of course, is the maximization principle, as Lopreato has called it, which is that people behave so as to maximize the representation of their genes in future generations. Of course, as we saw earlier, Lopreato reformulated this as the modified maximization principle.

In addition to van den Berghe and Lopreato and Crippen, the only sociologists who have enthusiastically accepted this basic sociobiological principle and made significant use of it in their research have been Lee Ellis (although to a limited extent), Satoshi Kanazawa, Rosemary Hopcroft, and myself.

In an extremely important book, *Crisis in Sociology: The Need for Darwin* (1999), Lopreato and Crippen identify a major crisis in sociology, saying that this once promising science "is now awash in the flotsam of extreme cultural relativism and multiculturalism, postmodernism, political correctness, and, permeating these and other isms, an ideological agenda driven by provincial concerns of race, class, and the many grievances of a radical brand of feminism" (1999, xii). They fear that this crisis is so severe that sociology risks being eliminated from academia altogether within the next few decades. What sociology needs is a general unifying paradigm, and they believe that sociobiology is it. They then proceed to show how this paradigm can make much sense of sex and gender, social stratification, and ethnicity.

Satoshi Kanazawa is a sociologist who has taken to evolutionary thinking like a duck to water. In an article written with one of his students (Kanazawa and Still 2000), Kanazawa invokes classical evolutionary principles to understand the immense overrepresentation of young men in crime, especially violent crime, all over the world. Young men are competing for status and resources in order to get access to mates, and those who commit crimes are those who otherwise have lost out in this competitive struggle. With the same student, Kanazawa proposes a *female choice theory* of monogamy (Kanazawa and Still 1999). This theory assumes that it is females rather than males who determine who mates with whom, and therefore whether monogamy or polygyny prevails in a society depends on what women want. Kanazawa and Still argue that women will choose polygyny when the resource inequalities among men are great, because it is better to be, say, the tenth wife of a wealthy man than the only wife of a man of modest means. But when resource inequality among men is relatively low, then women will choose monogamy because there is no advantage to be gained from polygyny. (For a critique, see Sanderson 2001c.)

Before discussing Rosemary Hopcroft's work, I need to make a detour by discussing the ideas of Jeremy Freese, who has been difficult to pin down in terms of exactly what he thinks of sociobiological arguments. Early on Freese was highly critical of these ideas. With Brian Powell he has attempted to test the well-known hypothesis of Robert Trivers and Dan Willard (1973) that parental investment in children of a particular sex varies by social status (Freese and Powell 1999). Parents of high social status will tend to invest more in sons than in daughters, whereas parents of low social status will tend to invest more in daughters than in sons. Although much research on a variety of preindustrial societies shows considerable support for the Trivers-Willard hypothesis, Freese and Powell wish to determine whether it will apply to the contemporary United States.

Freese and Powell's test uses nearly 25,000 eighth-graders and several thousand high school students. Their results show that high-status and low-status parents invested about equally in both sons and daughters. When there was a difference in the nature of parental investment by social status, it usually went in the opposite direction: High-status parents invested more in daughters than in sons (although the degree of differential investment was not large). On the basis of these findings, Freese and Powell claim that suspicion is cast upon sociobiology because one of its most important hypotheses has been shown to be defective.

More recently, Freese has seemed more receptive to Darwinian thinking. Freese and two coauthors surveyed literature on the potential relevance of biology to social inquiry (Freese et al. 2003). They looked at research guided by what is now essentially called evolutionary psychology, at research by behavior geneticists on the role of genetics in individual differences in behavior, and at the relevance of such proximate variables as hormones, especially testosterone, for social behavior. They are very much aware that sociology is far behind psychology and anthropology in incorporating biological variables into their explanations and conclude that sociologists need to do more in this regard. Their grand conclusion is that, "As science continues to reveal more about the biology of behavior . . . sociology should seek and support ways of understanding the interrelationship of biological and social influences that will allow our discipline to gain strength from these new developments rather than be diminished by them" (2003, 248).

Rosemary Hopcroft (2005) has carried out her own test of the Trivers-Willard hypothesis using a large sample of 10,000 Americans. She claims to find support for the hypothesis, but I am not so sure that her data actually point to this conclusion. To me, they suggest that in fact the differences in parental investment in sons vs. daughters by social class are quite small – much too small really to support Trivers and Willard. Hopcroft's data are no stronger than Freese and Powell's, and those researchers drew the conclusion that Trivers and Willard is not supported for the contemporary United States.

Hopcroft (2006a) has also studied the relationship between social status and reproductive success in one industrial society, the United States. Her findings, summarized crudely, show that higher-income men have slightly more reproductive success than lower-income men, but that for the women the pattern is just the opposite. In her sample, Hopcroft found that higher-income women had only about half the completed fertility of lower-income women.

I have space only to mention other sociologists who have taken Darwinism seriously in one way or another: Ullica Segerstrale, who has written an important book, *Defenders of the Truth: The Battle for Science in the Sociobiology Debate and Beyond* (2000); Michael Hammond (1999; 2003), who has done some provocative work on what he calls "arouser depreciation" and its relationship to social inequality, as well as on the neurological roots of Durkheimian solidarity; Richard Machalek, who has studied expropriative crime, social exploitation, and the formation of macrosocieties from a biosocial perspective (Machalek 1992, 1995, 1996; Cohen and Machalek 1988; cf. Machalek and Martin 2004); François Nielsen (2006), who has started to do work on the genetic contribution to academic achievement and social mobility (see also Nielsen 1994); Penny Anthon Green (1991, 1995), who has written on the biological foundations of revolution and class circulation; Thomas Smith and Gregory Stevens (2002), who have done research on the biology of interpersonal dependence, especially reciprocity and altruism; and Douglas Massey, who, in his presidential address to the ASA in 2001 stressed that sociology has not been as successful as it should have been because of three major conceits, one of which is the persistent elevation of the social over the biological (Massey 2002). Of course there is also my own work, in particular my Darwinian conflict theory (see below), which is the subject of many of the papers in this book.

And, in Europe, we find a number of sociologists who have been influenced by Darwinism, especially Peter Meyer, Tamás Meleghy, Heinz-Jürgen Niedenzu, Anna Rotkirch, J. P. Roos, W. G. Runciman, Michael Schmid, and Nico Wilterdink, all of whom are contributors to this volume. I should also mention Frank Salter, another contributor to this volume, a sociologist turned political scientist. He has done important work in a variety of areas bridging both human ethology and sociobiology (e.g., Salter 1995). Recently he has written an extremely important book on the biology of ethnic attachments, *On Genetic Interests* (2006). And in England there are a number of Darwinian sociologists, such as Christopher Badcock (1991).

DARWINIAN CONFLICT THEORY

Since it plays such a large role in the present volume, a summary of my own Darwinian conflict theory (DCT) was requested by the editors. DCT is a synthesis of two great social science traditions, the Darwinian evolutionary tradition that has now produced sociobiology and evolutionary psychology, and the tradition of economic and ecological materialism begun by Marx and developed and modified by Marvin Harris with his theoretical strategy of cultural materialism (Harris 1968, 1979; Kuznar and Sanderson 2007). Both of these theoretical traditions are materialist in the broadest sense, one focusing on the materialism of the body and brain and the other on the materialism of the physical environment and the struggle for survival and success. Obviously, therefore, DCT is a *materialist* version of social theory.

It is also a *conflict* theory. In sociology, conflict theories assume that humans are locked into various forms of competition with one another to survive and be successful, and that much of the structure of society is a product of such competitions. The best-developed conflict theory in all of sociology is that of Randall Collins (1975, 1988), whose theory stems primarily from the Weberian tradition (although with some Marxian elements) and makes no use of classic sociobiological principles. However, much of Collins's conflict theory is compatible with DCT, and DCT pushes Weberian conflict theory to a deeper level. Collins assumes that humans are naturally conflict-prone organisms, but he takes this as an unexplained given. DCT takes the conflict-prone nature of humans, and the particular forms of conflict they are most prone toward, as something that must itself be explained. It therefore biologically grounds sociological conflict theory.

It is critical to recognize that conflict theories do not take as their *explananda* only forms of social conflict. Conflict theories are so named because they draw on conflict as *explanans*. Humans with competing and conflicting interests also produce various forms of social cooperation, which is an important *explanandum* in DCT. DCT is applicable to all social phenomena – conflict and cooperation, stasis and change, micro and macro, and so on.

I first presented DCT in my book *The Evolution of Human Sociality* (Sanderson 2001a). Here I give a somewhat abbreviated version of the theory as it stood several years ago. However, DCT is a work in progress and thereby unfinished. I intend to modify and elaborate it in several successive installments, and in my response to critics in Chapter 17 of this volume I explain some emendations that have already been made.

1. Principles Concerning the Deep Wellsprings of Human Action

1. Humans as organisms have been built by natural selection, not only in their anatomy/physiology, but in their behavioral predispositions. This means that theories of social life must take into consideration the basic features of human nature that are the products of human evolution.

2. Like all other organisms, humans compete with other conspecifics to survive and reproduce. Since the resources necessary for survival and reproduction are inevitably in short supply, humans are caught up in a continual struggle to achieve these goals, and this struggle is inevitable and unceasing. Human social life is the complex product of this ceaseless struggle for survival and reproduction.

3. In the struggle for survival and reproduction, humans give overwhelming priority to their own interests and to those of their kin, especially their close kin.

4. Humans have evolved strong behavioral predispositions that facilitate their success in the struggle for survival and reproduction, the most important of which are:
   - Humans are highly sexed and are oriented mostly toward heterosexual sex. This predisposition has evolved because it is necessary for the promotion of humans' reproductive interests, i.e., their inclusive fitness. Males compete for females and for sex, and females compete for males as resource providers.
   - Humans are highly predisposed to perform effective parental behavior, which is behavior that will optimize the number of surviving offspring. Mating and marriage serve the function of reproductive success, and marriage is primarily a reproductive contract. Thus the family as a social institution rests on a natural foundation.

- The female desire to nurture offspring is stronger than the male desire, and the mother-child bond is the most basic familial unit. Such differences in parental solicitude have arisen as a result of the natural and sexual selection of different reproductive strategies for each of the sexes. Mating effort is greater in human males, parental effort in females. These differences in reproductive strategies have consequences for gender arrangements.
- Humans are naturally competitive and highly predisposed toward status competition. Status competition is ultimately oriented toward the securing of resources, which promotes reproductive success. Because of the natural and sexual selection of different reproductive strategies, the predisposition toward status competition is greater in males than in females.
- Because of the natural competition for resources, humans are economic animals. They are strongly oriented toward achieving economic satisfaction and well-being, an achievement that promotes reproductive success.
- In their pursuit of resources and closely related activities, humans, like other species, have evolved to maximize efficiency. Other things equal, they prefer to carry out activities by minimizing the amount of time and energy they devote to these activities. A Law of Least Effort governs human behavior, especially those forms of behavior that individuals find burdensome or at least not intrinsically rewarding. The Law of Least Effort is a major constraint on the behavior of humans everywhere; much behavior can only be explained satisfactorily by taking it into account.

5. None of the tendencies identified above are rigid. Rather, they are behavioral *predispositions* that move along certain lines rather than others but that interact in various ways with the total set of environmental contingencies within which humans find themselves. The behavioral predispositions tend to win out in the long run, but they can be diminished or even negated by certain environmental contingencies. At the same time, other contingencies can amplify these tendencies, pushing them to increasingly higher levels.

6. From the above it follows that humans' most important interests and concerns are reproductive, economic, and political. Political life is primarily a struggle to acquire and defend economic resources, and economic life is primarily a matter of using resources to promote reproductive success. But at the experiential level individuals have no conscious recognition that their behaviors are driven by these motives. People often experience economic and political behaviors as valuable in themselves and are often highly motivated to continue and elaborate such behaviors in their own right.

7. Many, probably most, of the features of human social life are the adaptive consequences of people struggling to satisfy their interests.

2. Principles Concerning Group Relations

1. Individuals pursuing their interests are the core of social life. The pursuit of interests leads to both highly cooperative and highly conflictive social arrangements.
2. Many cooperative forms of behavior exist at the level of social groups or entire societies. Cooperative social relations exist because they are the relations that will best promote each individual's self-interests, not because they promote the well-being of the group or society as a whole. The selection of cooperative social forms occurs at the level of the individual, not the group or society.
3. Cooperative forms of interaction are found most extensively among individuals who share reproductive interests in common, i.e., among kin and especially close kin. This is the basis for the family as a fundamental social institution.
4. Outside of kinship and family life, cooperative relations are most likely to be found among individuals who depend heavily on each other for the satisfaction of their basic interests.
5. When competitive and conflictive behavior will more satisfactorily promote individual interests, cooperative relations will decline in favor of competitive and conflictive relations.
6. People are unequally endowed to compete in the social struggle – some are bigger, more intelligent, more aggressive or ambitious, more clever, more deceitful, etc. – and as a result social domination and subordination are common and frequent features of social life.
7. Members of dominant groups benefit disproportionately from their social position, and frequently they are able to make use of subordinate individuals to advance their interests. Their use of these individuals frequently takes the form of economic exploitation or social exclusion.
8. Because they benefit from their situation, members of dominant groups are highly motivated to structure society so that their superior social position can be preserved or enhanced.
9. Social life is therefore disproportionately influenced by the interests and actions of the members of dominant groups.

3. Principles Concerning Systemic Relations within Societies

1. Human societies consist of four basic subunits:
    *   Individuals themselves as biological organisms, which we may call the *biostructure*.
    *   The basic natural phenomena and social forms that are essential to human biological reproduction and economic production, i.e., the ecological, demographic, technological, and economic structures

essential for survival and well-being; this we may call the *ecostructure*.

- The institutionalized patterns of behavior shared by individuals, especially the patterns of marriage, kinship, and family life; the egalitarian or inegalitarian structuring of the society along the lines of class, ethnicity, race, or gender; its mode of political life; and its mode or modes of socializing and educating the next generation; these patterns may be identified as the *structure*.
- The primary forms of mental life shared by the members of the society, i.e., beliefs, values, preferences, and norms as these are expressed in such things as religion, art, literature, myth, legend, philosophy, music, and (to some extent) science; these we may refer to as the *superstructure*.

2. These four components of societies are related such that the flow of causation is primarily from the biostructure to the ecostructure, then from the ecostructure to the structure, and finally from the structure to the superstructure; the flow may sometimes occur in the reverse manner, or in some other manner, but these causal dynamics occur much less frequently.

3. According to the logic of 3.2, it is clear that the forces within the biostructure and the ecostructure are the principal causal forces in human social life; the biostructure structures social life both indirectly, i.e., through its action on the ecostructure (which then acts on the structure and superstructure), and through its direct effect on some of the elements of the structure and superstructure. It follows that the superstructure has the least causal impact on the patterns of social life, but this impact is in some instances more than negligible.

4. The components of societies are related as they are because such causal dynamics flow from the deep wellsprings of human action. The biostructure and the ecostructure have a logical causal priority because they concern vital human needs and interests relating to production and reproduction.

5. Once structures and superstructures have been built by biostructures and ecostructures, they may come to acquire a certain autonomy. New needs and new interests may arise therefrom, and these new needs and interests, along with reproductive, economic, and political interests, may form part of the human preference and value structure characteristic of the members of a society, and thus become new environmental contingencies constraining the expression of human biological predispositions.

4. Modes of Darwinian Conflict Explanation

1. As is obvious from the principles stated in Section 3, Darwinian con-
    flict explanations are materialist in nature; these explanations may take
    any or all of three forms: biomaterialist, ecomaterialist, or polimaterial-
    ist.
2. *Biomaterialist* explanations explain a social form by direct reference to
    a basic feature of the human biogram. That is, an explanation is bioma-
    terialist if it links a social form to the human biogram without reference
    to any mediation of the causal relationship by some other social form.
    Example: Polygyny is a widespread feature of human societies because
    it springs from an innate desire of males for sexual variety and from the
    tendency of females to be attracted to resource-rich males. (*But note*:
    The *extent* of polygyny cannot be explained merely by invoking the bi-
    ogram.)
3. *Ecomaterialist* explanations explain a social form by linking it directly
    to the influence of ecological, technological, demographic, or economic
    forces, and thus only indirectly to a feature of the human biogram. *Ex-
    ample*: Hunter-gatherer societies frequently display intensive sharing
    and cooperation because these are behaviors that promote individuals'
    interests within the configuration of hunter-gatherer technoeconomic
    systems and natural environments.
4. *Polimaterialist* explanations explain a social form by linking it directly
    to the political interests or situations of the participants. Political inter-
    ests or situations ordinarily spring from the participants' economic in-
    terests, which in turn are ultimately derived from the character of the
    human biogram. *Examples*: Democratic forms of government emerged
    earliest in those Western societies with the largest and most politically
    organized working classes. Third World revolutions occur most fre-
    quently in societies where the state is highly vunerable to a revolution-
    ary coalition. *Let's keep going in circles...*

THE STILL UNFRIENDLY RECEPTION OF SOCIOBIOLOGY BY SOCIOLOGISTS

Despite the excellent work of biologically inclined sociologists, sociobiological
thinking has still made very limited headway in sociology. Lee Ellis (1977) predicted thirty years ago that sociobiology would absorb much of sociology by the
year 2000. It hasn't happened, not even remotely. Will it ever happen? This is a
very difficult question to answer, but if it does happen it will clearly not be soon.

There appears little doubt that sociologists have remained more opposed to
sociobiology than the members of their closely related sister disciplines, anthropology and psychology, although people in those fields often say that sociobiol-

ogy – or evolutionary psychology, as it is usually known in those disciplines – is still very much a minority point of view there as well. Most sociologists range from being either indifferent to sociobiology or downright hostile to it.

Why have sociologists been so persistently negative? Van den Berghe (1990) has suggested that sociologists don't and won't think evolutionarily for two main reasons: anthropocentrism and trained incompetence. Anthropocentrism is a major characteristic of the human species, social scientists included, who base most of their claims on the uniqueness of humans. Sociologists emphasize this uniqueness more than any other social scientists, and sociobiology is a major threat to sociologists' anthropocentric conceit. As for trained incompetence, van den Berghe notes that sociologists are taught as undergraduate and graduate students, not only to be oblivious to biology, but to be militantly and proudly ignorant of it. They spend many years being disciplinarily indoctrinated into the dogmas of environmentalism and antireductionism.

I would add that students of sociology seem to be especially vulnerable to such dogmas. It has been my experience in over three decades of university teaching that students who go into sociology, even at the undergraduate level, are individuals who are already predisposed to think in terms of social and cultural determinism. Many sociology students start out as psychology majors, and many of these have told me that the reason they switched to sociology was because of its emphasis on the role of society in conditioning the individual. They did not like what they regarded as the overemphasis of psychologists on the individual person and organism. Van den Berghe is right: Sociologists are the victims of trained incompetence. However, they have been remarkably willing victims.

But sociological resistance to evolutionary thinking also has a great deal to do with politics and ideology. Most people who go into sociology want to change the world, and that is their motivation for becoming sociologists. Such people are ideologically convinced in advance that human behavior has little to do with biology. They believe this, and they fervently want to believe it, because they see the acknowledgment of biological factors as indicating that behavior is resistant to fundamental change. So sociologists dislike sociobiology because they are severely threatened by it politically, and it must be said that sociology has become an increasingly politicized discipline over the past two or three decades.

There is another threat perceived by sociologists, though, that must be recognized. Most sociologists believe that their claim to importance is to show that social and cultural forces shape everything. They seem to feel that without this they have nothing to distinguish themselves and make themselves important. We might call this sociologists' "Durkheimian mandate": Social facts can only be explained in terms of other social facts. Stressing the importance of biology, they think, undermines this, and robs their discipline of its unique importance. Thus sociologists feel threatened disciplinarily. As van den Berghe (1990) has noted, sociologists use antireductionism as a territorial display especially against psychologists, whom they regard as their nearest intellectual rivals (but they fear the biologists even more).

Is there any hope? There are perhaps a few glimmers. There has been some increase in the number of sociologists who are now doing serious evolutionary work, as discussed in the previous section. Another potentially encouraging sign is the formation of an Evolution and Sociology section of the American Sociological Association. I say "potentially" because this section barely achieved the minimum membership for official ASA recognition (300), and it accomplished this only because many of the sociologists who joined did so as a favor to friends and fully intended to drop their membership after a short period of time. (As of this writing, membership has declined from 326 to 213, and I fear it will drop even lower.)

Before concluding, let me contrast the situation in sociology with that in psychology and anthropology. Considerable evidence suggests that psychologists and anthropologists are a good deal more sympathetic to sociobiology/evolutionary psychology than sociologists. Both psychologists and anthropologists are prominently represented as authors of books and articles written from an evolutionary psychological perspective. Evolutionary psychologists founded the major scientific society for Darwinian social science in North America, the Human Behavior and Evolution Society (HBES), and they are currently its most numerous representatives and leading figures. Several textbooks in evolutionary psychology have already appeared, as have two handbooks. HBES is not only thriving, but is growing significantly, and is clearly where the action is today. This organization is composed mostly of psychologists and anthropologists, and only a small handful of sociologists attend its meetings (I am one of those few).

The sad fact is that, not only have psychologists and anthropologists taken to the study of the biological foundations of behavior much more than sociologists, but even the majority of biologically oriented sociologists continue to strongly resist the classical neo-Darwinian paradigm, seeing it as a threat to sociology. Unsurprisingly, it is the younger sociologists who have been most inclined to adopt classical evolutionary psychological principles and to use them to guide their research. Kanazawa and Hopcroft are the most notable in this regard, although older sociologists such as van den Berghe and Lopreato (along with the latter's former student Crippen) have largely accepted the main claims of the sociobiologists and evolutionary psychologists.

And, of course, I have done so myself in my synthesis of neo-Darwinism with materialist social theory to create DCT. But only a minority of sociologists looking at the biological foundations of human society embrace sociobiology or evolutionary psychology, and some reject it emphatically. Steven Goldberg, for example, wants to pursue a biological theory of gender by staying at the level of hormonal differences between the sexes and without invoking evolutionary principles at all. Goldberg is like Chomsky in linguistics, who famously claimed that humans possess an innate language acquisition device but at the same time denied that this device had evolved by natural selection or that it was even adaptive. And a number of sociologists who have embraced an evolutionary perspective in its broadest sense continue to resist the more specific principles of evolutionary psychology, claiming that it has produced mostly "just-so stories" unsupported by convincing evidence.

So, let me finish with two grand conclusions. First, sociology is not the optimal discipline for the Darwinian study of human social life. People who go into sociology are primarily concerned with changing society for the better and they see understanding it as simply a means to that end. In this light, they resist biological explanations because such explanations do not resonate with their goals – indeed, are seen as highly antagonistic to them. The Darwinian action today is in psychology and anthropology. I urge sociologists who want to be Darwinians to join HBES and to present papers there. Sociologists aren't listening, and aren't likely to listen any time soon. (Unfortunately, HBES is dominated by psychologists, whose substantive foci are rather different from those of sociologists, and often quite narrow. But sociologists could help to expand the substantive foci of HBES.)

But perhaps this conclusion is too pessimistic. Therefore, let me state a second one, which is that, although I am a short-term pessimist, I am a long-term optimist. I predict that sociologists for the most part will persist in their repudiation of sociobiology, not forever, but very likely until it is too late. Sociology's reputation, never all that strong to begin with, will drop even lower and sociology will eventually become marginalized within the social sciences and within the academic world more generally. Many sociologists may wake up, but not until the damage cannot be undone. By the time sociologists finally begin to realize they have to take sociobiology seriously – that they must change or die – the core of our field will have been stolen away from us by the evolutionary psychologists, Darwinian anthropologists, behavior geneticists, and others currently hard at work exploring the biological foundations of human behavior. Sociology will not disappear altogether, but the field will shrink considerably and will have even less credibility within the academic world and with the educated public than it already has. My message to sociologists in 2007 is thus that we are sailing on the Titanic and it is late afternoon on April 14, 1912. Let's get the lifeboats ready before we hit that iceberg. I, for one, am not going to go down with the ship!

Part II

DARWINIAN CONFLICT THEORY AND ITS CRITICS

2

SOCIAL EVOLUTION AND HUMAN ACTION

A Commentary on Sanderson's Darwinian Conflict Theory

Michael Schmid

I have now followed developments in the theory of evolution for over 30 years and was pleased when I discovered at the beginning of the 1990s Stephen Sanderson's critical assessment of evolutionism,[1] which corroborated many of my reservations about the traditional program of explanation in evolutionary theory. I was also encouraged by the fact that Sanderson did not draw the consequence from his criticism that evolutionism should be rejected, as for instance Robert Nisbet counseled us to do, but rather set about to correct and improve the theory.[2] I should like to touch on these efforts at correction only in passing, so as to concentrate instead upon a commentary on Sanderson's book *The Evolution of Human Sociality* in which he outlines a Darwinian conflict theory (DCT).[3]

I think highly of this book first of all and especially because of its metascientific position[4]; thus I find very fruitful Sanderson's recommendation that sociological theory pursue a *unitary theoretical program* which conceives of all theoretical proposals in the social sciences as answers to common questions about the (among other characteristics, conflictual) forms of human social conduct and sets its face against all theoretical "eclecticism." Further, I share Sanderson's intention of constructing sociological theory as an *explanatory theory* whose point is an identification of a "logic of explanation"[5] and not merely descriptions, types, or (historical) narratives.[6] I am also in agreement with his criticism of functionalism, constructivism, and structuralism, because I too am convinced that all explanations of social evolution should move within the frame of a methodological individualism[7] and require to this end a *microfoundation in the theory of action*, which looks upon human action as necessarily canalized by situations as well as being "adaptive" or "optimizing."[8]

SANDERSON'S DARWINIAN CONFLICT THEORY
OF HUMAN SOCIALITY

In order to provide a guiding line for my commentary, I should like first to describe the content and the logical structure of the Darwinian conflict program of explanation.[9]

To begin with, what is the *explanandum* of DCT? If I have understood Sanderson's theoretical proposal rightly, then the point is for him the explanation of the structural characteristics of *Gesellschaftsformationen*, as Marx called them, or "social forms"[10] and their dynamics of development.[11] In order to cope with this explanatory task, the *explanans* of the theory is designed for complexity and consists of several components: At the start we find a *sociobiologically founded theory of action* which presupposes definite (bioprogrammatically anchored) *dispositions* to and *capacities* for action (and so a set of genetically determined preferences and needs), and which treats the actor as oriented to his own welfare and to being a selfish defender of his interests. The chief problem of an actor with this equipment consists in the *scarcity* of (material) resources and the *indispensability of social attainments*.

This twofold problem can be remedied only within the framework of diversely shaped group relations which can be cooperative as well as conflictual; in all cases these relations are characterized by the necessity to guarantee (the in most cases controversial) distribution of resources, which by reason of the conflicting interests in distribution (necessarily) leads to domination, exploitation, and oppression. Consequently, especially those actors have an interest in the maintenance of such relations for whom these relations guarantee a greater reward than to the disadvantaged or to those who have lost in the fight over distribution.

This intrasocietal fight over distribution ensues under conditions that may be understood as (internal and external) "constraints" on the action of individual actors and that form a kind of gradient "system of (ontological) levels"[12]:

- first comes the *biostructure*, which describes the genetically prescribed preferences and capacities of action that arise in the course of biological evolution;
- then, the *ecostructure*, under which Sanderson includes ecological, demographic, technological, and economic structures, which he would like to conceive of as *materialist structures*;
- then there are (built upon both the previous structures) *social* structures (kinship and family, politically or economically generated structures of distribution, etc.);
- and finally there is a *superstructure* to be considered, which comprises above all (autonomous) systems of interpretations.[13]

This complex composition of the explanans is bound up with a specific conception of the "content" and "structure" of a (conflict theoretical) explanatory argument:

- Biostructure and ecostructure are the "principal causal forces in human life"[14]; the "flow of causation" proceeds from bio- and ecostructures and extends to the overlying structures. The former structures are accorded a "logical causal priority"[15] because they refer to "vital human needs and interests" which serve the ineluctable (biophysical) reproduction of the actors and without which the existence of "social forms" would be inconceivable.

- The biologically programmed needs and capacities that serve survival have a dispositional character,[16] that is, they must be actualized by particular circumstances. It is the task of DCT to identify these circumstances and to formulate these as to how the existing material structures restrict and constrain these "behavioral predispositions" and thereby reproduce (or change) them.

- DCT endeavors to deliver "materialist explanations" in the sense that the "social forms" to be explained are traced *directly*, "without reference to any necessary mediation of the causal relationship by some social form,"[17] to biologically programmed interests, to ecostructural factors, or to politically (and that means differentially) assertable interests of dominance and distribution on the part of the actors. In this sense, DCT distinguishes among "biomaterialist," "ecomaterialist," and "polimaterialist" explanations.[18]

- Sanderson characterizes his explanations as, as I should call them, "microfoundational explanations."[19] The explanation of the existence and change of relations or "social forms" rooted in material conditions occurs *in all cases* by reference to the previously mentioned theory of action based on interests or needs and (bound up with this) "as results of the adaptation of individuals to their circumstances,"[20] whereby these attempts can also fail.[21] The collective effect of these efforts reacts restrictively and inadvertently on the future conditions of action for the actors. This defines a recursive dynamics between action and structure, and at least suggests a solution to the micro-macro problem as it has been discussed particularly in sociology.[22]

- Then Sanderson formulates a kind of "postulate of specification"; that is, the "logic of explanation"[23] favored by Sanderson operates as a "highly abstract theoretical strategy"[24] and must be *specified* in relation to historical circumstances in order to lead to testable conclusions.[25]

- By way of a closer characterization of the content of DCT, Sanderson variously emphasizes that "cultural explanations" (of any kind) do not belong to its set of conclusions; this thesis forms the basis of the conviction that "culture" is to be equated with "learning" and that the reference to "learning" (or even to "socialization") itself explains nothing, but, understood as at most a "capacity of culture,"[26] must for its part seek an (evolutionary) explanation. According to the thesis of Cosmides and Tooby, which Sanderson shares, there does not exist a "general learning mechanism," but only domain-specific problem-solving capacities which, brought about by the pressure of selection exerted by environmental requirements important for survival, are built into the biologically programmed equipment of the actor.[27] The object of Sanderson's theory of action, therefore, is exclusively the actor's specific achievements of adaptation to the environment.

QUESTIONS ABOUT DARWINIAN CONFLICT THEORY

One will certainly not refuse to accord this "new theoretical synthesis"[28] its due admiration, for it undoubtedly represents a great intellectual achievement and deserves to be appreciated as such. All the same, there remain a few (in part related) open questions which I should like to raise in turn and, as far as I am able, provide cursory answers to.

The Basic Explanatory Argument and Its "Logic"

I am happy to believe that there are behavioral dispositions that possess a genetic basis and an evolutionary past; but does it make sense to reduce the issue of (social, economic, and political) fights over distribution *directly* and *exclusively* to the actor's self-interest in evolutionary survival,[29] without taking into account the (highly variable) *forms of social organization* of the process of distribution whose operation and result equip various actors with diverse means of power (and corresponding opportunities of gaining and exercising power)? Or differently stated: Does DCT represent a sociobiological reductionism? If this is not the case,[30] as I think, then one need only give due emphasis to the evolutionary (or biological) past and anchoring of definite interests in optimization if one wishes to bring to the fore the (historically overarching) permanence and ineluctability of corresponding fights over distribution; and if, on the other hand, it is a matter of explaining the historically contingent course of such struggles and their finally unforeseeable concrete results, it suffices to assume the (*constant*) premise of (different) "interests"[31] in the combatants in order to determine the probably highly diverse *effects of situative factors* underlying the dynamics of distribution and struggle. In this way, sociobiological and social-scientific explanatory claims may be cleanly separated and the usual quarrels between representatives of both camps avoided, especially those about the question whether sociology (and also anthropology and every other social science) is reducible to sociobiological premises.

My next question concerns the advantage DCT promises itself in this connection from introducing completely heterogeneous factors of influence (such as actor-endogenous biograms[32]; situative-external distributions of resources; the contingent availability of technical equipment; and social, political, and economic structures of production and distribution) under the common head of "materialism"? Two specific questions arise here:

1. First, can DCT really inspect the conceivable and expectable interactive effects of these factors that are localized at diverse structural levels?
2. And why should the economic production and distribution processes of a society be assigned to its "ecostructure" rather than to its "social structure"?

I should be glad to see that Sanderson's favored materialist ontology[33] could distinguish between "material" resources and "social" externalities which reciprocally saddle actors, because I should otherwise fear that the difference between control processes which arise from the constraint of material scarcities and those controls which arise from *social relations* (and that means their underlying rights and duties) would remain theoretically disregarded.[34]

The present context also gives cause to pose a question about the explanatory role of Sanderson's "materialism." It appears to me that Sanderson vacillates in his assessment of the question how material structures affect the interests and opportunities of action of actors. Certainly he wishes to avoid an exaggerated "structural determinism"[35]; on the other hand, he holds fast at the same time to the thesis that the inner and outer constraints which influence actors hinder their acting "truly voluntaristically."[36] I think it would be of advantage if Sanderson could distinguish more clearly than he has done so far between the "energizing factors" of "interests" and "needs," to which he assigns a "logical causal priority" in the explanation of divergent "social forms,"[37] and the "constraining factors," which do not "produce" but rather "steer" or "restrict" or "confine" action. This would have the advantage that the quite divergent influences of these groups of factors would not be mixed together under the designation of "causal mechanism"[38] or designated jointly as "causes" independently of their different kinds of effects. I should like to insist on this interpretation, because it permits me to describe the logic of Sanderson's project more precisely: Obviously his DCT is concerned to investigate, on the assumption that actors have (biologically) fixed preferences and are moreover dependent upon asserting their interests against others, how diverse structures of distribution (defined by means of the "dimensions" of power, influence, access to sexual partners, money, social support, status and reputation, etc.) arise that limit and select their further opportunities of action. In this formulation it becomes apparent that his pattern of explanation is possibly less "original" than he supposes; to my eyes, it takes its place in the ranks of the mainstream program of an integral sociological explanation such as Robert K. Merton proposed in his day. This should not, however, hinder us in acknowledging Sanderson's merit in having in this way made an important contribution to the clarification of the question which "type of explanatory logic" sociological theory pursues.[39]

A final remark would be to ask why DCT looks upon it as urgent to renounce the investigation of learning processes and *learning effects*. On this I
have two questions:

1. Is it correct that forms of behavior cannot at all be explained by learn-
    ing only because the capacity to learn is itself a process in need of (bio-
    logical) explanation[40]? I regard this argument as not logically cogent.[41]
2. Can DCT afford such a conception when it is interested in the (re-)ac-
    tion of structural effects on the action of actors (for instance, on the un-
    desired effects of distribution stemming from competition and "cul-
    ture")? Must it not attend to the (learning dependent) changes of
    "needs" and "behavioral dispositions"[42] especially to the extent that
    these needs and dispositions are *not* sociobiologically anchored?[43] Or is
    in the end the suspicion right, in spite of the concession to the con-
    trary,[44] that DCT is interested in "needs" and "dispositions" only if
    these are ("ultimately"[45]) derivable from the genetic equipment of ac-
    tors?

If the understanding of evolution is extended to include learning processes (as,
for instance, Boyd and Richerson, Hallpike, Runciman and others have proposed), then Sanderson's DCT would possibly lose its (aggressive) "anticultural-
ist" verve, but whom would that harm? On the contrary, by renouncing this kind
of "theory politics," DCT could gain in substance in two respects: If learned
variability of action is shown to be important for actors' selection of the "social
forms" that they develop and stabilize, then DCT need not restrict itself to actions based on biological programming – namely, those which have to do with
emotions and reproductive behavior[46]; and secondly it would obtain that only
when actors are capable of learning is the fact that the consequences of their
actions possess unintended components important for the progress of evolution.[47] That is to say, DCT could incorporate the insight that the assumed "adaptiveness" of human action[48] is *logically* dependent on the learning capacity of
the actors.

The Evolutionary Logic of Explanation

DCT lays claim to outlining a "Darwinian perspective."[49] Is this claim justified?
Or more generally stated, wherein lies the actual "evolutionary" character of
DCT's explanations? It should be acknowledged that Sanderson has repeatedly
pointed out that he does *not* wish to represent a holistic, teleological, or progres-
sivist theory of evolution.[50] If, however, one searches for a *positive characterization* of his theory, one finds only the two hints that he is concerned with the
biological explanation of dispositions to action which condition sociality, and
that sociological theory has to explain "directional trends,"[51] the "general
lines"[52] of the course of history, or the "directional sequence of change,"[53] that
is, the succession of social forms.[54]

Especially the last-mentioned definition, which to my ears sounds Spencerian rather than Darwinian, goes back to Gerhard Lenski and applies the concept
of evolution to characterize in the first place the object of explanation, *but not* its
dynamics and, in consequence, the explanatory logic of the arguments of evolutionary theory. That is to say, in order to develop his explanatory argument,
Sanderson refers neither to the Darwinian two-in-oneness of "modification" and
"descent," nor to Campbell's extension of the explanatory mode to the tripartite
form of "variation," "selection," and "retention," nor to Runciman's (or Hull's
or Chattoe's) "theory of selection," or Dawkins's "theory of memes"; nor does
Sanderson apply a genetic algorithm, as is customary in recent formal models of
evolution, in simulation research, or in the Santa Fe Institute's "theory of dynamic complexity"; nor does he touch at any recognizable point upon related
explanations in population ecology.

Why not?[55] Or differently stated, is the evolutionary character of DCT sufficiently defined by the assumed *adaptive character of individual action* (under
the constant of biologically programmed "drives")?[56] How then does DCT differ
from (especially economic) theories of rational action which hardly lay claim to
defending a general theory of evolution? And would it not be more reasonable to
see in the "constraints"[57] that proceed from the existing equipment of resources
and capacities (of actors) a *selector* for the opportunity of successfully carrying
out certain variations of actions? Or does it not make sense to reconstruct Sanderson's "materialist" explanations as *explanations of selection* in order to maintain a junction with at least one basic idea of a "genuine" Darwinian program of
explanation?[58] This way of seeing things has the advantage of enabling us to
analyze the *mechanism of conflict* (or *the struggle for positional goods*) as *a
selection mechanism*, whereby it is worth considering (for one thing) that competitions for positional goods need not necessarily be solved by establishing
relations of domination,[59] and worth paying attention (beyond this) to the ways
in which such diverse mechanisms mesh with each other and with what collective consequences.[60]

A final question that suggests itself to me in this context is one concerning
the relation of Sanderson's material (world-) historical analyses and his DCT. It
can hardly be denied that the observable "evolutionary trends" and the directional constancy of world-historical developments[61] *by no means* necessarily
result from the conflict mechanisms which Sanderson treated in 2001, and that
in view of the fact that not only competitions over distribution but also the pool-
ing of efforts and uncontroversial (that is, apparently conflict-free) conventions
play a role in shaping structures (or historical developments), it is not plausible
to hope for the opposite. One possible interpretation, in my view, is that Sanderson's attempt to place evolutionary theory on the foundation of conflict theory
has little or nothing to do with his materialist historical analyses, and that he has
no systematic theory to offer for the explanation of "historical developments,"[62]
but rather at most a "reconstruction" of the course of world-historical development with the aid of a series of *single causal explanations*, which have the task
of tracing identifiable lines of development (such as the emergence of state

domination, of early agricultural societies, of capitalism, or of the "world system" of global domination and exchange relations) as more or less necessary
consequences of certain "constellations of events."[63] The method employed in
these sketches does not differ from the usual practice of (causal) historical explanation. I should be glad to concede that Sanderson wishes in this context to
counter structuralist fallacies (such as are to be found in Theda Skocpol) by
pointing out that all "evolution" should be explained on the basis of the action of
actors motivated by self-interest[64]; but I have not been able to discover how far
the thereby employed causal analyses are distinguished by a separate "evolutionary" character. The same also holds for Sanderson's DCT; in the final instance "evolution" invariably means (only) "development," but not that this development is to be explained with the help of distinguishable "evolutionary arguments." Or alternatively Sanderson proposes *no* evolutionary explanations of
"social forms" or "social transformations" and instead offers (similarly to the
structural analyses of Skocpol, Barrington Moore, Immanuel Wallerstein, or
Michael Mann) an (event related) *causal analysis of historically unique processes of emergence and change.*[65]

The Causal Analysis

At this juncture I should prefer not to enter into the extensive discussion on the
necessity and scope of causal historical explanations and, instead, confine my
reservations about their application, such as I find in Sanderson, to a few points.

To begin with, that Sanderson favors the resort to statistical analyses in order to test his hypotheses is, to my eyes, a desperate solution resulting from the
fact that DCT specifies *no* evolutionary mechanism and discusses *no* general
model (of fights over distribution) which could be tested by means of their logical implications (or prognoses and retrodictions). Instead DCT inquires after the
structural consequences of the basic biological equipment of actors or after an
(empirically) verifiable connection between distribution variables and proceeds
to formulate (mainly unconnected) hypotheses. To test these hypotheses, it takes
distribution data from history or ethnology and seeks an (empirical) confirmation for the assumed hypotheses in a (statistically guided) analysis.

The questionableness of this procedure is of course familiar:

First of all, statistical relations between distribution data (or random individual factors) do not constitute a proof that causal relations exist between
them[66]; moreover, I emphatically doubt that one distribution structure can be
explained by another. Unless structural *explananda* are related to a theory of
action that delivers information about the social problems of actors and their
eventual solutions, no "social causation" can be discovered at all. My complaint
is not that Sanderson sees this differently, but rather that he satisfies himself
with testing his theses by (statistical) causal analyses.

To identify causes, causal analyses incline to "comparative studies"; the fact
should be familiar, however, that such comparative methods (on which Sanderson, too, sets his hopes) are, independently of the number of "cases" considered,

possible and profitable only when all causal influences (or all "causes") of a contingent *explanandum* are known.[67] In sociology this is quite out of the question, for which reason its practical testing leads with great regularity to the result that the assumed causal hypotheses are obviously *false*.[68] This is not a great matter, since most of the hypotheses formulated by the social sciences are false; but owing to the peculiarities of causal analyses, we do not know what we have overlooked and *why* our assumptions are faulty.[69] That is, *on the basis of causal analyses, we can establish no fruitful heuristic method of research.* In my view, in place of the testing of single causal hypotheses should be set work with *action-based models about evolutionary mechanisms* and the testing of their logical consequences, which is possible without correlational (or causal analytical) procedures. At any rate, the scientific basis of a genuine program of evolutionary research does *not* depend on the latter methods.

And further: Causal analytical procedures trust in the validity of induction; therefore Sanderson insists on the availability of "parallel evolutions"[70] that should secure a "broader basis" for his reflections. The underlying thesis then seems to be that knowledge of several identical (or at least comparable) results implies something about the truth (or about the reliability) of the assumed theses. I look upon such hopes as illusory, because as Karl R. Popper showed long ago, no inductive procedure (either as a procedure of derivation or of testing) can ensure truth. Whether induction opens a way of detecting interesting hypotheses is, to say the least, debatable.

CONCLUSION

I believe that, against Sanderson's intentions,[71] DCT is systematically incomplete because it operates (almost exclusively) with (biologically) *fixed interests* and *only a single mechanism of distribution*, for which reason it is difficult for me to judge it as a general theory (of "human sociality"). The sense in which it should be regarded as an "evolutionary" theory remains undisclosed to me; it is "evolutionary" in at most its efforts to found explanation in *sociobiology*; but the relation between action theory and sociobiology appears to me to be in need of clarification. In addition, it must be noted that DCT is committed to a faulty theory of testing and renounces the development of a *model theory of evolutionary mechanisms* that would allow for the development of a heuristically fruitful program of research.

On the credit side may be entered that DCT points out once more that the formation of society is not an arbitrarily malleable event (for instance, through "culturally guided processes of definition"), but is subject to constraints that result equally from (biologically) given capacities and goals of action of actors, from the inescapable scarcity of their (social as well as material) resources of action, and from the adverse consequences of their collective actions, to which they must indeed always "adapt" themselves, with whatever uncertain success. That sociology may not omit to explain (microfoundationally) exactly these relations is also my conviction, which is why I always welcome Stephen Sanderson's DCT, notwithstanding its limitations, as a valued ally in the struggle to achieve the "broad theoretical synthesis"[72] that I too envisage.

ACKNOWLEDGMENTS

This article was translated by Jonathan Uhlaner.

NOTES

1. Cf. Sanderson 1990.
2. Sanderson 1990, 223ff.
3. Sanderson 2001a, 1, 143.
4. Cf. Sanderson 2001a, 1ff.
5. Sanderson 2001a, ix.
6. Cf. Sanderson 2001b, 14281ff.
7. Cf. Sanderson 2001a, 83ff, 332.
8. Cf. Sanderson 1988, 41ff; 1995, 381ff.
9. Cf. Sanderson 2001a, 143-57.
10. Cf. Sanderson 2001a, 151.
11. Cf. Sanderson 2001a, 152.
12. Cf. Sanderson 2001a, 144, where he emphasizes the multilevel character of his theory.
13. I do not understand why "feelings" belong to the "superstructure" (Sanderson 2001a, 151) and not to the "biostructure," as Antonio Damasio proposed?
14. Sanderson 2001a, 151.
15. Sanderson 2001a, 151.
16. Cf. Sanderson 2001a, 147, 148.
17. Sanderson 2001a, 151.
18. Cf. Sanderson 2001a, 151.
19. Cf. Sanderson 1995, 12-13.
20. Sanderson 2001a, 152.
21. As an implication of the distinction between "adaptation" and "adaptiveness" (Sanderson 2001a, 148f), there is failure and "maladaptation"; cf. Sanderson 2001a, 129f.
22. Sanderson enters into this part of his argument only cursorily; cf. Sanderson 2001a, 322.
23. Sanderson 2001a, 2.
24. Sanderson 2001a, 2, 152.
25. Cf. Sanderson 1988 and Sanderson 1995. In my terminology, DCT may be called a "theory of action" which is applied to concrete historical circumstances in the form of a specific "model."
26. Sanderson 2001a, 154.
27. Cf. Sanderson 2001a, 155f.
28. Sanderson 2001a, 143.
29. Cf. Sanderson 2001a, 146.
30. Cf. the context of the argument in Sanderson 2001a, 331-32.

31. Sanderson 1995 presupposes that actors are "satisficing," whereas Sanderson 2001a, 182 speaks of "maximizing." I am uncertain whether Sanderson has noticed the irreconcilability of the two assumptions.

32. Sanderson 2001a, 121, 198.

33. Cf. Sanderson 1995, 391. Sanderson pretends that "[this ontological assumption] cannot be empirically evaluated," which I do not accept. Whether something exists or not can be inferred from our theories, and theories can be tested; if they are false, then the purported facts may not exist.

34. Of resources (as such), sociology has *nothing* to say. In order to discover how these things affect the opportunities of action, we need to consult a theory of action which tells us what the *problems* of actors are and by help of what *rules* they apply their technologies in order to solve these problems.

35. Cf. Sanderson 2001a, 331.

36. Cf. Sanderson 1997, 99.

37. Sanderson 2001a, 151.

38. Cf. Sanderson 1995, 8.

39. Cf. Sanderson 2001a, ix.

40. Cf. Sanderson 2001a, 155. That learning processes operate in specific domains, as Cosmides and Tooby repeatedly maintain, is surely right, but does not solve the problem here broached.

41. If we let "the genetic basis of learning" be "p," "learning processes" be "q," and "learning effects" (that is, changes in behavior) be "r," then p . q $\rightarrow$ r in fact obtains. If, however, p = constant, then the variability of "r" is *completely* explained by the variability of "q."

42. Sanderson 2001a, 148.

43. This is the place to ask why, in contrast to Sanderson 1988, 45, or Sanderson 1995, DCT renounces the ambition of being a "theory of cultural evolution"? And does the reluctance of DCT to treat group selection depend upon this self-restriction?

44. Cf. Sanderson 2001a, 151.

45. In the philosophy of evolutionary explanations, it has become customary, probably following Ernst Mayr, to distinguish between "proximate" and "ultimate" explanations (cf. Sanderson 2001a, 1f) and to satisfy oneself "ultimately" only with the latter, whereby "ultimately" means that action is explained by recourse to its positively selected genetic conditionedness. I look upon this position as a metaphysical conviction which is reminiscent of Engels's historical materialist thesis according to which all phenomena of human life can be reduced "in the last instance" to economic causes; unfortunately such a thesis cannot be disconfirmed.

46. DCT obviously shares this restriction with (some versions of) evolutionary psychology. Perhaps Sanderson could agree with the possible identification of (a set of quite diverse) "learned" (or "imprinted") programs (or "heuristics" and "frames") of action, as authors like Vanberg, Gigerenzer, Kahneman, Tversky, and others have proposed, and which may play an equivalent explanatory role as (genetically evolved) "biograms."

47. Cf. Sanderson 1995, 398.

48. If this condition does not obtain, I can make no rhyme of Sanderson's thesis according to which "adaptation" is called the process "whereby individuals originate (or inherit or borrow) social forms" which serve their "interests" and "needs"; cf. Sanderson 2001a, 148.

49. Cf. Sanderson 2001a, subtitle and 143f, 151, 331f.

50. Cf. Sanderson 1988, Sanderson 1990, and Sanderson 2001a.

51. Sanderson 1990, 223.

52. Sanderson 1995, x.

53. Sanderson 1995, 4.

54. Cf. Sanderson 1988, 11, and Sanderson 1995, 4, where he speaks of "long term social change" and of "directional sequences of change." That by this the (directional) change of *social formations* is meant is emphasized by Sanderson 2001a.

55. Sanderson 1997, 194 looks upon the attempts of Campbell, Langton, and Runciman as "misguided," but we do not learn why.

56. Cf. Sanderson 1995, 392f.

57. Cf. Sanderson 2001a, 331.

58. Sanderson 1995, 387, explains that he does not regard the concept of "natural selection" as adequate for the explanation of social evolution. But as Toulmin, van Parijs, and others have shown, not every selection process must be a sexual-reproductive one in Darwin's sense.

59. That such conflicts over "positional goods" can be solved *only* by help of dominance relations may be taken to be a typically Marxist *déformation professionelle* which simply does not see that lotteries, auctions, market competition, or gifts also have solutions in store.

60. Sanderson 1988, 45f still distinguishes between "parallel," "convergent," and "divergent" evolution; but already here he does not pursue the question on the basis of which *mechanisms* these different forms of social change result. That there could be various mechanisms Sanderson discusses at most in passing; thus he acknowledges that, in addition to fights over distribution, there are also (antagonistic) "cooperations" (Sanderson 1995, 398), but he does not specify the circumstances in which such forms of distribution prevail against "conflicts"; in view of the repeated admission that cooperation exists (cf. Sanderson 2001a, 149, 238f, 265ff, 300) it remains unclear why his DCT equates the "driving force" of human sociability with the presence of conflicts. Additionally he devotes little attention to the investigation of the sociobiological foundation of the division of labor and exchange; cf. Ofek 2001. A (sociological) theory of action may furthermore know that there will be *diverse kinds* of conflicts (e.g., zero-sum games, "battles of the sexes," "mixed motive games"), from which I infer that Sanderson's conflict theory is in need of specification. I am also rather uncertain whether his proposal can be accepted that societal conflicts could always be interpreted as "competitions" with self-corrective effects on efficiency (cf. Sanderson 2001a, 37).

61. Cf. Sanderson 1997, 94.

62. Cf. the subtitle of Sanderson 1995. It would be of interest to learn how Sanderson's "general theory of historical development" comes to grips with Popper's refutation of historicism; in Sanderson 1990, 34, he obviously accepts Popper's objections, so far as nineteenth-century theories of change are concerned.

63. This is how, at any rate, I understand the talk of the "evolutionary logic" (Sanderson 1995, 18) of social developments.

64. Cf. Sanderson 1995, 382ff.

65. Cf. Sanderson 1995, 5. Thus I contradict Sanderson's thesis that every evolutionary analysis has to be an historical analysis (Sanderson 1995, 6).

66. Sanderson evidently regards high correlations as a valid indication of causalities; cf. Sanderson 2001a, 315. In fact, correlations can only be taken as a confirmation of causal relations when the "generative mechanism" is known; consequently by *defining* a mechanism as a "causal correlation" (cf. Sanderson 1995, 8), Sanderson somehow misses this point.

67. Sanderson 2001a, 314, sees that there is no complete catalog of causes and effects, but he does not revise his test theory.

68. Sanderson emphasizes continually that his tests explain only a part of the variance to be explained and speaks of the necessity for further research – but this is to say that the theses discussed are demonstrably *false*. That this fault cannot be remedied within the framework of causal analyses is documented by the evidently *interminable* debates about the "causes" of capitalism, of agricultural production, of feudalism, of states and revolutions, and so forth.

69. Sanderson seems to admit this (cf. Sanderson 2001a, 233, 270, 314) and also notices that many hypotheses, which are proposed to save questionable causal assumptions, are *ad hoc*.

70. Cf. Sanderson 1995, 68f, 381f; Sanderson 2001a, 39.

71. Cf. Sanderson 1995, 1.

72. Sanderson 2001a, ix.

3

METAPHYSICAL
MATERIALISM

Some Critical Remarks on Sanderson's
The Evolution of Human Sociality

Nico Wilterdink

Stephen Sanderson's *The Evolution of Human Sociality* represents one of the very few serious efforts to bring sociobiology (or, more broadly, neo-Darwinian evolutionary theory) and sociological theory together. The book is much more than just a plea for sociobiology by a social scientist. It deals, not only with aspects of social life that are supposed to be common to all human societies, but combines sociobiology with sociology in order to explain social variations and social change as well. On this account, Sanderson's book is original and innovative. It offers a new, synthetic perspective which promises to bring sociology a step forward.

However, this proposal for a new synthesis is, in my view, not successful in all respects. Though it distances itself from any simplistic biological reductionism, the alternative it offers is neither wholly clear nor entirely convincing. This has to do, I think, with Sanderson's overly polemical stance against "culturalism" and his corresponding defense of "materialism" as the basis of the human sciences. This black-white opposition of materialism and culturalism, I will argue, is misleading, and it hinders a proper understanding of the interconnections between different aspects and levels of human social reality. For this reason I am inclined to call Sanderson's materialism metaphysical in the Comtean sense: a conviction not based on empirical observations that impedes rather than helps scientific understanding. My critique will focus on two main points: (1) Sanderson's distinction of four "basic subunits" in human societies, and (2) his implicit assumptions about the causal connections between biological dispositions, individual actions, and social outcomes, particularly as applied to human sexual and reproductive behavior. I will argue in this paper that on both counts Sanderson's

42

theoretical perspective has shortcomings, and I will suggest better answers to the questions that are raised in this connection. In this way I hope to contribute to a better understanding of the actual and potential contributions of behavioral biology and Darwinian evolutionary theory to our insights into the problems that are central for sociology.

FROM BIOSTRUCTURE TO SUPERSTRUCTURE: SANDERSON'S EXPLANATORY SCHEME

Sanderson (2001a, 150-51) distinguishes four "basic subunits," or explanatory levels, in human societies:

- The *biostructure*, consisting of individuals "as biological organisms," and referring particularly to "the deep wellsprings of human action" that are the outcome of biological evolution and that can only be explained by their functions for human survival and reproduction.
- The *ecostructure*, i.e., the ecological, demographic, technological, and economic structures essential for survival and well-being.
- The *(social) structure*, i.e., the institutionalized patterns of behavior concerning, in particular, family and kinship, social inequality, and political power.
- The *(cultural) superstructure*, i.e., the beliefs, values, and norms shared by the members of a society.

The biostructure is the deepest level in the sense that it contains the necessary conditions for phenomena on the other levels, whereas the cultural superstructure is dependent on the levels beneath it. In Sanderson's words, the "four components of societies are related such that the flow of causation is primarily from the biostructure to the ecostructure, then from the ecostructure to the structure, and finally from the structure to the superstructure; the flow may sometimes occur in the reverse manner, or in some other manner, but these causal dynamics occur much less frequently" (2001a, 150). On this basis, three types of sociological explanation are distinguished, all of them of a "materialist," i.e., nonculturalist, nature: *biomaterialist* explanations, in which social phenomena are caused by elements in the biostructure; *ecomaterialist* explanations, which refer to causation by the ecostructure; and *polimaterialist* explanations, which locate the causative factors in the (social) structure, but primarily in political interests and goals. The distinction follows the logic in which biological characteristics have causal priority, but it also implies a rejection of biological reductionism: Higher layers have a certain relative autonomy with respect to the deeper ones.

This conceptual scheme is, of course, reminiscent of the Marxian dichotomy of the economic base and the spiritual superstructure. More directly, it is inspired by Marvin Harris's threefold distinction of infrastructure, structure, and superstructure (Harris 1979; 1993). Sanderson largely takes over this typology, to which he adds a fourth, "deeper" level of biological species traits. His explanatory scheme may be regarded as an attempt to synthesize Harris's cultural materialism with behavioral biology. With Harris's model and the original Marxian scheme it has both attractive features and basic weaknesses in common. The attractive side is that it gives a neat ordering of a wide array of human phenomena and suggests general guidelines on how to explain them. The problematic side is that the grounds for this ordering and these guidelines are not very firm. I see three fundamental problems.

First, the distinction of four societal "subunits" is questionable since it draws quite arbitrary lines, suggesting divisions that do not correspond to any observable reality; it brings together under one name elements of reality that can and should be distinguished and, on the other hand, it separates elements that conceptually belong together. Thus, insofar as the "ecostructure" refers to humans' natural environment (including climate, wild plants and animals, soil and water), it is not a subunit of human society, but, indeed, is its environment, to which it must adapt. Economic relations, on the other hand, which Sanderson also regards as belonging to the "ecostructure," are aspects of social relations and cannot be separated, therefore, from the social structure. Technology, which Sanderson also places in the "ecostructure," refers to socially shared and learned knowledge and is therefore, according to a common sociological definition, part of culture (cf. Lenski, Nolan, and Lenski 1995, 42; Lenski 2005, 63). More generally, the distinction between "culture" and "social structure" implied by Sanderson's model is problematic since human social relations ("structure") always involve norms, learned preferences, knowledge, and symbols – in short, culture. This general point can also, and has been, leveled as a critique of the Marxian distinction of the "real structure," consisting of the forces and relations of production, and the spiritual or ideological superstructure, the realm of the mind. It is hard to see how people can produce material things without having ideas, knowledge, and thoughts about how to do that (cf. Elias 1971, 149-56). Knowledge and ideas are not separate from but part of the production of material goods. The "materialism" in Marxist historical materialism is an unclear category, and the same is true, I would argue, for Sanderson's materialism, which continues this tradition.[1]

Second, Sanderson gives no clear argument for his statement that the causal chain is predominantly from the biostructure through the ecostructure and the social structure to the cultural superstructure. The biostructure, if it is defined as "individuals themselves as biological organisms" (2001a, 150), crucially depends on the social relations individuals have with one another (the social structure), as well as on the ways they have learned to cope with their environment (which is part of their culture): Human individuals "as organisms" can only survive in groups that have patterned social relations and common cultural traits. Similarly, and related to that, demographic patterns and developments, which are defined as part of the ecostructure, are strongly influenced by social-structural changes. Thus, the demographic transition in Western societies, i.e., the strong population growth and subsequent decrease of the growth rate since the late nineteenth century, can be explained by its connection to modernization processes in which intertwined changes in technology, production, education, relations between men and women, state organization, family structures, and moral norms all played a part (Chesnais 1992).

A third problem is that, in contrast to the proclaimed evolutionary approach, the four components are conceived in static terms. This makes it difficult if not impossible to assess how they are causally connected. The metaphor of "deeper" (more basic) and "higher" (more dependent) levels of reality becomes more useful if the phenomena thus distinguished are conceived in dynamic terms, as processes: The processes on the deeper level precede and condition but do not determine the processes on the higher level. A relevant and clear distinction to be made on this basis is that between changes in the human genetic structure and changes in human culture; or, in other words, between biological and sociocultural evolution.[2] Biological evolution is the more encompassing process; it preceded, and created the conditions for, human sociocultural development which is relatively autonomous in relation to (i.e., cannot be reduced to) biological evolution (cf. Spier 1996; Trigger 1998; Wilterdink 2003). Sociocultural characteristics of human societies, once developed, in turn had an impact on natural selection processes and, as a consequence, on biological or "genic" evolution. The process of hominization that resulted in modern *Homo sapiens* was a gene-culture coevolutionary process (E. O. Wilson 1998, 128), or one in which both processes were intertwined. These interconnected processes are still going on, though the tempo of sociocultural change is much faster than that of biological evolution, particularly since the beginnings of agricultural food production about 11,000 years ago. We may say that sociocultural processes have become more autonomous with respect to biological evolution in the course of human history as humans learned to control natural forces more effectively, including the natural forces in their own bodies. A recent step in this "expanding anthroposphere" (Goudsblom 2002) is the development of knowledge by which humans are able to manipulate their own genetic structures. We can only guess what the consequences of this new cultural development will be.

My criticisms are not intended as an argument for a return to a culturalist perspective, which takes culture (norms and values, religious beliefs, discourses, etc.) as given and explains cultural traits, in a near-tautological fashion, only by connecting them to other cultural traits. Sanderson is fully right and convincing in his criticism of such a position. He is also right, I think, in pointing out the significance of biological, precultural human species traits that may be the basis of various culture-mediated human actions and social relations, even though these traits cannot fully explain them. However, the connections between biological dispositions, individual actions, and the social outcomes of these actions are somewhat more complicated than may be derived from Sanderson's book. This I will try to show in the next section by focusing on human sexual and reproductive behavior.

SEXUALITY AND REPRODUCTION: CONNECTIONS BETWEEN
BIOLOGICAL DISPOSITIONS, INDIVIDUAL ACTIONS,
AND SOCIAL PROCESSES

In order to explain human social phenomena one may start with biological dispositions that are supposed to be determined, to a large extent, by the human organism's genetic structure and to have a function for survival and reproduction. This does not imply, however, that the social phenomena in question are a direct reflection of the (supposed) biological dispositions, or that they have a direct function for survival and reproduction. The distinction between the "ultimate" explanation of behavioral phenomena in functional evolutionary terms and their "proximate" causation by environmental stimuli is crucial, but even this is not sufficient to account for human actions and social processes. Distinctions have to be made between (a) biological dispositions that are explained ultimately by their functions for survival and reproduction; (b) human actions that are to be explained primarily in terms of more or less conscious motives (goals, desires, intentions, preferences), learned knowledge and capacities, and situational stimuli and constraints; and (c) social processes that are the intended and unintended consequences of human actions and that have feedback effects on subsequent actions and, therefore, on human survival and reproduction. Biological dispositions, individual actions, and social processes are causally related in nondeterministic ways. A crucial question in the relation between (a) and (b) is how biological dispositions are translated, transformed, and molded into actual preferences through social learning processes. The central question in the relation between (b) and (c) is how the actions and interactions of many interdependent human beings lead to social outcomes that are largely unforeseen and unintended (cf. Elias 1978). Sanderson does not enter into these questions, at least not explicitly and systematically, thereby simplifying the connections between biological dispositions, individual actions, and social processes. Though he rejects biological determinism, his statements on various aspects of human social life often go a good ways in that direction – too far, in my view.

This can be illustrated by Sanderson's analysis of human sexuality and reproduction. The basic evolutionary explanation of sexuality (or, more specifically, heterosexual mating) is that it exists because it serves the genes' reproduction. On this basis Sanderson (2001a, 178-93) claims, in line with the tenets of sociobiology and evolutionary psychology, that variations in human sexual behavior and sexual preferences, particularly between men and women, can be explained by their functions for the maximization of genetic reproduction chances. Thus, men are usually attracted to young women with certain bodily characteristics (such as a waist-to-hip ratio of about 0.7) since these are indications of fecundity. Women tend to prefer men who signal strength, vitality, or certain special abilities, be it physical strength, intelligence, verbal capacities, power, status, or income, since such attributes are signs of genetic fitness that will enhance the chances of genetically fit offspring and also indicate the possession of resources that can be used to support offspring. Women are more choosy than men in engaging in (hetero)sexual relations since they can get only a limited number of children and have to invest much more than men in each child. Men, more than women, desire sex with different partners since this will enhance their reproductive chances (they are "by nature polygynous," Sanderson 2001a, 246, writes), whereas women tend to seek a stable sexual relationship that will bind the father to the support of their children. Men are emotionally jealous when they find their partner having a sexual affair with another man, since this immediately diminishes their reproductive potential, whereas women tend to be more jealous when they find their partner to be affectively (rather than sexually) involved with another woman, since this is a threat to the continuation of his support for their (actual and potential) children.

These propositions are sound derivations from evolutionary theory, and they are corroborated by some empirical evidence (e.g., Buss 1989, 1994; cf. Freese, Li, and Wade 2003, 238-40). Yet they leave a lot of questions open. They hardly consider individual and collective variations in sexual preferences and behavior within the same sex-age categories. Empirical evidence suggests that these variations are considerable and that there is usually a strong overlap between the observed preferences and behavioral traits of men and women within a given group or society. For instance, Buss's investigation of sex differences in human mate preferences "in 37 cultures" does not only show sex-related differences in averages but also considerable variation within the sexes and overlap between them. Moreover, *both* sexes in all samples in this investigation considered "kindness" and "intelligence" as the most desirable traits in potential mates (Buss 1989, 13).

The evolutionary explanation of sexual behavior and desires as serving genetic reproduction goes astray when homosexuality is considered. More generally, biological-evolutionary theory is unable to account sufficiently for the wide variety of sexual norms and practices among human groups and societies. A universal tendency in human societies is that of male-female pair-bonding and its normative regulation and ritual affirmation in what is called the institution of marriage. On the basis of Darwinian evolutionary theory this might be explained as a consequence of the male reproductive interest in sexual exclusiveness, a guarantee for biological parenthood (or, in other words, as a male device to control female sexuality), combined with the female reproductive interest in getting support and resources for actual and expected offspring. However, this does not explain the strong *variation* in marriage rules and customs and, more broadly, in sexual morality and sexual practices among human societies and groups.

Given the universal genetic interest in maximum reproduction, why is it, for example, that groups in different societies proclaimed and put into practice norms and ideals of chastity and sexual abstinence? Was the West for a long time a "sex-negative society," as Sanderson (2001a, 185) writes, and if so, why? How could "the sex-negative religion of Christianity" (2001a, 185) become so influential in Western societies? And how and why did prevailing sexual norms and practices change over time? Why, for example, were these norms and practices in the Victorian Age so different from those in the European Middle Ages (cf. Duby 1994; Betzig 1995), and why did they change radically again in the twentieth century (Wouters 2004)? In order to answer such sociological questions, one cannot stick to a "biomaterialist" (or even an "ecomaterialist" or "polimaterialist") explanation. Apparently human sexual orientations and practices are much more culturally malleable than Sanderson suggests.

Even if human sexuality could be explained by the genes' "interests" in reproduction, this does not mean that people have sex "in order to promote their reproductive success," as Sanderson writes (2001a, 147). Proximate reasons for sexual behavior (bodily pleasure, expression of feelings of personal affection, material rewards, conformity to social expectations) are usually very different from ultimate evolutionary functions. Animals enter into sexual mating without being aware of its function for reproduction. Only humans have developed, as part of their culture, knowledge about this connection: Therefore they can use the wish to get a child as a conscious motive for sexual mating. But it is on the basis of this same knowledge that they are able to *disconnect* purposefully sexuality and reproduction. As we know, this is what people have done for ages and particularly since the demographic transition that started in Western Europe about a century and a half ago. The disconnection of sexuality and reproduction has been facilitated by technical inventions, such as contraceptive pills that found widespread application since the 1960s. It is particularly since that decade that sex is often regarded as a goal in itself, an activity just for the pleasure it brings, or as the emotional affirmation of an enduring intimate relationship.

In order to maintain the assumption that human beings always strive for the maximization of their genes' reproduction, Sanderson argues that the limitation of the number of offspring by contraception is a strategy to enhance reproductive success: When parents have fewer children, they can invest more in each of them and thereby strengthen the children's survival, status, and reproductive chances. The main cause of the decline of fertility in modern societies was the decline of infant mortality, to which people adapted by birth control. The "biomaterialist argument," Sanderson firmly states, is "the only viable explanation of declining fertility" (2001a, 176). This conclusion is highly questionable for several reasons. To begin with, a substantial and growing proportion of the adult population in Western societies choose *not to have* children; in particular, women who wish to give priority to their own professional careers often prefer that option (Rossi 1987, 42). Reproductive success is not the same as social success, and people compete for social rather than reproductive success, as childless "career women" exemplify. People with children usually try to enhance their children's *social* success, and the limitation of the number of children may be interpreted, to some extent, as a strategy to do so; but this is different from enhancing their own, or their children's, *reproductive* success (Barkow and Burley 1980; Vining 1986).

If people in modern prosperous societies would be really intent on maximizing their genes' reproduction, they would produce far more offspring than they actually do: The high level of material prosperity and social and medical care would enable them to have an extraordinarily large number of healthy children, many more than in the poorer societies of the present or the past. Actually the fertility rate (i.e., the average number of children a woman will have during her lifetime) in most highly industrialized countries today is far less than two, which means that the population is declining or will decline in the near future unless immigration compensates for this trend.[3] In contrast, population growth is relatively high in most poor countries; in terms of biological reproduction, these countries are the most successful ones. The population of the world's poorest continent, Africa, more than quadrupled in the period 1950-2005 (from 224 to 906 million), whereas Europe's population grew only 33 percent in this period (from 534 to 728 million), and is expected to decline in the next fifty years.[4] According to a recent United Nations estimate, the total population in the "more developed" regions of the world will remain almost constant between 2005 and 2050, despite immigration, which means that their share in total world population will drop from 18.6 percent to 13.6 percent; the population of the "least developed" countries, by contrast, will nearly double in this period, which means that their share in total world population will rise from 11.9 percent to 19.1 percent.[5]

A negative correlation between wealth and income on the one hand and birth rates and population growth on the other was first observed in the second half of the nineteenth century, when social Darwinists (among them, Darwin himself[6]) began to worry about the fact that the lower classes within industrial societies grew absolutely and relatively in numbers because of high birth rates and declining mortality. With the general expansion of education and the growth of incomes in industrial societies in the course of the twentieth century, demographic class-related differences largely disappeared, and population growth slowed down. At the same time, declining mortality rates in poorer countries pushed population growth in these countries and in the world as a whole upward, which in turn contributed to the growing wealth gap between rich and poor countries.

A strong positive relation between access to resources and survival (individual fitness) on the one hand and reproductive success (inclusive fitness) on the other is characteristic of living organisms in general, and is an essential mechanism of evolution. It has been continued by humans during the greater part of their history, when it took the form of a positive correlation (particularly among males) between wealth, power, and status on the one hand, and the number of surviving children on the other. Since the nineteenth century, however, this relation has been radically reversed: first within industrial societies, subsequently on the global level. More clearly and more dramatically than anything else, this demonstrates how far humans, as a result of sociocultural developments, have removed themselves from the evolutionary past in which their basic biological traits were formed.

Human sexual and reproductive behavior is a clear case in which it can be shown that, on the one hand, assumptions about biological dispositions are indispensable as a basis for explaining behavior and its social consequences, and, on the other hand, the causal relationships between these dispositions, actual behavior, and social outcomes are nondeterministic, variable, and changing over time, depending on conditions produced by humans themselves. Humans distinguish themselves from other animals in that they are much more active and effective in changing their environment, which includes the natural (living and nonliving) world, man-made artifacts, and the social world they form with one another. This is connected to distinctly human species characteristics, in particular the extraordinary capacities for learning and symbolic communication, which are the biological basis for the formation of cumulative culture.

Changes in the environment by human action are only partially the result of planned, intentional, collective action. Social developments in the long run are the largely unintended results of the actions of vast numbers of competing and cooperating individuals with their own intentions and interests. Population trends illustrate this: They are the unplanned outcomes of actions and decisions on the micro (individual and family) level, with unintended social consequences. The collective trends may lead to feedback responses, for example policy measures intended to increase or decrease the birthrate.

In the analysis and explanation of such collective trends, we are quite far removed from biological dispositions and genetic interests. If this is already true for demographic trends, it applies even more to topics that are central to sociology, such as trends in social inequality, migration flows, crime rates, industrial relations, or the institutions of the welfare state. Yet even for these topics, evolutionary biology is not irrelevant; it may have a place in sociological explanations, as Sanderson has shown. But in order to give it a proper place, one has to keep to a central assumption which justifies sociology as a relatively autonomous science: that human beings are cultural animals, equipped with social brains with which they have changed and continue to change, through cooperation and competition, intentionally and unintentionally, their environment and themselves far beyond the ordeals of their genes.

NOTES

1. Marxist "historical materialism" is different from the tradition of philosophical materialism originating in Greek antiquity, which holds that all of reality consists of nothing but matter, to the exclusion of nonmaterial spirits, gods, souls, and minds. There is a historical connection between these two kinds of materialism, particularly through the "dialectical" relation of Marxian theory with Hegelian idealism. After Marx, Engels and other Marxists tried to incorporate philosophical materialism into an all-encompassing Marxist philosophy. Today, the notion of materialism in philosophy seems to be somewhat outdated since, according to modern physics, matter is not the basic reality but a changeable form of energy.

2. This is, of course, a well-known distinction. It is also used by Sanderson in his work on social evolution, including his most recent book (Sanderson 2007c). But it is telling that he speaks of "social" instead of "cultural" or "sociocultural" evolution, though the latter terms express the difference with biological evolution more clearly. Strictly speaking, "social" evolution (i.e., evolutionary changes in the relations between

members of the same species) overlaps with both biological and cultural evolution (Wilterdink 2003, 55-56).

3. The fertility rate of all "developed" countries taken together is estimated at 1.58 in 2006, that of the entire world 2.58, and that of the "least developed" countries 4.08 (UN-FPA, *State of the World Population 2006*, URL www.unfpa.org).

4. Sources: *Encyclopedia of Population*, 2003; United Nations, *World Population Prospects*, 2005.

5. Source: see note 3.

6. In his *The Descent of Man* (1871); cf. Hermans 2003, 185ff.

4

DARWINIAN CONFLICT THEORY

Alternative Theoretical Strategy or Unifying Paradigm for Contemporary Sociology?

Rosemary L. Hopcroft

In his book *The Evolution of Human Sociality*, Stephen Sanderson presents Darwinian conflict theory as an alternative to older sociological theoretical traditions. Rather than being a specific theory of one particular phenomenon, it is a theoretical strategy or grand paradigm, giving ultimate answers to sociological questions. The theoretical strategy is premised on the idea that humans and human behavior are a production of evolution by natural selection. It is therefore explicitly reductionist: "Macrolevel phenomena are ultimately to be explained in terms of microlevel factors" (Sanderson 2001a, 152). Sanderson gives us a series of propositions based on this premise. These propositions concern the nature of individual predispositions, relations between groups, the makeup of human societies, and how societies change. To support his Darwinian conflict theoretical strategy, Sanderson draws on a great deal of anthropological and cross-cultural evidence on reproductive behavior, sex and gender, marriage and the family, economic systems, social stratification, and politics and war.

I have two problems with Sanderson's Darwinian conflict theoretical strategy. First, it is presented as a marriage of micro and macro, Darwinism and Marxian historical materialism, that can be used to explain aggregate societal phenomena. However, the propositions of this theoretical strategy are purposefully presented as "broad-grained" ideas that must be fully fleshed out with particulars of individual cases. This means that very few specific hypotheses about the relationships between measurable factors can be made using the approach; thus to my mind Darwinian conflict theory is not a theoretical strategy at all, but a series of orienting statements (Homans 1964). In my view, the real theoretical strategy Sanderson uses is sociobiological and evolutionary psychological – a *micro-level*, not a *macro-level* – paradigm. This micro paradigm, which can be broadly called a Darwinian paradigm, readily lends itself to producing testable hypotheses. That being said, Sanderson's propositions or orienting statements are a useful guide to macrosociological research.

Second, I suggest that Sanderson's book is incomplete. In making his case for his paradigm, Sanderson draws primarily on the work of anthropologists, historians, and psychologists. This means that his evidential focus is on past societies, preindustrial societies, or psychological studies of individual preferences and behaviors (in both preindustrial and contemporary societies). Notably absent are large-scale, empirical studies of contemporary industrial societies – the stuff of the vast majority of contemporary sociological research in the United States. Most of this research is motivated by no theory, or by small-scale theories of particular social phenomena. Yet if Sanderson's DCT is to be the grand paradigm that he suggests it is, then it should be able to explain and account for the empirical findings of contemporary sociological research. I contend that this is possible, at least using the Darwinian microtheoretical principles on which his perspective is based. There is a vast quantity of empirical findings in contemporary sociology that can be organized and unified by these principles. Currently, mainstream sociology is where biology was before evolutionary theory – an empiricist, classifying discipline. I further suggest that perhaps Sanderson should write a second book where he organizes and unifies the empirical findings of contemporary sociology using Darwinian principles, along the lines suggested in this paper.

In what follows, I amplify the evidence for the Darwinian paradigm using contemporary sociological research from two areas – marriage and the family and social stratification. Most of this evidence is drawn from empirical studies using data collected on the United States, but the Darwinian paradigm is likely to be applicable to studies using data collected in other advanced industrial societies as well. There is of course some overlap with points Sanderson makes himself.

KIN SELECTION AND THE SOCIOLOGY OF MARRIAGE AND THE FAMILY

The premise underlying Sanderson's DCT is that human physiology and psychology have evolved by natural selection. Thus, Hamilton's rule (Hamilton 1964), which applies to nonhuman organisms, also applies to humans. Hamilton's rule states that a costly action should be performed if

$$C < R \times B$$

where C is the cost to the actor, R the genetic relatedness between the actor and the recipient, and B the benefit to the recipient. Costs and benefits are measured in fertility – reproductive success or number of surviving offspring. So altruism to genetic relatives is not altruism per se, but genetically selfish behavior.

This means that individuals who share genes are likely to behave in a helpful and kindly fashion to each other, because by doing so they help ensure their own genetic reproduction. Those individuals who do help their genetic relatives are likely to leave more descendents than those individuals without this behavioral trait, and thus this trait is selected for and becomes universal. Helping genetic relatives is referred to as *kin selection*. For sociologists, biological kin selection can explain the altruistic behavior of parents toward their children, as well as the bonds that often bind members of nuclear and extended families. These bonds include the bonds between husbands and wives, who share genetic interests in their joint (and/or future) children and are therefore motivated to cooperate to promote those interests.

As Sanderson notes, just as with all other species, kin-based altruism is always contingent on circumstance (Hrdy 1999), which means that not all people are likely to be altruistic to all of their relatives all of the time. But it does mean that altruistic behavior of individuals to their genetic relatives will be apparent, on average. For example, while it is true that some human mothers in some circumstances kill their offspring, most human mothers do not and instead love and care for their children. Nonkin can and do care for each other, but they are less likely to do so than kin. Kin-based altruism explains why the family, a relatively small group of individuals with overlapping genetic interests, is the most enduring and cohesive social group across all known human societies (Brown 1991; Lopreato and Crippen 1999, 172).

Contemporary sociological research has identified many of the proximate mechanisms through which kin-based altruism can operate, including conscious motivations, acceptance of particular values and roles, self-identity, and emotions and feelings. The goal of kin selection need not be conscious, and usually individuals are only aware of the proximate mechanisms. That is, people are likely to be aware of the fact that they helped their children because they loved them, or because they wanted to be a good parent, or that they learned how to be a parent by watching their own parents, and so on, but they are not likely to be aware of their deep biologically driven motivations rooted in kin selection. In fact, in many cases of parenting, such as saving a child from toppling down a staircase, parents won't "think" at all, they will just do (Massey 2002).

The principle of biological kin selection can explain the findings from the contemporary sociology of marriage and the family that "marriage is good for you" (Waite 2000). Married people live longer, healthier lives, and are less likely to suffer mental illness than unmarried people. This can be explained by the beneficial effects of cooperation and altruism between married partners, and, when children are involved, between children, parents, and other relatives who often pitch in. Kin selection can also explain why children help create stability in the family (Manning 2004). Children create shared genetic interests in the family, as both father and mother have an equal genetic stake in their children. This encourages cooperation between parents (and other relatives) and joint investment in children. Research shows that the stabilizing effect of children on a couple's relationships occurs with or without legal marriage (Manning 2004). This is again consistent with the kin selection principle. There does not need to be a formal legal tie between parents for both parents to cooperate and invest in their joint offspring.

In the United States, divorce (and/or separation) disrupts this joint investment in children, and divorce has been shown to have negative effects on children (Amato and Cheadle 2005; Carlson 2006). Remarriage does not ameliorate these problems. Children brought up in other arrangements receive less education and have lower occupational achievement than children brought up by their biological parents or even by their mother alone (Cherlin and Furstenberg 1994; Biblarz and Raftery 1999; Case, Lin, and McLanahan 2001; Furstenberg, Hoffman, and Shrestha 1995).

Questions about the adaptiveness of contemporary fertility behavior (e.g., Vining 1986; Hopcroft 2006a) do not threaten the more general point of biological kin selection and its centrality in all human societies. Whereas evolutionary psychologists suggest that individuals may be kin selectors while not genetic fitness maximizers (Pérusse 1993), and sociobiologists stick to their guns about fitness maximization (Betzig 1993), these debates within the evolutionary community do not have to be resolved for sociology to find the principle of biological kin selection useful to explain sociological findings, as discussed above. Regardless of precisely how adaptive current fertility and parenting behaviors are, the physiological and psychological apparatus to promote kin selection is in place (for example, the biochemical basis for mother-infant bonding and for emotions). So are the physiological and psychological apparatuses to promote gender asymmetry.

Gender Asymmetry

The principle of altruism to one's genetic relatives because it promotes reproduction of one's genes has implications for gender differences in parenting behaviors. This is because of sexual reproduction. Among sexually reproducing species (such as our own), one sex typically shoulders a greater burden of the biological cost of parenting. In our species, as in many others, it is the female (although there are exceptions). The female provides the larger (and rarer) gamete, and must bear the biological costs of carrying a fetus to term, undergoing childbirth, and then the physiological costs of nursing. The male's biological contribution to the offspring is by comparison trivial – a few of the tiny and abundant male gametes. What this means is that from a biological point of view, the female's investment in any child is much greater than the male investment. The high costs of childbearing for females means that each child represents a greater proportion of total possibilities for gene replication for the female than for the male. For the female, then, from a biological perspective each child is more precious than for the male.

Evolutionary psychologists suggest that these differences in genetic interests have led to distinct male and female psychologies with respect to mating and parenting behavior. From the female point of view, given that the male's fixed investment in offspring is so small, it is in her reproductive interests to find a male as a mate who is willing (and able) to invest in nonbiological ways in her offspring. Even so adamant a critic of biological explanations of social behavior as Stephen Jay Gould concedes as much: "This principle of differential 'parental investment' makes Darwinian sense and probably does underlie some different, and broadly general, emotional propensities of human males and females" (Gould 2000, 121).

These different emotional propensities of men and women can explain sex differences in criteria for mate selection. Women typically prefer mates who offer love, commitment, resources, and status (Buss 1989; Buunk, Dijkstra, Fetchenhauer, and Kenrick 2002; see also Sanderson 2001a, 179), as this amounts to a promise to help (and an ability to help) in the childrearing process. Even women who earn a great deal of money themselves are interested in men who earn at least as much as they do (Blumstein and Schwartz 1983; Buss 1989; Buss, Abbott, Angleitner, Asherian, and Biaggio 1990). Sociologists Blumstein and Schwartz (1983, 326) note that women "still want their partners to achieve. When they enter the world of work, they do not want him to leave. Women want to look up to, or at least directly across at, their male partner if they are to respect him." Sociological research in the United States shows that males are also interested in resources in a mate, but not as much as females (Brattner and Raley 2004). Marriage timing has long been determined by the economic position of men, not women (Oppenheimer 2000; Sweeney 2002). Males are comparatively more interested in youth and beauty in a mate, as these are correlates of the ability of a female to successfully bear children.

The evolutionary psychologists contend that these *psychologies are independent of actual child-bearing behavior,* given modern technology and effective contraception. That is, even when no child is likely to be forthcoming, females will still prefer higher-status over lower-status males as long-term mates, all else equal, and males will still prefer younger and more beautiful mates. These psychologies together can explain the typical pattern across all cultures of women marrying up in age and status, while men marry younger women, on average (Buss 1999).

Given societal contexts, this evolved psychology can also explain changes in the patterns of marriage and the family. For example, there is cross-cultural evidence to suggest that women are less likely to prefer a mate with material resources when they have their own resources to support themselves (Eagly and Wood 1999). In the contemporary United States, however, this does not seem to be the case. Women still highly value resources in their mates (Bratter and Raley 2004). The correlation between husband's earnings and wife's wages has increased (Sweeney and Cancian 2004), suggesting that neither men nor women are valuing their partner's earning ability less (England 2004). There is evidence that males have become more interested in resources in their mates (Bratter and

Raley 2004), and families have become more egalitarian given the increasing incorporation of women into the paid labor force (Davis and Greenstein 2004). In terms of education, marriage has increasingly become a union of equals (Schoen and Cheng 2006). This trend is more true of the United States than other advanced industrial societies (Kalmijn 1998).

But the disjuncture in the priority placed on the earning capabilities of men and women persists. Male employment status and earnings remain important for marriage formation in contemporary developed societies (Oppenheimer 2000; Sweeney 2002; Goldscheider and Sassler 2004; Carlson, McLanahan, and England 2004), and there is a greater likelihood of divorce when wives earn more than husbands (see Sayer and Bianchi 2000 for a summary of studies). The absence of female earnings does not have the same effect, on average, on marital stability. In the American family, husbands are still disproportionately major providers for the family (Raley, Mattingly, and Bianchi 2006), and fathers on average still spend more hours in paid work than mothers (Nomaguchi, Milkie, and Bianchi 2005).

Age preferences of men and women are one reason why unmarried households in the United States are much more likely to be female-headed than male-headed, because divorced men are more likely to remarry than divorced women. Women's chances of remarriage drop quickly as they age. Marriage and divorce patterns resemble a recycling of marriageable men, where highly educated, high-earning men go on to remarry more often than comparable women (Blumstein and Schwartz 1983, 32).

Gender asymmetry in reproduction can explain the typical pattern of women being more committed to their children and more likely to care for their children in difficult circumstances, such as when the child is disabled (Cohen and Petrescu-Prahova 2006). It can explain why "women provide for children's needs, whether or not the women are married to their children's fathers. For men, marriage defines responsibilities to children. At divorce, men typically disengage from their biological children" (Seltzer 1994, 235). It can also explain why it is mothers who typically end up with custody of the children after separation or divorce.

It is important to note that the stuff of most sociological theories – *values, norms, roles, etc., remain important and are not superseded by biological factors*. For example, in the United States the value of marriage is an important predictor of whether an individual marries or not, and the value of marriage has declined for men over the last 30 years (Goldscheider and Sassler 2004). Partly as a result, marriage occurs more infrequently and at later ages than it used to. The rise of cohabitation in place of legal marriage has been a notable trend in both North America and Europe. This can be explained by a variety of changes in the material and social environment in both places – the existence of effective birth control, the rise in divorce rates, the lengthening of the amount of education needed to obtain stable employment, and so on. Social embeddedness theories argue for the importance of culture and social structure in explaining differences in marital and family behavior across cultures, for example, why cohabitation in the United States tends to be brief, whereas in Sweden it tends to be much longer (Cherlin 2000).

Yet none of these points – the importance of values and material and social environments – is incompatible with biology. The persistence and universality of some form of pair-bonded couple (whether formally married or not) across diverse social and material environments can be explained by biology. The variation can readily be explained by the existence of a human biopsychology that promotes pair-bonding in conjunction with particular social and economic conditions. The pair bond is a human universal; how it takes place depends on society and circumstance (Brown 1991). Similarly, the importance of kin has changed in various ways as families have become more mobile and geographically separated. But why people are typically altruistic to their kin is explained by the biological concept of kin selection.

DARWINISM AND SOCIAL STRATIFICATION

Darwinian principles also can help explain the findings of contemporary research on stratification by sex, class, and status.

Stratification by Sex

The asymmetrical investment of males and females in offspring helps explain stratification by sex. Both parents share fifty percent of their genes with their offspring, but females are always 100 percent sure that their children are their own, whereas for men there is always an element of doubt. This is called the problem of *paternity uncertainty*. Given this element of uncertainty, it is always more in male reproductive interests to control female sexuality than vice versa (Hrdy 1997; Sanderson 2001a, 182). Parents, aware of the male interest in paternity certainty and having an interest in ensuring that their daughters find good long-term mates, are motivated to attempt to control the sexuality of these daughters in order to improve their value on the marriage market. This promotes the double standard in sexual practices, where boys are given a great deal of freedom in sexual matters while girls are not. At its most extreme, it promotes patriarchy and the complete male control of female behavior, sexual and otherwise (Dickemann 1979; Smuts 1995).

The double standard underlies many cultural and institutional practices that mandate rigid control of women's freedom of movement, and particularly control of female sexuality. One way to deny women's freedom of movement is to deny women economic independence, either through forbidding the female ownership of property, or forbidding the education of females. Once again, material and social environments are very important in determining when and how this occurs. Women's rights are most likely to be curtailed in situations where males monopolize the means of production, most notably in agrarian societies. Where women are able to have control over the means of production, in hunter-

gatherer and horticultural societies, for example, as well as in advanced industrial societies, they have often been able to ensure individual freedoms and
rights for women (van den Berghe 1979; Daly and Wilson 1983; Sanderson,
Heckert, and Dubrow 2005).

A biological underpinning for the sexual double standard does not mean
that highly sex egalitarian societies are not possible. Throughout most of human
evolutionary history, human societies were characterized by highly egalitarian
relationships between men and women. These egalitarian societies were founded
on an economic equality where both males and females contributed in significant ways to subsistence. There is no biological reason why such highly egalitarian societies could not occur again.

Darwinian principles have other implications for stratification by sex. One
famous hypothesis from evolutionary biology, the Trivers-Willard hypothesis,
can be applied to differential investment by parents in sons and daughters. The
hypothesis, applied to other species as well as humans, suggests that high-status
individuals will have more sons among their offspring and low-status individuals will have more daughters. In a stratified society, the Trivers-Willard hypothesis further suggests that low-status individuals will allocate more resources
to daughters, high-status individuals more to sons. Tests of both components of
this hypothesis using contemporary data have been mixed, with some finding
support for it and others no support. Mueller (1993) and Betzig and Weber
(1995) have given evidence for male-biased sex ratios among the children of
male elites. Chacon-Puignau, Cristina, and Jaffe (1996) and Gibson and Mace
(2003) have found more girls born to economically distressed mothers. Catalano
(2003) has shown a lower overall sex ratio in economically distressed 1991 East
Germany compared to West Germany at the same time. Mealey and Mackey
(1990) found more boys born to high-status mothers and first wives among nineteenth-century polygynous Mormons. Hopcroft (2005) found evidence that
males with high occupational status have more sons among their biological offspring than males with low occupational status. Yet, other studies have not con-
curred. Essock-Vitale (1984) and Mueller (1993) have not seen a Trivers-
Willard effect in the children of some socially elite men. Studies of the economic status of pregnant women in a Canadian hospital (Marleau and Saucier
2000) and the social backgrounds of college students (Ellis and Bonin 2002)
have not found support for a sex ratio adaptation. Similar mixed results have
been found for the resource allocation component of the Trivers-Willard hypothesis (e.g., Freese and Powell 1999; Hopcroft 2005). More research using
random samples with complete data on both male and female fertility, as well as
better information on resource allocation to offspring, is needed here.

In past research, I have also used evolutionary reasoning to explain the pattern of interaction between young men and women in experimental situations,
and the common pattern of young female deference to males (Hopcroft 2002). I
have suggested that young female deference may have been sexually selected as
a trait because it advertises youth and controllability, both of which are characteristics males prefer in a mate. Similarly, the lack of male deference may have

been sexually selected as a trait because it advertises high status or dominance, a characteristic females prefer in a mate. I have tested and found support for several hypotheses drawn from this theory, both experimentally and using survey research from a variety of cultures (Hopcroft 2002, 2006b).

Stratification by Class and Status

As Sanderson notes, the principle of genetic selfishness can also help explain the emergence of economic inequality in societies beyond the hunter-gatherer level of subsistence (Lenski 1966; Lopreato and Crippen 1999), and the drive of some groups and individuals (typically males) throughout history to accumulate economic surplus at the expense of others.

In contemporary industrial societies, drives for power and wealth by individuals are also observed, if on a smaller scale. Much of this has been done legally and, especially when accompanied by innovation and creativity, has served to benefit the larger society. Sometimes such efforts are less beneficial. Institutional regulations such as licensing practices, particularly those that restrict the labor supply in particular occupations, boost earnings of individuals in those occupations (Weeden 2002). Such regulations may be seen, at least in part, as a strategy by members of the occupation to help maintain their earnings levels. Sometimes individuals have fleeced their companies and defrauded investors and employees alike. The more notorious of these have conducted themselves as befits preindustrial autocrats, indulging in excess and handing out favors to their friends and family members. As throughout history (Betzig 1986), males have used their advantages in income and wealth to gain access to women. The dalliances of rich and powerful men in the contemporary world are well known.

Just as in previous societies, wealthy and powerful individuals have used their resources to benefit themselves and their families. The importance of the family in the transfer of social status across generations is well accepted. The literature on social mobility documents how over the last century men have been able to pass their socioeconomic status on to their sons (and sometimes their daughters). This basic rate of immobility (net of structural mobility or change in the nature of jobs available) has remained constant over the past hundred years or since data collection began (Erikson and Goldthorpe 1993; Breen and Jonsson 2005). Rates of occupational mobility, net of structural mobility due to change in the nature of available jobs, are also fairly similar among advanced industrialized countries, and have become more so recently (Breen and Jonsson 2005). Undergirding this stable rate of mobility is the constant activity of the family (particularly in the training and education of children) to ensure occupational status is passed on across generations (Entwistle, Alexander, and Olson 2005). Just as would be predicted using Darwinian principles, mothers appear to be highly important in this process: "The farther alternative family structures take sons away from their mothers, the more the intergenerational transmission process breaks down" (Biblarz, Raftery, and Bucur 1997, 1319).

Similarly, contemporary wealth transfers across generations in the family are another foundation of stratification in contemporary societies (Spilerman 2000). As wealth has become more widespread across all segments of society, such transfers have become more important as a determinant of the living standards and class position of a family. Wealth transfers from parents to children even before death can be quite extensive. A study of data from the 1992 Health and Retirement Study (McGarry and Schoeni 1995) found that 13.8 per cent of adult children were given at least $550 in the last year, with the average transfer being $3,061. Such transfers from parents to children can influence children's educational attainment, ability to own a business, and financial security, and in many ways promote the well-being of offspring (Spilerman 2000). There is evidence that transfers of wealth from parents to children are less when parents are divorced (Furstenberg, Hoffman, and Shrestha 1995), and this may be part of the mechanism for the reduced ability of divorced parents to pass on status to their children (Biblarz, Raftery, and Bucur 1997).

CONCLUSION

In critiquing Sanderson's paradigm, I have emphasized its Darwinian microfoundations rather than its macro implications – more Darwinian and less conflict, you might say. I have tried to show how those Darwinian principles can make sense of a great deal of contemporary American sociological research in two important areas – marriage and the family, and stratification. The emphasis on the Darwinian microfoundations helps explain not only how and why conflict occurs as often as it does, but how cooperation and altruism also occur all the time, most notably within the family. Darwinian principles can be further used to explain and unify findings in many other areas of contemporary sociological research, notably crime and deviance, race and ethnic relations, sociology of emotions, mathematical sociology and experimental games, social network research, sociology of religion, and historical sociology and demography, although space does not permit me to elaborate on this here. The Darwinian paradigm cannot only explain and unify many of the findings of contemporary sociological research; it can suggest avenues for future research in all these areas. More research is needed, for example, on male fertility and its relationship to income and status.

While I have critiqued Darwinian conflict theory here, I would like to reiterate my support for the approach in general. As a set of macrosociological orienting statements, it is probably the best sociology can hope for. At the same time the Darwinian micro principles on which it is based form the best hope of a unifying, general paradigm for sociology.

5

SOME REFLECTIONS ON SANDERSON'S EVOLUTIONARY APPROACHES

Christoph Antweiler

Although social evolutionism became unfashionable in cultural anthropology (less so in archaeology) after the mid-1970s, there has been a renewed interest in issues of social and cultural evolution since the late 1980s and early 1990s. This is evidenced by several monographs by anthropologists, sociologists, archaeologists, and historians (e.g., Corning 1983, 2003; Ingold 1986; Hallpike 1986; Adams 1988; Sanderson 1990, 1995, 1999a, 2007c; Maryanski and Turner 1992; Snooks 1996, 1997, 1998; Bogucki 1999; Johnson and Earle 2000; Carneiro 2000, 2003; Turner 2003; Pluciennik 2005; Christian 2005). There have also been special issues of journals devoted to social evolutionism (e.g., two quite different issues of the journal *Cultural Dynamics*: Antweiler and Adams 1991 and Ingold 1991) and several edited books (e.g., Rambo and Gillogly 1991; Feinman and Manzanilla 2000).

At last, we now have some good accounts of theories of social evolution aimed at both scholarly and student audiences (e.g., Sanderson 1990, 2007c; Trigger 1998; Carneiro 2003). This renaissance of interest in social and cultural evolution is not only an English and American affair. There is also new work in German-speaking countries and in the Netherlands (e.g., Antweiler 1988 and Bierstedt 1997 on selectionist models; Müller and Schmid 1995 on evolution-istic social change theories; Lang 1998 on the importance of evolution for the definition of culture; Wimmer 1996 on political evolution; Claessen 2000 on structural evolution and the state; Goudsblom and Wilterdink 2000; Schelkle, Krauth, Kohli, and Elwert 2000 on sociostructural models; and Aschke 2002 on communication).

Since the late nineteenth century quite different things have been discussed under the headings "social evolution," "cultural evolution," "sociocultural evolution," or "societal evolution":

1. the evolution of the capacity for culture (especially among humans);
2. the long-term change of humanity's culture as a whole;
3. the transgenerational change of specific collectivities, e.g., ethnic groups;
4. specific patterns or directional trends regarding 2 and 3, e.g., areal expansion, diversification, the general increase in societal complexity, and the effects on natural ecosystems; and
5. the explanation of the phenomena described under 1 to 4.

Most contemporary work on the causes of transgenerational social change in the evolutionary guise is from archaeologists, whereas nowadays there are only a few contributions by cultural anthropologists or sociologists, and only the rare contribution by an historian. Stephen King Sanderson's (1995, 1999a) "evolutionary materialism" is an example of such work by someone who is a sociologist.

Sanderson addresses all five of the abovementioned facets of social evolution. His is an explicitly pluralistic model, but Sanderson does not want to create an eclectic one. He aims at a coherent model and therefore he combines historical sociology and Immanuel Wallerstein's (1974a, 1974b, 1980, 1989) world-systems analysis with a refined version of Marvin Harris's (1977, 1979) cultural materialism, and with elements added from Gerhard Lenski's (1966, 1970, 2005) materialist evolutionism, Robert Carneiro's (1970, 2000) circumscription approach, and Michael Mann's (1986) work on political evolution. More recently, Sanderson has sought to expand and deepen his approach and has embedded his evolutionary materialism in a broader perspective that he calls Darwinian conflict theory (Sanderson 2001a).

A definitive strength of Sanderson's work is that it represents a truly explanatory theory. Instead of presenting mere metaphors, as we see in the bulk of postmodern and poststructuralist theory production today – e.g., on globalization, identity, and hybridity – he really tackles the issue of explanation. Sanderson presents a theory of history that explains both change and continuity. He aims to explain parallel courses of history as well as trends of increasing complexity or efficiency of social systems ("progress"). Even if Sanderson himself might not agree, I would regard his approach as eclectic, but eclectic in the best sense of the term.

A further strength of Sanderson's work is the clear exposition of the main argument. In all his work, Sanderson not only outlines his arguments in clear prose, but in explaining his theoretical strategy he provides many precise statements that are, at least in principle, empirically testable (e.g., Sanderson 1995, 3-16). In this regard, Sanderson's work contrasts with large parts of the literature in the field of social science evolutionistic theorizing.[1]

Although I see mainly positive points in Sanderson's approach to social evolution, even a good model can be improved. I see two lacunae in Sanderson's work, one regarding cultural universals and one involving social institutions. Sanderson's approach could benefit from looking at pancultural patterns in a more precise way. It is surprising that the work of George Peter Murdock, the famous comparativist and originator of the modern concept of human universals (Murdock 1945), is almost completely missing in the literature cited by Sanderson. Murdock's work is cited only with respect to specific questions, but not regarding universals. The same holds regarding the detailed work of Donald E. Brown, probably the leading figure in the modern anthropological study of human universals (Brown 1991). Human universals are traits or characteristics found in all societies. Brown characterizes universals in a recent definition in the following way: "Human universals – of which hundreds have been identified – consist of those features of culture, society, language, behavior, and mind that, so far as the record has been examined, are found among all peoples known to ethnography and history" (Brown 2004, 47). Other authors conceive universals as confined to recent cultural traits.

Universals are transcultural similarities within the sea of cultural variants. Anthropologists have discovered enormous cultural variation, but not all of the possibilities imaginable in an "ethnographic hyperspace" are realized. Many conceivable cultural variants are nowhere to be found: Cultural diversity is limited and it is patterned. Sanderson provides us with a list of universals similar to Murdock's. But Sanderson's list is much shorter, including only 43 universals, abbreviated from Murdock's original inventory of 73. That seems somewhat haphazard, since there is no argument provided by Sanderson for his selection. Furthermore, we should not forget that Murdock's list is only one of several such inventories of human universals before and after him. Both Clark Wissler (1965, orig. 1923) and Charles Hockett (1973) have provided their own lists. Sanderson's way of handling universals is similar to other authors using Murdock's list – changing it without giving empirical or theoretical arguments for the changes. So it should be mentioned that Murdock's list, despite its many problems, was not an outgrowth of mere speculation but based on a vast amount of empirical cross-cultural data incorporated into the *Human Relations Area Files* (HRAF).

Sanderson assumes that universals are evidence of a biological root of humanity. But universals are traits existing in all human societies, not necessarily in all human individuals. Thus, cultural universals and biopsychic universals are causally connected, but they should not be confounded. Cultural universals are called "cultural" because they are *ubiquitous on the level of cultures* (societies).[2] They are present in every culture, but not in every individual. To treat both types of universal under the heading of "human universals" as one and the same phenomenon is a confusion often made, especially in evolutionary psychology. A case in point is the work of Steven Pinker, which I otherwise admire in many respects (Pinker 2003, 601-08; cf. critiques in Buller 2006, 208ff., 457-71, and Antweiler 2007). Biological explanations may hold for many or most universals, but several universals have to be explained by other factors (Meyer 1990b; Brown 1991, 88-117; Antweiler 2007, Chapter 6). The main explanations of human universals are manifold: (a) adaptedness of an evolved human psyche, (b) diffusion (Rogers 2003), and (c) sheer practical circumstances of life in a material world. Universals do not come as a simple category, and there are several specific types of universals. One specific type is represented by *implicational universals* (*if-then universals*), which exist if a specific instance is given in a culture. Furthermore there are newly emergent universals, especially in complex societies since about 10,000 years ago. These would not be truly diachronic universals in the strict sense of Brown's definition (universal in all cultures and all times), but are nevertheless important because of their newly acquired global reach. An example would be the use of all-purpose money. Once it was developed, it rapidly spread to and became universal in all societies of its type.

A consideration of universals is imperative for every theory of long-term change in human societies in order to avoid the trap of Eurocentrism. Cross-cultural data provide a good test-base for generalizing assumptions of social theory. We have to differentiate between true diachronic universals and new or part-time universals. Even if many universals have some evolutionary basis, the assumption of universals is theoretically independent of biology. Thus, universals should not be simply equated with human nature, the human biogram, or "anthropological constants." The empirical referent or target of universals is societies, not individuals.

The second major lacuna in Sanderson's work, seen from an anthropological or sociological perspective, is the almost total lack of any discussion of social institutions and their role as factors and effects in long-term societal change. This is evident by a look at both the text and the indexes of Sanderson's books. Some aspects of institutions are mentioned in the texts under other terms, but mostly only in passing. Especially notable for their absence are religion and mass media (on the latter, see Hejl, Chapter 16 this volume). Religion is a critically important institution in all societies, and mass media are of special significance in "ultrasocial systems," i.e., highly complex modern societies.

Finally, I will only mention some more minor hints concerning how Sanderson's approach could be improved. One point is that Sanderson tends to reduce culture to the realm of behavior. In order to understand the dynamics of culture, especially long-term change, we need to delve into cultural realms beyond behavior, namely thoughts and material culture. It is important to specify the dynamics of extrasomatic material culture. We know that culture that is manifested in artifacts or in anthropogenic landscapes has specific dynamics compared to culture manifested only in behavior or in the minds of humans. The different realms of culture are differently related to selective pressures. The selective consequences of thoughts, emotions, and acted-out behavior are differently related to effort: input of information, energy, material, and risk. Thus we should build separate minimodels about the transgenerational changes in these respective cultural realms. Another critical point in Sanderson's work is that, at least implicitly, ultimate explanations are regarded as better than proximate explanations. Both should be seen as essential types of explanations and both should be pursued with equal vigor.

In conclusion, Sanderson's materialist social evolutionism can be seen as a genuine contribution to an encompassing theory of social change in combining natural-history explanations with historical factors. My specific criticisms show that Sanderson's approach is a theoretical argument with precise assumptions which can be modified in specific parts and amended by minimodels for specific issues and processes of long-term societal change.

NOTES

1. In making these assessments I should perhaps state my own biases. I am a cultural anthropologist but, having a background in palaeontology and a long-standing interest in organic evolution, I may not be so typical for an anthropologist. If most cultural anthropologists are "culture vultures," to use Sanderson's terminology (borrowed from George Homans), I am probably only a "culture dove." Culture may be only analytically separated from nature. Like Sanderson, I follow a materialistic stance.

2. Human universals are not to be confused with the specific structural notion of a universal pattern (infrastructure, structure, and superstructure), general dimensions of societies as conceived by Marvin Harris.

6

WHY SHOULD MARVIN HARRIS MEET CHARLES DARWIN?

A Reply to Sanderson's Critique of Cultural Materialism

Khaled Hakami

"Good intentions do not guarantee good theories."
Anonymous

SANDERSON'S GOOD INTENTIONS

Although cultural materialism is the strategy that I have found to be "the most effective in my attempt to understand the causes of differences and similarities among societies and cultures" (Harris 1979, preface), it is obvious that this paradigm (like every other one) has some shortcomings. Since the very beginning, Harris was not only criticized from outside but also from within the materialistic community. This historical (and necessary) process is in no way a special feature of cultural materialism. As in every major paradigm in anthropology, time does not stand still, and there are always scientists who wish to elaborate the existing ones or to make them even fitter. This is an essential part of Kuhn's "normal science." Hence, there is nothing to argue about the fact that Stephen Sanderson, a thoroughgoing scientist and one of the most prominent sociologists within the scientific community at the moment, wants to reformulate the cultural materialist program. Actually, he is not the first to do so. R. Brian Ferguson (1995), for example, is one of the leading figues of the opposition within the paradigm (Frank Elwell 1991 might be another).

But there is a big difference between Ferguson and Sanderson. The latter is not just interested in giving cultural materialism a more precise and historical shape, as Ferguson is, but in recombining it with another major scientific paradigm. For Sanderson (2007b, 226) "the problem with Harris's thinking was not that it was materialist, but that it was not materialist enough. It needed to move in a more biologically materialist direction, by embracing the principles of sociobiology." There we have it: Two old and traditionally opposed strategies should be brought together under the banner of Sanderson's own paradigm, called *evolutionary materialism*.

Combining two paradigms is a hard thing to do, but it is in no way a "mission impossible," because, as Harris himself points out, there are parts of the cultural materialist research program that do fit other paradigms as well. With dialectical materialists, for example, cultural materialists share some theoretical principles, but they have different epistemological principles. With sociobiologists it is just the other way round – the epistemological principles are very similar, while the theoretical principles seem to be incommensurable (see Harris 1979, 141). This is where Sanderson comes in. As he fancies cultural materialism *and* sociobiology, he tries to overcome these theoretical differences by arguing for some biological determinants within the concept of infrastructure. As the cover of one his latest works *The Evolution of Human Sociality* suggests (showing pictures of Marx and Darwin), he would like to combine the materialist approach, based on the principles of Marx, with biology, based on the principles of Darwin, in order to make the materialism even more materialistic and the social sciences even more scientific. In Sanderson's words, Marvin Harris should "meet Charles Darwin."

To me, Sanderson's thoughts on the specific problems of cultural materialism and evolutionism in general are very interesting, but his arguments on the modification of the cultural materialist program are not really convincing. To be sure, there is indeed a need to reformulate the cultural materialist program in some sense (and on some critical remarks Sanderson is perfectly right) but not by adding some nonrelevant biological determinants to the given theoretical principles. However, this is not my main point. One is basically wondering why Sanderson, by claiming to be an evolutionist, is starting a quarrel with a more "diachronic oriented functionalist," as Harris never was a sophisticated evolutionist. In fact, I would like to show that Sanderson is messing with the wrong guy.

SOCIOBIOLOGY SELECTED AGAINST

The history and the main principles of sociobiology are widely known among scientists and need not be discussed here in detail. What is worth mentioning is the fact that many of the traditional critics of sociobiology did not refer to those basic principles at all. Some argued that sociobiology grew out of a Western ideology (see Sahlins 1976, Part II) that is based on the interests of the political right and tries to justify various social inequalities (see Lewontin, Rose, and Kamin 1984). In principle it is not necessary to defend a theory against such objections, as these do not have the status of a logical judgment: History alone doesn't explain anything but is to be explained. Moreover, even if this argument were true, and the sociobiologists' theories bear similarities to the capitalistic ideology or are derived from it, the argument would not falsify sociobiological theories (for a detailed summary of this objection see Sanderson 2001a, 132). To argue the opposite is to commit the genetic fallacy.

On the other hand, some of the critics of sociobiology have made additional remarks as well, and the best examples from anthropology are Marvin Harris and Marshall Sahlins. It seems to me that Sanderson, in criticizing those two (especially the latter), is making the same mistake he attributes to his critics, namely, to pour out the baby with the bathwater. Neither can sociobiology be falsified by an historical or ideological argument, nor could the whole criticism by using an argument from the other side of the ideological spectrum. No doubt, Sahlins thought about the ideological and political implications of sociobiology (1976, Part II) but at the same time tried to demolish kin selection theory in a purely scientific manner. And the same is true for Harris. But Sanderson's reply to those kinds of scientific criticism is short, insufficient, and unconvincing, as we will see.

The foundation of Harris's theory of cultural materialism is that a society's mode of production (technology and work patterns, especially in regard to food) and mode of reproduction (population level and growth) in interaction with the natural environment have profound effects on sociocultural stability and change. In a nutshell, cultural materialism is "based on the simple premise that human social life is a response to the practical problems of earthly existence" (Harris 1979, preface). But that is only half of the story. This principle, which of course is Harris's famous Principle of Infrastructural Determinism, ontologically reflects the so-called "biopsychological needs" that every cultural materialist is familiar with.

Needless to say, especially the third biopsychological need – people are highly sexed and generally find reinforcing pleasure from sexual intercourse – is the one Sanderson seems most interested in (even the actions of sociobiologists can be predicted). He agrees with Harris that "reproduction has a crucial impact on social life," but is quick to add "in a more fundamental biological way than Harris has been willing to acknowledge" (Sanderson 2001a, 146). For Sanderson (2001a, 147) Harris's biopsychological needs "only make sense in terms of sociobiological principles. Why should people be so highly sexed, and why should most be oriented toward heterosexual sex than toward any other? The answer can only be, because heterosexual sex, and lots of it, works to promote one's inclusive fitness." But is this really the only answer? Surely not. First, Harris does not argue for any hierarchical ordering of these four needs, and therefore the third need is as important as any other. Second, these needs do not reflect a deterministic principle. They are just the framework within which the determined processes unfold. Third, there is no necessary connection between the factual statement that people have sex and the *assumed* concept of "inclusive fitness." It is neither a logical deduction nor as self-evident as Sanderson suggests. No doubt, searching for new constants in human nature is a reasonable enterprise, but as every scientist knows, constants cannot explain variables. So even if the statement of Sanderson were true, there would be room to argue that this concept explains nothing more than why people have sex. But of course the concept of "inclusive fitness" implies much more than that – it seeks to explain constants and variables, and there the problems begin.

One of the most fundamental criticisms of the sociobiological perspective was formulated by C. R. Hallpike (a critic Sanderson fails to mention at all). Hallpike's intention is to show "that it is impossible to apply Darwinian principles to the evolution of human societies because they are inherently of the wrong type to be applied to socio-cultural systems" (Hallpike 1986, 32). After reviewing different forms of sociobiological explanations, he turns to the concept of "inclusive fitness," which is, in fact, the hallmark of that paradigm. Beside this specific concept, which stresses individual reproductive success in relation to close kin, Hallpike argues that there are two additional concepts basic to this theory, namely "altruism" and "selfishness," and two scientists who were the main advocates of these concepts, William Hamilton (1964) and Robert Trivers (1971). Hamilton was, without doubt, the more radical of the two. Along with the original argument, which was derived from the study of animals, he concludes that in human societies too the attempt of individuals to increase the fitness of their own genes by aiding their close relatives is a major determinative factor. This argument, as one can imagine, was unsustainable, even for other sociobiologists. There were too many cases where this principle could not be applied to human behavior. Trivers, on the other hand, advanced the argument that reciprocity even between nonrelatives may be of selective advantage, too. There is no space to lay out the theory of Trivers here in detail, but it can be said that his theory of "reciprocal altruism," which Sanderson's theory relies on (see Sanderson 2001a, 178, 266, 270) is certainly much closer to the facts of human cooperation than that of Hamilton. However, what at first sight could be interpreted as having explanatory power by an advanced sociobiologist turns out to be a fundamental weakness from the point of view of a social scientist. Because, as Hallpike (1986, 67) points out,

> the very reasonableness of the theory means, ironically, that the predictive value of inclusive fitness theory with regard to altruism and selfishness in human society is reduced to about zero. For we now have the predictions that in some circumstances people will give benefits to, or "invest in," their kin, and that in others they will give benfits to non-kin. No doubt, this is quite true, but it amounts to nothing more than the affirmation that *all* the various forms of human reciprocity are biologically possible, in so far as some argument of natural selection can, on the basis of these theories, always be constructed to "explain" any act of reciprocity reported by social scientists.

In short, that which explains everything at the same time explains nothing. If all the "weight of the evidence" (Part V of his book) Sanderson is citing only makes sense in light of this weak principle – and it seems so – then there is nothing much left. And if this is all the theory of inclusive fitness is contributing to an understanding of human behavior, then it is unnecessary as a scientific axiom and faces elimination – or, in the sociobiologists' own terms, "is selected against" – through Occam's razor – just as easily as the dialectics of the Marxists.

While Trivers's reformulation seems like a kind of desperate rearguard action in light of the naive assumptions of Hamilton, Hallpike's arguments are in any case consistent with what other major scientists have stated before him. First, to argue that biological principles are inadequate to explain the range of human behavior is not to argue that humans are not biological or natural beings. The social scientist merely states that biology is but a broad framework that constitutes a set of constraints but does not have determinative effects on the social sphere, as the sociobiologists suggest. A long time ago George P. Murdock left no doubt about this: "It is of the utmost importance to note, however, that although heredity [or any biological principle] probably establishes the broad outlines of the universal pattern, it in no way determines the content of the latter. Heredity may enable man to speak, but it does not prescribe the particular language he shall employ" (Murdock 1932, 203). Second, to see culture as something qualitatively distinct is not to sit in one boat with some "culture vultures." Culture is just the expression of a new qualitative step in the evolution of humans, and should be thought of as an evolutionary mechanism, rather than as something completely detached. (There is, of course, no Kroeberian cultural determinism going on.) Third, to say that cultural behavior is socially rather than biologically determined is not to give favor to some wishy-washy kind of determinism. Determined processes in the sphere of societies are as strict as in other spheres of nature.

THE USE AND ABUSE OF HUNTER-GATHERERS

Social evolution starts with the appearance of hunter-gatherer societies, and for most sociobiologists this type of society is the gateway to the social sciences. Reasonably so, because if they can show that "our contemporary ancestors" behave in essence as we do, namely, behave "in a rational and self-interested manner" (in Sanderson's words), then there is reason to assume that this (biologically determined) fact did not change since ancient times. To be sure, Sanderson is not one of the outdated sociobiologists who argues that any form of adaptation should be related directly to the so-called EEA (Environment of Evolutionary Adaptedness), but he is still in the camp of the "Darwinian social scientists" who take pains to cite as many proximate causes (and therefore cover as many sociocultural phenomena) as possible to make their ultimate cause – the concept of inclusive fitness – even fitter. But that doesn't work. The problem is not the citation of proximate causes (psychological, economic, or whatever), but the underlying concept of "inclusive fitness" as an ultimate cause. Here, in the case of the ultimate cause, nothing has changed since the time of the first sociobiologists. And Sanderson's application of cultural materialism, too, can be seen as nothing but the attempt to add more powerful proximate causes to sociobiological theory. But by doing to Trivers what Trivers did to Hamilton, Sanderson is still making a retreat, as the best proximate causes will not help if the ultimate cause is scientifically unsustainable. Sociobiology still stands or falls with the validity of its major concept. So let us go back to the original discussion, which is closely related to the question of "human nature" and the EEA, and therefore to the study of hunter-gatherer societies.

First of all, Sanderson challenges Sahlins's notion that kinship is culturally rather than biologically constructed, by asking, "Is Sahlins denying that most of the members of a household or lineage are genetically related? It would be absurd to do so" (Sanderson 2001a, 272). But it is not. (By the way, is this all Sanderson is able to argue against Sahlins?) Hunter-gatherer societies in particular have a high fluctuation of individuals and no consistent groups (and especially no consistent kin groups) over a substantial period of time. In many cases people live, not with their nearest kin, but with people of other groups, without showing any change in their "altruistic" behavior. Members of hunter-gatherer societies are not "most altruistic towards their own offspring" as Sanderson (2001a, 272) suggests, but equally altruistic to all members (and especially to all offspring) of the present group. But again, even if it is true that most members of a hunter-gatherer group are genetically related or that they favor their direct offspring, where is the logical deduction or the empirical evidence for the concept of inclusive fitness? What should be demonstrated Sanderson takes simply as given. If he had himself lived with a hunter-gatherer society, as I have, he could have seen the original affluent society and the inadequacy of kin selection in action.

Moreover, for Sanderson, most of the hunter-gatherer societies today are truly *hunter*-gatherers (and not *gatherer*-hunters), as their diet consists primarily of game. And this is where "optimal foraging theory" comes in, which, for Sanderson, is the key link to the Darwinian conflict model. So the argument (which is obviously based on a formalist notion of economy, as he is ready to admit; see Sanderson 2001a, 250) has its own logic: If societies rely mostly on hunting and the success of hunting could be measured by individual hunting strategies, in other words brought down to the level of individual cost-benefit decisions, then there would be a more or less direct link to individual reproduction. But Sanderson does not present his evidence correctly. The most meaningful dual classification of hunter-gatherer societies is not the one between mostly gatherers and mostly hunters, but between primary and secondary hunter-gatherer societies, as most of these today are secondary hunter-gatherers. Secondary hunter-gatherers are a historical product, and their existence can only be understood by stressing their relations to existing agricultural societies (of which they are actually a product, through specialization). This social form should therefore be explained in terms of historical processes and there are several (historical) reasons why secondary hunter-gatherers have their specific diets. However, that the vast majority of primary hunter-gatherers (in fact, there are just a few left) are primarily gatherers is a fact. Hence, the former can tell us very little about "human nature" compared to the latter. During my field research among a primary hunter-gatherer society (the Semang) in the south of Thailand, and by comparing them with other primary hunter-gatherers, I realized that, with their focus on hunting and game, the different versions of optimal foraging theory (including Sanderson's own) are weak for these cases and with it the whole Darwinian model, primarily derived from the study of nonhuman animals.

METHODOLOGICAL AND SCIENTIFIC PRINCIPLES

The whole discussion, in some sense, can be brought down to a single point. Why is it that the variation in individual behavior (biologically determined or not) cannot explain the range of variation of cultural and social institutions? One possible answer could be that there is something more than just individuals. Sanderson, however, is clear about the point in saying that "those who advocate group selection reify the group." In saying so, he puts himself in the camp of the methodological individualists – not a surprising act for a sociobiologist. Sanderson argues that the only form of group selection that can logically exist is one in which the members of a group are the recipients of benefits that result from individual-level adaptations. Hence, something like the group does not exist as an entity in itself. Just like species in biology, groups are only abstractions without any kind of behavior of their own. To be sure, groups can have needs and wants, Sanderson readily admits, but "these needs and wants are ultimately only the needs and wants of their constituent members" (Sanderson 2001a, 149).

There is nothing new in this. Nearly all scientists who are in some way oriented toward biology (or psychology, natural allies, in fact) tend to be methodological individualists. Necessarily so, because biology and psychology only deal with individuals. And again, Murdock (1932, 207) was aware of that fact. For him, this kind of approach "is powerless to explain the development of culture." To say that man is "unique" in some sense, however, frightens many scientists – for understandable reasons, as humanists argue exactly the same point. But by "unique" humanists imply that culture cannot be studied scientifically, that man is really something "special." Social scientists are far from that, however. All social scientists are saying is that man, through culture, differs from the rest of the animals not only in degree, but in *kind*. That is all.

Many critics, though, have pointed out that this position is unscientific, as one is referring to a nonphysical component. Those who argue that all social and cultural phenomena should be considered reducible to physical entities (such as the individual) are known as "physicalists," and even for modern physicalists like Tim O'Meara (see Harris 1997) or Sanderson, "methodological individualism" therefore is the chariot. But to say that something is superorganic is not to say that something is metaphysical and "to say that sociocultural things are abstractions is not to say that they are not real" (Harris 1997, 413). Social scientists are just insisting on the fact that, at a specific point in human evolution, a new qualitative stage came into being. It is that simple, as we deal with main differences in quality, (biological) organic principles cannot explain the (social and cultural) superorganic, just as the other way round. Just as a biologist would rightly object when a physicist or chemist would explain the organic only in inorganic terms of matter and energy, social scientists will rightly defend their objects of study against biologists. In essence, the relationship between the superorganic and the organic is exactly the same as between the organic and the inorganic. The superorganic rests on the organic, and the organic rests on the inorganic, but they cannot explain each other sufficiently. That is why the social sciences should be "studied by their own students with their own methods and instrumentalities" (Murdock 1932, 207).

From my point of view, however, this matter is not just a kind of philosophical question; it can be argued in a scientific way. The main scientific principle which reflects that fact is the well-known principle of quantity and quality, which every natural scientist is familiar with. This principle can be argued ontologically as well as phylogenetically. To begin with the former, we can say that, compared to subhuman species, "man has no new kind of brain cells or brain cell connections" but rather a brain that has "steadily increased in size until it reached a critical mass, which allowed the human species to cross the Rubicon, giving rise thereby to both language and culture" (Carlson 1926, quoted in Carneiro 2000, 12927). Phylogenetically, it is just the same, as Carneiro points out: "Similarly we can say that social evolution is largely the struggle to increase structure in proportion to size"(Carneiro 2000, 12927). In both cases new structures and functions are established that are irreducible to their components. As the new ability of the brain cannot be explained by the unchanged quality of a single brain cell, so we cannot explain the new quality of a chiefdom by means of the quality of an autonomous village, though a chiefdom consists of several villages – just as a new qualitative change in a chemical substance, produced by an increase in the number of its atoms, cannot be fully explained by the quality of its single units.

But Sanderson, like Tim O'Meara (1997) and James Lett (1997, 111) before him, is unwilling to accept the consequences of that fact. For him, "any so-called adaptation at the level of a group or society is but a statistical aggregate of individual adaptations." And he goes on to argue that the mistake of some methodological holists (ironically within the sociobiological community) "is the failure to draw a very simple distinction between behavior *that evolves because it benefits the group* and behavior *that has the consequence of benefitting the group*. They [the group selectionists] provide no evidence to show that the former is occurring; in their examples, the latter is in fact occurring, but only because the groups in question are aggregations of individuals. The group benefits simply because the individuals within it benefit" (Sanderson 2001a, 128). But by proposing the principle of quality and quantity, and in light of the fact that sociobiologists can only cite some *apparent* occurrences of "inclusive fitness," one can reverse the argument and argue that in some cases of group behavior individuals benefit in such a way that their behavior can be interpreted *as if* resulting in increased fitness. However, the problem remains that there is no way of measuring the assumed benefits other than by observing the behavior that they are said to determine. The sociobiologists thought of the accurate Darwinian principles as their strength, but as they try to put them to use by hook or by crook these principles at the same time are their soft spot. Because, as Hallpike (1986, 36) points out, for example, "There is no significant resemblance between the *mutation*, the basic source of variation in the Darwinian scheme of things, and *social* invention, which is purposeful, responsive, and can be diffused." And no biological principle can explain this fact without becoming unfalsifiable.

As many anthropologists have pointed out, something like social institutions or cultural innovations can survive for many generations and lie beyond the influence of individuals. No single Kwakiutl elaborated the potlatch, no single Kachin developed a complex alliance system, no single Australian bushman set down a section system, and no single Trobriand invented the kula ring (which is reflected in the fact that no single Trobriand knows how the kula ring actually works!). "Societies … are 'more than' the individuals who created them" (Sanderson 2001a, 152). Yes, indeed! But the "more than" Sanderson is speaking of is what social science is all about. It reflects nothing less than the fact that not only is a group or society a qualitative entity in its own right, but holism implies that it is also a major determining factor. As every person is born into an existing culture and into existing institutions, the individual is "little more than the agent of social and historical forces" (Murdock 1932, 206). In any case, holistic perspectives have proved to be much more useful in interpeting social behavior than anything else.

NATURAL SELECTION AND TRUE EVOLUTIONISM

The principle of quality and quantity, as we have seen, is an overall scientific principle; it does not belong to a single specific discipline. Sociobiologists, however, with their incomplete understanding of science, tend to define (social) science only in terms of the theoretical principles of biology. But, by doing so, the "Bermuda Triangle" of O'Meara, Lett, and Sanderson is missing the point. A long time ago, Leslie A. White left no doubt about the meaning of science: Science is *sciencing*, and this concept is related to a specific set of epistemological principles, not to specific phenomena or to a specific scientific discipline. It is in some sense a striking irony, then, that physicalists (or sociobiologists in general), with their radical scientific attitude, do not recognize overarching principles derived from the natural sciences (and, more ironically, it is surprisingly difficult to find methodological reductionists among modern physicists). Among other things, this is due to the fact that the sociobiologists confuse – as we will see specifically in the case of the principle of natural selection – main principles with some special articulation of these principles.

By invoking this most powerful tool of the biologist, Sanderson is sure of the fact that "social groups and societies in and of themselves cannot be adaptational units, i.e., cannot be the units on which selection operates – because they cannot and do not exist apart from concrete flesh-and-blood individuals ... [and] because groups cannot have a critical trait of individuals, viz., consciousness and a brain" (Sanderson 2001a, 149). But is this really the case? Yes, for biologists it is, because natural selection in biology is operating only on the individual organism. No, because biologists have a very limited and therefore incomplete notion of natural selection. Natural selection can work on everything, not only on individual organisms. As Robert L. Carneiro (1992, 113) has shown, the principle of natural selection is – just like the principle of quantity and quality – a so-called master principle.

True enough, most social scientists, in the past or in recent times, avoided the term *and* the concept. There were just some tough-minded people who spoke of "cultural selection." Biologists, on the other hand, were convinced that natural selection is a very special principle, uniquely biological. But as Carneiro has shown, there is no need for giving the horse another name, nor to lose this concept to the biologists. For him, the concept of natural selection "is just as valid, fruitful, and essential in explaining cultural evolution as organic evolution" (Carneiro 1992, 117). As a master principle it works on any kind of phenomena. "The domain of nature in which the process has operated may be different, but the process itself is basically the same" (Carneiro 1992, 117). Natural selection can operate on single organisms as well as on institutions, beliefs, and cultural traits. The *principle* of natural selection, therefore, is an overarching one, and its biological meaning is just a *special qualitative formulation* of it. The difference is even more obvious if one admits that the units of selection do not have to be originated by chance, as in biology. Inventions, for example, are purposeful entities, but they, too, can be selected for or against. Why, on the contrary, should we assume that a trait (or anything else) should be declared immune from natural selection purely on the basis of its origin (Carneiro 2003, 177)? What follows from this is that this principle is not logically related to biology and therefore to the reproductive success of individual organisms. To stress this principle, one does not need to mention a biological feature at all.

The same is true for the concept of evolution. As in the case of natural selection, Sanderson has a very limited notion of evolution. For him, evolution (social or not) has to be understood in – and only in – Darwinian terms. But as the Darwinian notion of natural selection is only a special formulation of the master principle, so is the Darwinian notion of evolution just a special case of an overarching principle of evolution. As Carneiro points out: "Important as Darwin's contribution was to it, [his theory] was nonetheless restricted in scope. ... [F]rom this recognition [descent with modification] to recognition of a profound and universal transformation, proceeding at many levels towards greater complexity and increased integration, it is a large step. And this step was taken by Spencer alone" (Carneiro 1981, 201).

The problem is this: All those who stress only the Darwinian notion of evolution (they could be called the "functionalists") only deal with the concept of adaptation, because the biological notion of natural selection is intimately bound up with it (a good example of this is Harris's understanding of the phenomenon of "war" as just a social means of responding to population pressure in order to assure a social equilibrium). But adaptation is just one feature of evolution, and not the only one. To the Spencerian evolutionist, however, it is clear that evolution is defined as a process of successive differentiation and integration in the direction of increasing complexity and that adaptation, though a basic feature, should be thought of as just an agent of evolution. Adaptation alone is incapable of explaining the major transformations in "the evolution of human sociality" (see Carneiro 2003, 180).

Claiming to be an evolutionist, the real addressee of Sanderson therefore should not be Harris, but Spencer, or rather the most loyal follower of Spencer in anthropology, namely, Carneiro. There is, I would argue, as far as the understanding of social evolution is concerned, a quantum leap between Harris and Carneiro. As Ferguson has rightly argued, Harris's understanding of cultural materialism is weak at the level of historical time. But the same is true for the highest level of social abstraction, the level of social evolution. His cultural materialism is weak there, too. To be sure, Harris had his vision about how social evolution unfolds, and he was one of the first to argue for a diachronic approach to culture. In fact, however, Harris was much more concerned with synchronic features of societies and wrote only a few things about social evolution. His only book that is primarily concerned with social evolution, *Cannibals and Kings*, is the best example of an ecological functionalist doing pseudoevolutionism by stringing together some synchronic studies.

And here Harris and Sanderson are sitting in the same boat. Even when it is articulated differently, it is obvious that they both have a Darwinian notion of evolution (even if the former sees the principle as analogy, while the latter puts it to use as homology). Both concentrate their research on the mentioned middle-range level. Their concepts are therefore weak at the historical time level, as well as at the highest level, the level of social evolution. This is because both stress adaptation as the main feature of social existence. From a Spencerian point of view, then, neither of the two is doing true evolutionism at all, but just a restricted version of it.

THE DARWINIAN MONKEY

As cultural materialists are known for their polemical attitude, I too can engage in polemic. So, polemically speaking, one could argue that if we get the "Darwinian monkey" off Sanderson's back, there is nothing left but pure cultural materialism. And in some sense that is exactly what Marvis Harris argued in responding to a letter Sanderson wrote to him in 1994:

> Yet there is nothing in the EM [Evolutionary Materialism] paper that remotely resembles a critique of CM's [Cultural Materialism's] basic theoretical principles with respect to their limited applicability; nor do you advance any new set of theoretical *principles* from which the asserted advantages of EM follow. To add to the confusion [it] doesn't test substantive theories, but continues to list general theoretical *principles* that can be matched almost without exception with the basic theoretical principles of CM. ...
>
> Perhaps I am missing something. Enlighten me (quoted in Sanderson 2007b, 196-97).

Up to now, Harris's qualification has proved to be correct. And, up to now, nobody has been enlightened by Sanderson. Though Sanderson was not a staunch sociobiologist at the time he wrote that letter, things haven't changed. To be sure, he is arguing a straightforward materialism and evolutionism and faces the challenge to a science of culture without making a compromise with antiscientific paradigms. For this "good intention" I pay tribute to him. But defending a "natural science of society" (in Spencer's words) is not equivalent to defending it with the right arguments. His aim to push the theoretical principles of cultural materialism "to a deeper level" (Sanderson 2007b) failed and made things even worse. The application of biological principles to the existing materialistic ones was but a step in the wrong and, finally, unscientific direction, as we have seen. So if we put the biological baggage aside, evolutionary materialism is, as Harris pointed out, just cultural materialism with a new name, and Stephen K. Sanderson therefore would be ... well, just Marvin Harris, and not the founder of a "powerful new theory."

7

COOPERATION WITHOUT COERCION?

Responses to Sanderson's Conflict Perspective

Peter Meyer

In this chapter I am going to confront Sanderson's theory with some questions, particularly with regard to the origin of coercion and cooperation. The first part will address some problems with Sanderson's use of the term "materialism," whereas the second part will look into some of the underpinnings of conflicts of interest. In contrast to Sanderson's materialistic notions of human society, it seems to me that a complete appraisal of conflicts of interest has to take the interests of currently living individuals, their ancestors, and their descendants into account, as a famous quotation from the English conservative theorist Edmund Burke accentuates. According to him:

> Society is indeed a contract. . . . [But] the state ought not to be considered as nothing better than a partnership in trade of pepper and coffee, calico or tobacco, or some other such low concern, to be taken up for a little temporary interest, and to be dissolved by the fancy of parties. . . . As the ends of such partnership cannot be obtained by many generations, it becomes a partnership not only between those who are living, but between those who are living, those who are dead, and those who are to be born. Each contract of each particular state is but a clause in the great primeval contract of eternal society (Burke and Hamer 1999, 368; quoted in Corning 2005, 422).

Turning to the origin of cooperation, Sanderson points to Durkheim's and Parsons's notions that the pursuit of self-interest would eventually "lead to the use of force, fraud, anarchy, and in general to the Hobbesian war of all against all. Therefore, selfish behavior had to be restrained by norms and values" (Sanderson 2001a, 103). As for the evolution of society, Durkheim insisted that society is a reality *sui generis*, a social organism that exists apart from any of its members" (Corning 1982, 364). Durkheim wanted to explain society in terms of its coercive effects upon individuals (Corning 1982, 370). Despite Durkheim's insistence, the crucial question is whether we accept his holistic reaction to the evolution of society from coercion, or whether we would rather appreciate that the evolution of cooperation dates back to ancestral times, when the human species evolved as part of the more embracing primate taxa.

COOPERATION AND KIN SELECTION

Provided that we accept kin selection theory to be sufficient for understanding everyday interactions between people of the same extraction, we need to understand what happens if outsiders, particularly men or women from different tribes or ethnic groups, are recruited as marriage partners. Due to genetic problems in the human species, as well as in other species, marriages between closely related kin will in general have detrimental genetic consequences for people (Bischof 1985; Meyer 1990b). This is the reason why many ethnic groups established systems for exchanging marriage partners even if the people concerned had no idea about genetics at all. Kin selection theory applies to people with a common background, but why would partners from different ethnicities be prepared to comply with rules from an incorporating society? Regarding kin selection theory, even partners from the same extraction are going to have different interests, and this is even more true for partners from different ethnic backgrounds.

With respect to the evolution of cooperation, I contend that many theorists agree that cooperation evolved because it was favored by natural selection since "moral sentiments" helped produce mutual sympathy between kinsmen, as Adam Smith argued some time ago (Raphael 1991), or because of the more general benefits for survival, as Peter Corning and some other authors suggest (Corning 1998, 2003; Richerson and Boyd 1998; Boehm 1989). Obviously Smith, who preceded Darwin by several decades, had similar ideas in mind regarding the origin of cooperation. In this regard I agree with Sanderson, according to whom cooperation arose as part of the evolution of inclusive fitness strategies. There is, however, a crucial point in this argument, namely whether kin selection theory favored the evolution of cooperation between kinsmen, precluding nonkin from social interactions. In this regard it is interesting to examine Daly and Wilson's (1988) findings according to which some 690 homicides occurred in Detroit in 1972. Among those, only 127 victims were relatives of their killers, and only 32 were consanguineous (genetic) relatives (Daly and Wilson 1988, 19).

Even though marriage may be regarded as an important form of cooperation, this cultural institution does not prevent people from killing their spouses. As Daly and Wilson point out in detail, the vast majority of homicides occur between strangers, unrelated acquaintances, or married couples. This is quite in line with suggestions from kin selection theory, according to which the killing of kinsmen should seldom occur. When a kinsman is killed by someone from another kin group, people from the victim's group generally feel that they must take revenge for their kin. This type of situation sparked dangerous types of conflict between people in the famous case of Romeo and Juliet, as well as in many similar types of social situations. Therefore, the question arises whether coercion is a necessary concomitant of any type of society?

Let me emphasize once again that kin selection theory may in fact shed light on the evolution of different kinds of conflict. What I do doubt, however, is Sanderson's use of materialism as the proper ontology for a theory of conflict. Although I agree with Sanderson that kin selection theory may be a good starting point for conflict theory, it seems to me that mentalistic approaches are fully compatible with evolutionary theory as well. In other words, I am suggesting that a multitude of human behaviors, such as tendencies for within-group obedience, preparedness for blood-revenge, and readiness for human sacrifices in numerous societies, are not only human universals but may be more easily accounted for in terms of a slightly different approach.

Unlike recent postmodernist theories and their insistence on the "strong programme in the sociology of scientific knowledge" (Fuller 2000, 191), E. O. Wilson, as well as the German epistemologist Hans Albert, censure the denial of the natural foundations of human behavior in sociology. According to Albert (1999), most phenomena in sociology can be accounted for by biological approaches, and thus there is no fundamental difference between the natural and the social sciences. Obviously, Sanderson's book concurs with most of these appraisals but does not harmonize with some of the reservations pointed out in the following section.

MENTAL STATES AS ELEMENTS OF
MATERIALISTIC APPROACHES

With regard to evolutionary biology's general background, Wilson explains in his *Consilience* (1998) that any science starts from metaphysical assumptions. Regarding ideas of a complete understanding of nature, we as human beings do not have any methods at our disposal to fully understand nature as such. Instead, we may follow Wilson's (1998, 76) suggestions and accept that "reductionism" is the crucial method for understanding the most variegated aspects of nature, based on the additional assumption that nature is organized by physical, biological, and other laws (Küppers 1986, 168). In this regard it is important to understand that there are no metaphysical distinctions between genes for genetic reproduction and those singular genes producing consciousness or even self-consciousness in the human species. Following Wilson, it seems that the human brain includes some 100 billion neurons and synapses, and there are about 3,195 genes specifically designed for the brain's evolution (Wilson 1998, 132).

Further insights are also provided by MacLean (1994, 108), according to whom neuronal processes are transformed into psychic emanations: "All psychic emanations are without substance. In regard to colors, for example, we understand many of the neural mechanisms involved in inducing the experience of colors, but the colors themselves do not exist in the entire universe; they exist only as products of the subjective brain." It seems to me that psychic experience is a form of information produced by neuronal processes, but nonetheless appertaining to a novel and emergent hierarchical level. All in all, evolutionary theory predicts that nature consists of material causes, i.e., "regularities among events" (Eigen and Winkler 1981, 162), as well as from various hierarchical levels the laws of which cannot be predicted by lower-level phenomena (Wilson 1998, 76).

Turning finally to the evolution of consciousness, it is particularly interesting that this phenomenon may also be understood in terms of evolutionary reasoning. According to Edelman and Tononi (1997, 225),

> consciousness is linked to certain biological structures. . . . According to the qualia assumption, subjective-qualitative aspects of consciousness cannot be understood in terms of scientific methodology, just because their nature is subjective. . . . This does not mean, however, that the necessary and sufficient conditions for consciousness cannot be explained in scientific terms, but only that characterizing these conditions is not the same as their production in the first place.

Similar to these authors, Dan Sperber (1991, 27) explains that "token mental states . . . are identical to token neural states, though mental types need not be identical to neural types."

With these reservations in mind, it seems to me that a mentalistic approach enables us to include individual mental states, as well as various types of social interactions, and that therefore we may account for some of the human universals designated in the introduction in this manner. Having considered these aspects of materialistic cum mentalistic conflict theory, I am now turning to other parts of Sanderson's theory.

COOPERATION: A MIXTURE OF SYMPATHY AND COERCION

As for the evolution of cooperation, Sanderson dwells upon Hamilton's rule, according to which cooperative relations exist because they are the best way "to promote each individual's selfish interests, not because they promote the well-being of the group or society as a whole" (Sanderson 2001a, 149). According to Maynard Smith and Szathmary (1995, 259), Hamilton's idea is simple: "The basic idea is that, by helping a relative, an individual is propagating its own genes, or, more precisely, copies of those genes. It was hinted at by Darwin, and expressed in genetic terms by Haldane (1955). However, its precise formulation, and its application to animal societies, we owe to Hamilton." Regarding Hamilton's rule, Sanderson puts special emphasis upon individual "selfishness" that extends to close kin. But beyond kin relations, people tend to be more conflictive, and in the long run one may expect some type of stratification to arise from nepotistic interactions. In fact, numerous sociobiologists agree that nepotism is or was part of social relations in most regions of the world. Maynard Smith and Szathmary point out that (1995, 261)

> if an individual can produce, say, two offspring on its own, but a group of individuals can raise three offspring if they cooperate, then it pays each of them to cooperate. Such synergistic effects are often invoked to explain cooperation. For example, perhaps lions are social because group hunting is more efficient than hunting alone. . . . The snag, of course, is that it takes two to cooperate. It is important to distinguish two situations, which we call the rowing and skulling games. The skulling game is identical to the Prisoner's Dilemma. If both players cooperate, they are better off than if both defect, but, unfortunately, whatever the other player does it pays to defect, so "rational" players end up defecting.

Also, Peter Corning suggests that it is advisable to prefer Maynard Smith and Szathmary's "win-win-proposition" because "cooperative groups may gain mutual advantages for their members, so that the net benefits to all participants outweigh the costs" (Corning 1998, 24). And he continues:

> From a functional perspective, if cooperation offers sufficient benefits it may be in the interest of some individuals to invest in coercing the cooperation of others. Inclusive fitness provides one possible explanation for punishment as a successful strategy in social groups. . . . But group selection may also provide a mechanism. The enforcement of cooperation in the "public interest" might have a significant fitness-enhancing value for groups that are in competition with other groups (Corning 1998, 24).

In a similar manner, Richerson and Boyd lay stress upon differences between human individuals and social insects. Whereas individuals in many insect species are genetically nearly identical, human ultrasociality could have evolved through the coevolution of culture and genes. In Richerson and Boyd's (1998, 73) words, "Cultural evolutionary processes drove the evolution of human ultrasociality by cultural transmission." According to them, cooperation with kin is deeply rooted in human psychology. Dwelling upon Alexander's notion of indirect reciprocity, perhaps reciprocity can encourage cooperation among large, diffuse networks of cooperators.

   However, some individuals may be looking for selective advantages which according to these authors may be subordinated to "punishment." In this regard they base their argument upon Tooby and Cosmides's (1989; Cosmides and Tooby 1989) notions, according to which human individuals possess an "innate decision-making module" devoted to detecting cheaters on social contracts.

   Further doubts are also voiced by Crippen, who contends that group selection "cannot be dismissed entirely from discussions of human sociobiology" (1994, 312). However, even more forceful are Wilson and Sober (1994), who seem to be dismissive of individual selection. They base their objections on what they feel is the erroneous conception of the gene as the fundamental unit of selection (Wilson and Sober 1994, 589). According to them, "individualism in biology and in the human sciences both fail for the same reasons. As far as human evolution is concerned, group-level functional organization is not a "by-product" of self-interest in humans any more than it is in honeybees." Therefore, they feel that "it is legitimate to treat social groups as organisms to the extent that natural selection operates at the group level" (Wilson and Sober 1994, 598). As an example, Wilson and Sober discuss the Hutterites, who are "as explicit as they can possibly be that their members should merge themselves into a group-level organism" (Wilson and Sober 1994, 604). In sum they suggest that this sectarian movement is not something found only in sixteenth-century Europe, "but reflects an evolved human potential to construct and live within such group-level organisms" (Wilson and Sober 1994, 605).

Despite these differences, there is yet another aspect of genetic interests directly relevant for the evolution of cooperation, namely the development of gender differences. Since sexual reproduction is the crux of all social systems even among the most diverse types of species, and since in human societies men and women play different reproductive roles, their respective contribution to the production of offspring is quite different too. Underlying these sex-related roles is the so-called fitness variance, according to which parents on average may expect more offspring from their sons and fewer from their daughters (Voland 2002). Regarding the impact of sex roles on human cognitions, Wang (1996, 13) points out that cognitions are dependent upon age, gender, fecundity status, and expected inclusive fitness effects: "The age- and perspective-dependent choice patterns found in the present study argue against an all-purpose rationality view-point, and indicate that human cognitive mechanisms are sensitive to the internal biological status of the information-processing organism." Regarding cognitive states, they seem to be guided by the dynamics of the respective organism's specific biological status.

From this point of view, there are no "fixedly altruistic or selfish humans. They are complex, cryptic, and deceptive in behaviour" (Peritore 1998, 79). It is true that the Hutterites are a "group level organism" (Wilson and Sober 1994, 605), but, from an evolutionary point of view, individual compliance with any group "always involves large amounts of pressure or coercion" (Peritore 1998, 21). It seems that deception will be comparatively rare in tightly knit groups because they are made up of persons with a similar background. Similar views are also pointed out by Sanderson (2001a, 149). According to him, the evolution of constraints may be expected from the ways people are descended from each other because, usually, parents exercise an influence on their offspring.

STEPS FROM ALTRUISM TO THE MODERN WORLD

As pointed out by Trivers (1971) and other sociobiologists, reciprocal altruism was the basis for cooperation between nonkin in ancestral times. Despite the prevalence of small groups, there were also incentives to expanding groups to larger size. Due to hunting and defense strategies, sizable groups were favored by natural selection. With respect to hunting, Corning (1998) states that the amount of time each animal spent avoiding and defending against predators declined dramatically as group size increased, i.e., reciprocity provided more benefits than kin selection did. Also Richerson (1997) points to increased benefits as being favored by gene-culture coevolution, extending even beyond original kin groups. This is also acknowledged by E. O. Wilson, according to whom individuals must pay tribute to more embracing groups (Wilson 1998, 230). In this regard he points to the impact of religions, which motivate individuals to adjust to symbolic rewards granted by religious authorities (Wilson 1998, 326).

As pointed out above, gender differences are among the most relevant aspects of social life. With regard to the maintenance of cooperation between people, the exchange of marriage partners between populations is a decisive step. Drawing on Westermarck's insights, Brown (1991, 118) suggests that in general "there is a lack of erotic feeling between persons who have been living closely together from childhood."

Moreover, it seems that despite the many benefits of living in closely knit populations, marriages between partners from the same ethnic origin are comparatively less fertile (Shaw and Wong 1989, 234; Brown 1991, 121) as compared to intermarriages between unrelated partners. Despite this general rule for the preference of intermarriages, obviously there are exceptions, such as breaches of this rule among pharaonic dynasties. Regarding natural selection's impact on intermarriages, it seems that people will in general adhere to these rules and tend to deviate only in exceptional situations. Finally, it should be stressed that unless people have clear ideas about kinship and understand differences in social status, intermarriages as in pharaonic dynasties could not be accounted for. Last but not least, marriages are an important aspect of cooperation, but occasionally they give rise to different types of conflicts between populations.

COOPERATION, RECIPROCITY, AND MORALITY

Evolutionary biology provides numerous insights into the general causes underlying the origin of patterns of cooperation. In this regard it is interesting to note different types of reciprocity as they evolved over time. According to Alexander (1986), direct types of reciprocity may be distinguished from indirect types. As he has pointed out (1986, 106), "humans use consciousness, self-awareness, foresight, and conscience to estimate long-term costs and benefits, and to make decisions about short-term pleasures or accepting short-term pains."

Similar to some animal species, direct reciprocity is part of human behavior; however, indirect reciprocity seems to be much more important. Indirect reciprocity exists "whenever rewards and punishments come from individuals and groups other than those directly involved" (Alexander 1986, 107). Also Badcock (1991, 86) suggests that patterns of reciprocity are among the fundamentals for any type of human society.

An interesting description of reciprocity's impact on human society is presented by Polly Wiessner. According to her portrayal of !Kung San economy, this hunter-gatherer economy employs a form of reciprocity they call *hxaro*, which is a "social system for reducing risk" (Wiessner 1982, 62). People in the Kalahari desert use this institution in order to store "social obligations," not as economic contracts "but rather as bonds of mutual help" (1982, 68) that will be activated at a later date if the region might be drought-stricken.

With regard to the evolution of reciprocity it is not surprising that a number of reports suggest that people "might possess an evolved, universal cognitive algorithm for detecting cheating in situations of social exchange" (Machalek and Martin 2004, 466) and that "people are better at remembering the faces of cheaters than those of trustworthy people" (2004, 466).

There is, however, still another sphere that is directly relevant for the emergence of reciprocity, namely when people experience the killing of close kin (Boehm 1989, 930). As Fornari points out, "blood revenge is set in motion not so much by murderous lust but by family affection" (quoted in van der Dennen 1995, 392). Much like Fornari, Hans Kelsen suggests that taking revenge is a human universal, particularly when close kin have been slain. It is important to convince dangerous rivals, he says, that there are extremely high (often unacceptable) costs associated with killing members of alien kin groups.

Last but not least, in an evolutionary setting it is most interesting to realize that people concerned with defending themselves are likely to decide involvement in violent strife based upon kinship considerations (Wang 1996). Obviously, moralistic systems are being activated in order to check whether the norms of reciprocity have been observed by partaking individuals.

Since in modern societies people are mostly nonrelatives, Richerson and Boyd (1992, 172) suggest that human "eusociality is based on reciprocity." However, since "cooperation is unlikely in sizable groups," Richerson and Boyd show how the introduction of punishment changed individual considerations: "Although nobody lives forever, social groups often persist much longer than individuals. When they do, individuals can expect to be punished up until their very last" (1992, 185). Leaving aside further concomitants of fighting, I am now turning to some causes underlying the preparedness for fighting among human individuals.

Another social institution to be addressed here is ostracism. According to Gruter and Masters (1986, 1), ostracism is a "process of rejection and exclusion observed in the human" as well as in other species. Obviously, this practice contradicts assumptions of kin selection theory insofar as this theory suggests that kinsmen should support each other in most situations. According to numerous studies, ostracism is started by persons "who disrupt the cooperative system of a group" (Barner-Barry 1986, 133). As pointed out by various experts in the field, ostracism has been practiced in many societies, including the Pathans of Afghanistan, the Montenegrins in the Balkans (Gruter and Masters 1986), by various Amerindian peoples (Meyer 1999), as well as in many ancient societies in Europe and other parts of the world.

Regarding the origin of warfare, people often resort to fighting in order to take vengeance on outsiders who for whatever reason killed their ancestors. Very often in the history of warfare, it is the ancestors who exact militant action against their foes; however, their descendants' current interests probably concur much more with those of these former adversaries. Viewed against this background, waging war in order to take vengeance for a slain kinsman is not necessarily an expression of a "reification of the group," as Sanderson assesses this action (Sanderson 2001a, 128). In this regard there is an ongoing dispute between proponents of Milgram's (1974) assumptions, according to which natural selection has provided people with a general inclination to obedience, whereas Sanderson insists "that disobedience is frequently rather than rarely encountered" (Sanderson 2001a, 311).

CONCLUSION

It seems to me that Sanderson's insistence on a materialistic approach to conflict theory contradicts recent advances in evolutionary theory. According to these findings, human consciousness is based on the physical laws of nature, as well as on the emergent properties of nature. Max Weber's insights into the antagonistic teachings of religions should therefore be included in a more general theory of social conflict. Among sociologists, it is well-known that Randall Collins and Michael Mann share this appraisal of Weber. It was also argued that despite some of the shortcomings of Durkheim's approach (Tooby and Cosmides 1992), in general most people are obedient, and occasionally they "reify" their group allegations and, hence, wage war against adversaries who previously had killed their ancestors.

To sum up, morality, as well as the institution of blood-revenge and other aspects of humanity, would not exist at all unless mental states provided human beings with information on their ancestors' former existence, as well as their struggles in the past. This is the case because people adhere to "indirect reciprocity" (Alexander 1986), taking upon themselves responsibilities from their ancestors. It seems that much violent strife cannot be accounted for by a purely materialistic approach, and it seems that a mentalistic approach does a better job of explaining this type of behavior. This is also in agreement with Adam Smith's point that sympathy plays a decisive role in conflictive situations; whereas people usually behave according to the principles of kin selection, they do this for different reasons. For instance, they reciprocate on the one hand their ancestors' obligations, or they may on the other hand ostracize their own kin if they "disrupt the cooperative system of the group" (Barner-Barry 1986, 143). However, in most situations people are neither "fixedly altruistic or selfish. Humans are complex, cryptic, and deceptive" (Peritore 1998). All in all, kin selection theory may in fact provide causal reasoning for the evolution of human groups, but Adam Smith was correct too when he "censured Hobbes's neglect of sympathy, a natural source of cooperation" (Raphael 1991, 11). Society is not feasible without "sympathy," or without constraints imposed by ancestors.

8

DARWINIAN CONFLICT THEORY AND HUMAN CREATIVITY

Heinz-Jürgen Niedenzu

Sanderson's Darwinian Conflict Theory (DCT) claims to provide an explanatory strategy that can explain the major phenomena of human existence and the formation of social structures better than other existing sociological theories. According to Sanderson, this is accomplished by means of a synthesis of diverse heuristic perspectives that are judged to be fruitful (Sanderson 2001a, 1, 144). Sociobiology is regarded as the ultimate form of materialist social theory, in which all forms of materialist and conflict theoretical approaches must be anchored (Sanderson 2001a, 143). Thus DCT represents a methodological reductionism to a single "first principle" (Sanderson 2001a, 144), and its causal explanations run accordingly from "below" to "above"; "the flow of causation is primarily from the biostructure to the ecostructure, then from the ecostructure to the structure, and finally from the structure to the superstructure" (Sanderson 2001a, 150). At the same time, the theory recognizes very well the socially constructed character of human societies and a certain autonomy of their superstructures (Sanderson 2001a, 151), although these processes are conceived to take place not arbitrarily but within the pregiven conditions with which they must be compatible. The central problem of the theory, in my view, despite Sanderson's concessions, lies in this: Sanderson does not assign in his theory any systematic place to human constructivity and creativity, which are the distinguishing features of human societies. It seems therefore that the psychological, social, and cultural processes, which have their own logic and occur independently of the sociobiologically conceived conditions, are accorded only a marginal importance in his theory's explanations.

I shall attempt to show some of the problems with the explanatory claims of DCT in a necessarily condensed argumentative form. After a short retrospective of its development in the discipline of sociology, I discuss whether and to what extent the contemporary reception of this theory in the social sciences takes up the full potential of its stimulus. Following this, I discuss the question of whether the theoretical architecture of DCT contributes to a sounder foundation for sociological knowledge.

THE ATTRACTION OF THE DARWINIAN THEORY
IN THE NINETEENTH CENTURY

The early phase of European sociology (the "long nineteenth century" from the French revolution to the First World War) can be understood from the point of view of the history of science as an oscillating search for suitable conceptual-theoretical means for the description and analysis of the construction of order and change in societies (Hejl 2000, 167). Both dimensions of society thereby came into view, namely, on the one hand, society as a structural and functional object susceptible to abstract description and, on the other hand, society as an historical-empirical phenomenon.

Turning to the concept of evolution, Darwin's work, along with the older evolutionary thought of Herbert Spencer, became a source of both inspiration and discussion for sociologists (Engels 2000, 112-39; Weingart 2000, 146-55). The first generation of German-speaking sociologists was not at all shy about coming into contact with the categories and models of biology; however, except for a few representatives from the selection-oriented theory of social biology (Weingart 2000, 155-59), this "Darwinian sociology" did not pursue a reductionist strategy at that time. From the very beginning, the discussion of Darwin's theory of evolution was marked by ambivalent positions, ranging from terminological loans and selective adoptions, through conceptual-metaphorical appropriations, to total rejection (Engels 2000, 122-31; Hejl 2000, 202-06; Baldus 2002, 316-20). This treatment became manifest in the naturalization of the picture of humans ("anthropology"), although the distinction between inherent and acquired characteristics as the foundation of needs and dispositions to action was maintained from the beginning. The more recent discussions of nature vs. nurture were already present in sociology's early phases and also in the metaphorical applications of models of the organism and the evolutionary idea of society (Francis 1981, 215-16). In this way, it manifested disciplinary independence, and the applicability as well as the suitability of the scientific method became an object of sociological study. Only with the works of classical sociologists such as Weber, Simmel, and Durkheim was the way finally prepared for establishing the independence of the discipline and the development of an increasingly culturalist understanding of sociological investigation.

MAKING SOCIOLOGY INTO A SOCIAL SCIENCE IN THE TWENTIETH CENTURY

In contrast to these early phases of sociology, in twentieth-century sociology there are hardly more than a few borrowings from discussions in biology. Thus, for instance, in mid-century Gehlen (1993 [orig. 1940]) attempted an overarching anthropological description of humans, attempting to integrate the biological knowledge of the time within a comprehensive philosophical view. Paradoxically, Gehlen's taking into account man's biological constitution leads to an extreme culturalist description in which a rupture is discerned between the human biological constitution (drives, needs) and the cultural mastering of life (consciousness, action). According to Gehlen, the biological dimensions are under the control of higher cultural and symbolically encoded systems of orientation and institutions (Gehlen 1963, 21, 52-60), where the biological explanation of individual action, social processes, and social structures is no longer accorded any real importance. It seems that Gehlen's ahistorical approach is responsible for this result that renounces the application of all process-related perspectives. Furthermore, Parsons's theory also takes pains to include and integrate the biological substrate in its architecture, but here too the effort is finally without consequence, since the control of human behavior is exclusively the result of superordinate systems (Staubmann 2001, 151-52). In sum, man's biological nature is deprived of any direct significance with respect to the shaping of the individual as well as of society and, again, the culturalist view prevails.

It may be observed that sociology in the twentieth century became self-absorbed and more or less exclusively culturalist, which hindered its catching up to and incorporating the views of other disciplines. This tendency resulted in an approach in which actions and systems of action are analyzed exclusively as mental-cultural phenomena (*Versozialwissenschaftlichung der Soziologie*, Meleghy 2003a, 121, 24; Meleghy 2003b). By contrast, DCT can be understood as an attempt to rectify the culturalist slant of modern sociology through the integration of fresh knowledge from modern biology. In principle, this enterprise is most welcome. The problem, however, is whether the sociobiological imagination of man can be adopted as a model for sociology. As pointed out above, it seems that a sociobiological description of man underplays human creativity and constructivity. It confines itself to a narrow image of humans so that the evolutionary model as such, particularly its effective mechanisms, remains largely excluded from explanations of social processes and the formation of structures. DCT therefore runs the risk of adopting the sociobiological account of human behavior with its static preconditions and underplaying or making theoretically secondary the creativity and constructivity of human life in its historical and material significance.

THE EVOLUTION OF A NEW CONTROL MECHANISM

With regard to epistemology, sociobiological notions run the risk of underexposing a major step in the development of social life forms. According to modern knowledge, human society and culture in their historical shapes can be grounded in variants that are not established upon a metaphysical or extramundane reality, and hence must be made comprehensible as organizations emerging from natural history (*Anschlussorganisationen*). The organization of human society is distinguished from animal societies by the fact that it is a form of intellectual and sociocultural organization, constructed and reconstructed in continual processes through symbolic media, that is, mostly through conceptual thought and language (Dux 2000, 20). The social form of organization of human society is not unambiguously given by nature as it is for other animal species known to us, but is indisputably subject to human influence, to the power of action as well as to ecological influence. Fundamental for this kind of social life is man's intellectual-constructive capacity, which may be described formally as a biological precondition in the form of a program that is open in content. The diversity of human forms of social organization, both in respect to their structure and in their historical perspective, is a manifestation of this extraordinary constructive capacity.

The crucial problem is: How, on the one hand, can this capacity for meaning-guided action be placed within meaning-neutral evolutionary processes that are anchored in a general evolutionary process, while on the other hand we insist on the autonomy of the cognitive capacity, which manifests itself according to its own logic and in ever new forms, at times even acting contrary to evolutionary mechanisms and imperatives?

Obviously there are degrees of freedom within the natural determinants. Nevertheless, the constructive character of types of human societies, as well as the resultant consequences, forms the ultimate and the primary ground for all objects and questions of sociology and the justification for its independence as a discipline. Given this background, how can the stimulus of the Darwinian theory of evolution be taken into positive account? How does DCT treat the problem of the human constructive capacity and its medial-symbolic unfolding? What place does this theory have in the construction of sociological theory?

THE RICHNESS OF THE DARWINIAN THEORY

Darwin was very well aware of the difference between naturally predetermined social organization, founded on hereditary social instincts, and socioculturally organized patterns of life, founded on the transmission of Lamarckian rules (social virtues). With regard to the formation of cognition, language, and social capacities, he pursued a naturalistic argument that aimed at the selection of variants. At the same time, he noted that just these intellectual and linguistic capacities place humans in the position to respond actively to changes in their environment without having to develop physical adaptations. In fact, he saw the real qualitative difference between humans and many animals residing in the human capacity for morally guided action. This presupposes two things: first, the uncoupling of humans from the mechanism of natural selection and, second, the presence of novel degrees of freedom that developed only in the course of social evolution (Engels 2000, 101-08). Thus we have the paradoxical situation that the mechanism of natural selection sets in motion a gradual (not teleological) process which brings forth a new biological species with new potentials, in which further processes of moral and sociocultural development influence this biological selection mechanism itself or are able to repress its effective force.

Therefore, it is decisive for the understanding of the theory of evolution that the relation between individual organisms and their environment be reconceived. All too often environmental selection is placed one-sidedly in the foreground, and the organism is seen in a passive role: The forces of external selection affect organisms in their variants without the latter being able themselves to influence the selection. Paradigmatic for this way of seeing this relation is the example of differently colored butterflies in which the more darkly colored insects enjoy survival advantages under certain environmental conditions, such as air pollution in industrial areas. Yet, at the same time, Darwin recognized an active testing of possibilities by the organism itself. Those tests are bound up with the fact that many characteristics of the evolutionary process are generated as blind variations precisely because they are accidentally generated. Therefore, they need not have any adaptive advantage and may contain a scope of possible choices for the individual organism. The relation between individual organisms is treated by Darwin under the heading of sexual selection, in which the characteristics of other organisms have naturally arisen independently of the internal preferences of the choosing organism, namely as blind, accidentally occurring variants. There are, therefore, two sides to the process of adaptation: First, selection through environment, which occurs on the grounds of parameters external to the organism (natural selection, sexual selection) and, second, selection which occurs on the grounds of an organism's internal evaluation of given variants. The latter can include a preference expressed externally in the form of choice behavior (sexual selection) but can also include a choice or formation of a behavioral strategy against the background of hereditary variability. In this way, the relation between organism and environment is not a rigid one, but rather includes a testing behavior on the part of the former organism. It seems that, in the case of all higher animals, such adaptive structures and performance spectrums are built up within processes of play.

In the course of evolution, this active, organism-internal process gains an ever greater importance through the growing capacity of the brain, and the moment of "intentionality" in choice acquires a correspondingly greater importance in the process of selection (Baldus 2002, 321-24). Greater cerebral capacity, the development of understanding and (self-)consciousness, enable both a growing, cognition-based flexibility of reaction toward external pressures of selection and a growing capacity for reflection in the treatment of organism-internal conditions and possibilities of action. At least among human beings, environmental parameters as well as preferences can increasingly become the object of hypothetical treatment; moreover, the category of utility thus becomes dependent upon subjective and experiential valences and self-ordered preferences. Regarding natural selection, the theory of selection understands the blindly occurring emergence of this kind of creative capacity as an adaptive advantage with respect to contingent environmental processes, but it is also, particularly among human beings, the source of new contingencies in the form of surplus production and the condition for the possibility of unnecessary, poorly adapted, or altogether nonadaptive forms of behavior, thought, and sociocultural structures. In this regard, the brain is more than a fitness-maximizing organ; its function goes far beyond that. In this way, internal selection simultaneously produces, on the one hand, order through the lessening of complexity (by, for example, generating criteria of selection such as systems of preferences or institutional structures) and, on the other hand, instability by bringing forth unexpected or new alternatives, which in turn lead to new complexities and contingencies and drive on sociocultural evolution (Hejl 2001, 43-46; Baldus 2002, 324).

With respect to the history of evolution, organism-internal processes come increasingly to mediate the relation between organism and environment. This means that a constructive rather than purely passive role accrues in the process to organisms. The hereditary transmission of adaptive characteristics and forms of behavior are only one side of evolution; before such transmission can occur at all, the active organism must apply these characteristics and forms of behavior to contingent problems relevant to survival. Hereditary material is thus not translated into action according to a direct one-to-one correspondence but must pass through organism-internal processes of experiment and filtering that grapple with the possibilities and necessities of application. At the same time, it is precisely the redundancy of cognitive innovation and cultural characteristics, that is, the creation of variation, that enables the active organism to make flexible responses to a contingent environment. According to Hejl, the intentionality of human action, the constructive capacity for action within the medium of conceptual thought and language, can probably be formally embedded in the genome or the organization of the brain as its structural material foundation, but not in its substantial material manifestations and, so, also not in its individual, historical, cultural, and social contexts (Hejl 2001, 36). For this reason the inherent and potentially autonomous logic of sociocultural phenomena cannot be adequately covered by sociobiology. Moreover sociocultural evolution cannot be reduced to biochemical evolution, although the former has developed out of the latter in the form of an emergent organization (Dux 2000, 53-54; Baldus 2002, 318-19).

The shortcomings of sociobiology lie in an unclear treatment of the problem of the creative character of evolutionary processes and their manifestations, which one-sidedly overemphasizes the process of externally induced selection and adaptation (Reichholf 1994, 1; Hejl 2001, 49-50; Sanderson 2001a, 128). As far as sociocultural phenomena are concerned, man's constructive capacity has in the meantime been taken into account by, for instance, Wilson, who, in contrast to his previous views, now concedes the human mind a more independent role between genes and culture, without having therefore to break the connection between genes and culture. According to Wilson, the place of imprinting and determination is taken by predispositions and a realm of free play in the sense of conditions for possibilities and epigenetic rules (Sanderson 2001a, 143, 148; Richter 2005, 530-33), but now as before the guiding question of the maximization of fitness dominates his explanations. Regarding sociobiology, it seems not to be the diversity of cultural phenomena that appears to be in need of explanation; instead, it seems to lay its efforts at proving the compatibility of this diversity with fundamental sociobiological theses. From the perspective of sociobiology, it is not the *diversity* of cultural phenomena that needs to be explained; rather the task is to demonstrate that this diversity is compatible with fundamental sociobiological theses. Whereas in the reflections of the classical social sciences, social and cultural particularity came to the fore and is analyzed within an historical framework, the biological point of view is interested in ahistorical universals (Sanderson 2001a, 125-26, 130-31). This is why sociobiology has had a hard time fitting maladaptive cultural behavior, characteristics, and social structures into its explanatory schemes. If sociobiologists are prepared to acknowledge this issue (Richerson and Boyd 2005), then they would immediately be confronted with questions about the theoretical rigor of sociobiological explanations in general.

The limitations of sociobiological analyses that have here been broached have consequences for the place of sociobiology in a comprehensive paradigm. In the second and concluding part of my paper, I shall illustrate this point by means of the theoretical architecture of the Darwinian conflict theory.

THE EXPLANATORY CLAIMS OF THE DARWINIAN CONFLICT THEORY: BETWEEN NATURALISM AND CULTURALISM

Without the infrastructure of a realist understanding of human motives and interests, the constructive capacity (which Sanderson, after all, acknowledges) is given too great a weight in attempts to explain sociocultural structures and thus an overemphasis that brings with it the danger of purely culturalist explanations and hence a relativism of the "everything-is-possible" variety. Against this, DCT offers a clear strategy: For sociocultural phenomena, only biomaterialist explanations, which refer to innate structures of motivation and particularly to reproductive interests, enjoy ultimate causation, whereas ecomaterialist and polimaterialist explanations are assigned a subordinate or derivative importance, because they operate exclusively at the level of proximate causation. However, proximate causal factors may in fact contradict ultimate causation. Similar to the Marxian dialectic, a tension then arises between biological imperatives and sociocultural solutions which in the evolutionary perspective (that is, in the long run) can be resolved only in favor of the biomaterial conditions, that is, of evolutionary heredity in the sense of the imperatives of the maximization of reproductive fitness.

In this model, sociobiology is assigned the role of specifying the strategies for coping with survival that have been inherited and developed in the course of evolution and their fields of application. Some examples would be sex-specific interests, strategies for increasing social power, forms of social structure (hierarchies, insider-outsider), and territoriality, all of which stand in the service of reproductive interests. Now, regardless of whatever objections one may have as to the details of this anthropological description, it is not, in my opinion, the critical point. The critical point is the theoretical architecture with its specific linkage of diverse levels of explanation. I shall now briefly illuminate this problem by a comparison, first with Norbert Elias's model of evolution, and then with Gerhard Vowinckel's model of level linkage.

Starting Point for Explanations: Ultimate Elements or Figurations?

Norbert Elias conceives his model of the "great evolution" (Elias 1987, Chapter III) as an attempt, spanning several specific disciplines, to work out the general characteristics of the evolutionary process. According to this view, cosmic, inorganic, and organic evolution are marked by a single, unitary principle: The movement from smaller units to greater units. The greater units of integration that come into being through this process have new emergent properties. In distinction to inorganic material, where the integration of atoms into molecules is reversible in that, after the disintegration of the original unit, the component units again possess their original properties, units of organic material (for instance, cells integrated into groups of cells or organs) have two distinguishing characteristics: The newly formed unit of integration develops differentiations in the sense of functional specialization, and it is organized into hierarchical patterns. Consequently, the integration is irreversible; disintegration of the unit means the end of the components because these are capable of survival only within the greater unit owing to the specialization of functions. Evidently Elias orients himself according to a model of individual organisms in which, with the death of the organism (the unit of integration), its components disintegrate into their inorganic elements, since alone they are no longer viable.

Elias sees a similar principle at work in animal groups as well as in human societies. Doubtlessly, there may be logical gaps in Elias's extension of this principle to supraindividual and social phenomena (Niedenzu, 2003), a point that cannot be pursued here. Still, interestingly, there is an inference that Elias draws concerning an appropriate epistemological strategy and methodology. According to him, the more that comprehensive units of integration with internal differentiation and hierarchical structuring of their components develop, the more explanations must proceed on the level of the interplay of the interlocking components as well as on the next level of smaller units of integration as components of greater such units. Analytical explanatory models that take as their starting point the characteristics of the smallest components and, therefore, pursue a methodological reductionism, are subordinated to synthetic explanatory models that proceed from the constellation of interlocking components. In Elias's view, the isolated characteristics of these component units do not lose their general value for an understanding of the organism as a whole; on the contrary, this must always be taken into account. But in relation to the process arising from the constellation, they are less important for the comprehensive explanation.

In further following this approach, Elias uses the example of the European civilizing process to show how the development of the absolutist state in France arose from a figuration-conditioned dynamic among smaller units that led to a more comprehensive integrated unit afterwards. With respect to the people included in this process, they possess natural motives, wishes, and strategies that are an important part of this process, but only the figurational constellation as such molds and selects these psychobiological conditions in a particular direction. According to Elias it is this sociogenetic process that effectively selects the affective structure. In this way, action that is founded in a rational process of decision is for Elias only the result of a specific historical-figurational process and not an already genetically precoded kind of thought.

How can Elias's theoretical architecture help us to address the problems of DCT? In my opinion, the preeminence that DCT gives to biomaterialist explanations of sociocultural phenomena and develops in an individual-reductionist manner cannot be maintained because it is too one-sided. Ecomaterialist and polimaterialist explanations, which refer more than biomaterialist ones to historical-figurational constellations, should be more than mere ancillary constructions to be used when biomaterialist accounts do not directly apply. Unlike in DCT, it seems to me that at these levels – economic and political – the fundamental motivational outfitting of formative processes is taking place. Therefore, it is necessary for our theoretical models to capture better the peculiar logic of sociocultural processes and their corresponding importance for explanations. In the next section I should therefore like to briefly review Vowinckel's reflections on an alternative model for setting diverse, simultaneously effective levels in relation to each other.

A Model of Level Linkage

Regarding human beings, biological evolution has brought forth a form of life whose survival depends, to a much greater extent than in all other known animals, upon the interplay of three analytically distinguishable levels of control. According to Vowinckel (2001, 2003) those levels may be called the biotic, the psychological, and the social. All behavior is well rooted in biotic preprogramming. This does not operate directly but needs an autonomous epigenetic unfolding with respect to the possibilities and demands offered by the environment. This active-creative process of translation occurs in humans in the mode of conceptual thought and language. None of these levels can act alone and for themselves without consideration of the others, and the corresponding processes of biogenesis, ontogenesis, and sociogenesis can thus be enlisted independently as the explanation of the human capacity for action. According to systems theory, any individual level, regarded as an operatively closed system, is marked by its own peculiar process-related logic, which is simultaneously bound up in indissoluble interdependence with the other levels, because each level always has the two others as its relevant environment of selection. The autonomy shows itself in the criteria of selection specific to each level. At the biotic level, fitness maximizing genetic information is selected, then passed on and manifested in the outfitting for needs, body language patterns, adaptive learning capacity, and intelligence as a creative-constructive element. At the psychological level, patterns of thought, feeling, and action are selected that offer highly subjective rewards with reference to the prevailing environmental conditions. These are built upon preprogrammed, but individually developable, needs and inclinations in which the bioevolutionary criterion of fitness plays no role in the striving after satisfaction, that is, in which the corresponding actions are not oriented toward reproductive success. At the sociocultural level, higher systems of individual action, organization, and orientation are selected that provide a stable framework of order for individual interests ("care for the self") generated by evolution through integrating diverse interests and power potentials within constellations, which then tend to become independent of immediate interests.

It seems that the selection criteria of bioevolution, ontogenesis, and sociocultural evolution can steer the development of individual behavior in different or even opposing directions, and so in turn, through reciprocal action and reaction, change the environment and with it the selective conditions of the processes occurring on the other levels. Therefore, the reciprocal dependence seems to be indissoluble, for only it can produce the capacity for survival. In this connection, however, the different rates or speeds of adaptation must be taken into account. Whereas the passing on of genetic information is tied to the change of generations, psychological modeling is a short-term process tied to the individual lifespan, and social-cultural knowledge again can be handed down and applied independently of the succession of generations and particular concrete individuals. Conditioned by a biotic preprogrammed potential for learning and intelligence, temporarily faster and more short-term adaptive flexibility to changing circumstances may come about at the psychological and sociocultural levels, which at the same time shields the biotic level from the pressure of bioevolutionary adaptation. A purely biological or biomaterialist explanation is therefore adequate only where behavior remains untouched by biographical experience, that is, where behavior is not reorganized cognitively (that is, as social) in the course of life.

CONCLUSION

Vowinckel's reflections appear to me to provide a suitable foil with which to throw new light on both the relations of levels and the problem of creativity. As opposed to DCT, Vowinckel recognizes no explanatory preeminence of a narrowly understood biotic level with its imperative needs, but conceives the biological foundation rather as simultaneously expressed in three subregions: genetic predispositions in the strict sense; cognitive-psychological processes of translation, which doubtless have an ontogenetic-processive and preprogrammed acquisition succession, but are nevertheless open with respect to content, activated only by socioculturally determined learning processes and can be made useful at different levels; and finally the region of sociocultural processes, where cognitive capacities find their formative expression in various organizations and worldviews.

It seems to be decisive that the organism's coping with the challenges of life must be ensured by a constructive-creative activity; that is, its biological constitution provides need-patterns, problems, and paths of solutions (for instance, the basic motive of reproductive interest), but that these must be treated actively, worked on, and absorbed. Constructive activity does not take place in a space emptied of biology, but remains coupled with preconditions and is therefore not arbitrary. Everything must be secured through the organism's own means. Thus, the development of cognition follows a successive structure that has emerged through evolution, but (and this is a central point) the stages of the acquisition process do not follow a biological automatism but rather depend on sociocultural settings. Sociocultural structures again are diverse, but in all their formations the problem of reciprocity comes to the fore and they are all constituted normatively. Differently stated: Basic motives, the cognitive-psychic translation process, and social ways of life are, from the point of view of biology, equal fields in a single biological structure and can affect survival only through their interplay. According to Vowinckel, decisive however is the manner of functioning: Action must set all three fields into motion in the mode of conceptual thought and language.

As for the explanatory potential of sociobiology, this seems to be limited: Basic genetic equipment changes only over long periods and these changes, moreover, need not always affect behavior. Moreover, selection on the biotic level can be blocked by processes at the psychological and sociocultural levels, since these can respond more swiftly to changes in environmental conditions and thus the adaptive pressure on the genetic equipment can be diminished. At the same time, human beings can resist this adaptive pressure. With respect to the relation between the psychological and the sociocultural levels, Elias's reflections are again interesting. The structures developed at the sociocultural level are longer-lived and exert a greater and stronger influence on the ontogenetic processes of motives and affect modulation than the latter on the former, which ought to be an admonishment against one-sided individual-centered explanations. Constructivity and creativity may be found in all these fields, but because of their temporal structure and systemic effects, the events at the psychological level of translation and within a sociocultural framework have more explanatory power for sociology. Basic motivational structures set the problems that must be treated at the psychological and sociocultural levels. However, the archaic structure of needs is unable to provide direct explanation of concrete sociohistorical patterns of treatment of the latter levels. What it can do is raise the important question whether specific sociohistorical patterns and strategies are compatible with it and whether they can remain stable in an evolutionary perspective.

In conclusion, it may be said that the demonstration of compatibility with bioevolutionary preconditions is an important and necessary corrective against the biology-blind sociological theories of society. The dialectic of framing conditions versus human constructivity, as well as the dialectic of creativity and the imperatives of the organism and their symbolic-medial treatment, however, still have not been definitively answered with DCT. Without a closer consideration of the processes of translation, the mediation of naturalism and culturalism cannot be achieved and the historical dimension of human social systems cannot be made accessible to a theoretic sociological logic.

ACKNOWLEDGMENTS

This article was translated from German by Jonathan Uhlaner.

9

STRUCTURALISM AND SOCIOBIOLOGY

The Missing Link

Tamás Meleghy

In his book *The Evolution of Human Sociality*, Sanderson undertakes a quite ambitious attempt to develop a general theoretical frame of reference for the study of social phenomena on a Darwinian foundation. To this end, he discusses in great detail and very critically the most important theories of the sociological tradition. Many approaches he rejects in principle; others he more or less tidies up. Thus his own frame of reference emerges step-by-step as a theoretical synthesis of what he looks upon as the usable parts of the analyzed concepts.

Among the traditional theories that Sanderson examines is the structuralism of Claude Lévi-Strauss. His judgment of this theory is annihilating and is, in sum, that structuralism is on the one hand dubious for logical reasons that have to do with the functional character of the argument, and on the other hand empirically false.

This chapter will attempt to show that Sanderson's view is only partially justified and that it is worth taking a closer look at structuralism. The author comes to the conclusion that Lévi-Strauss's structuralist program anticipates certain aspects of Sanderson's concerns and could therefore be counted among the precursors of his approach. Complemented by sociobiology, Lévi-Strauss's program could make an important contribution to a Darwinian theory of sociality.

SANDERSON ON STRUCTURALISM

Sanderson focuses his criticism of Lévi-Strauss's structuralism on its linguistic approach to the understanding of social processes. Society for Lévi-Strauss is, as Sanderson argues, a kind of language or text. The task of the social scientist is accordingly to decipher or decode this text. Determined by the tendency of the human mind to think in oppositions, the "social grammar" is constructed according to a system of binary oppositions. Examples of such oppositions are high-low, man-woman, and sacred-profane. In Lévi-Strauss's view, the "social grammar," the totality of the deep structures of society, develops through the reciprocal linkage of binary oppositions.

The diverse social grammars, however different they may be, are in the structuralist view not somehow arbitrary but rather formed by the unconscious laws of the human mind. Sanderson objects that Lévi-Strauss, and with him all other structuralists, has neglected to show what determines these laws. As he puts it, "One looks in vain in the writings of Lévi-Strauss or of any other structuralist for even the slightest hint at the natural laws that might determine how the mind works in any particular time or place" (Sanderson 2001a, 42).

The best method of evaluating a theory is, according to Sanderson, to confront it with empirical reality. What is necessary is not a reflection on concepts, but rather a testable theory. In his view, Lévi-Strauss's explanation of the various forms of cannibalism offers us such a theory.

The starting-point of Lévi-Strauss's reflections are observations of practices having to do with cannibalism. As Lévi-Strauss remarks, human flesh is prepared differently by different cannibals. Some tribes roast the flesh over an open fire, while others boil it in water in a fireproof pot. Further, there are tribes that eat only members of their own tribe, and others that consume exclusively members of alien groups. How is this to be understood? According to Lévi-Strauss, these different practices can be traced back to the social grammar, constructed by four systematically interconnected binary oppositions. The four relevant oppositions are

them:us
nature:culture
roasting:boiling
exocannibalism:endocannibalism

In each pair, the right side represents the more highly rated alternative. "We" are better than "they," culture is higher than nature, boiling is higher than the more natural roasting over a fire (because it requires a cultural artifact, the cooking pot), and endocannibalism, the consumption of members of one's own tribe (we, us) is higher than the eating of strangers (they, them).

In accordance with the logic of this "social grammar," the eating of strangers (them) and the roasting of meat (nature) belong together; that is, exocannibalism and roasting should occur together. The eating of members of one's own tribe (us) and the boiling of meat (culture) form a different unit; that is, endocannibalism and the boiling of meat should be practiced together.

This is Lévi-Strauss's structuralist theory of cannibalism. Can this theory be corroborated by the facts? The prospect, according to Sanderson, is not good. In 1969, the theory of cannibalism was tested by the anthropologist Paul Shankman using a sample of 60 cannibalistic societies (Shankman 1969). The results were as follows: Of the observed exocannibalistic societies, 10 practiced roasting and 15 boiling; of the endocannibalistic societies, 9 practiced roasting and only 2 boiling. Furthermore, human flesh was also smoked and baked – methods of preparation which Lévi-Strauss completely failed to take into account. In light of these results, Lévi-Strauss's theory of cannibalism is (so Sanderson contends) simply false (Sanderson 2001a, 44). Cannibals, one could add, simply do not adhere to Lévi-Strauss's reconstruction of their "social grammar," or else the "grammar" that he assigns to them is not really theirs.

Sanderson also discusses Lévi-Strauss's famous work on the structure of marriage and kinship (Lévi-Strauss 1969). There he interprets the diverse forms of marriage and kinship as a kind of communication, that is, as forms of the exchange of women between diverse descent groups. This form of communication can, according to Lévi-Strauss, be compared to other kinds of communication such as the exchange of messages, goods, and services. That the exchange of women is a matter of communication is often overlooked, according to Lévi-Strauss, because the rhythm of this process is much slower than that of, for instance, the exchange of messages.

In Sanderson's view, Lévi-Strauss's explanation of these phenomena is functionalist as well as structuralist: functionalist, because Lévi-Strauss traces the forms of exchange back to the result effected by this communication, that is, to the solidarity generated among members of societies that goes beyond the narrow bounds of kinship; structuralist, because the forms of marriage and kinship are traced back to the general tendency of the human mind to think in binary oppositions; for example, in the categories of "us" and "them" (Sanderson 2001a, 41, 237).

Both ideas, according to Sanderson, are untenable. The structuralist explanation simply does not work, and functionalists confuse the question about why a social form develops with the question about what this social form effects. A functionalist explanation is therefore not an explanation at all (Sanderson 2001a, 228, 148).

COMMENTS ON SANDERSON'S CRITICISM

In my opinion, Sanderson's criticism of structuralism is only partly justified. Here we must distinguish two areas. The one concerns the idea of a social grammar constructed through binary oppositions. This idea exerts an indisputable fascination and forms the core of modern semiotics (Eco 1979). The human inclination to think in binary oppositions is undeniable. It stands in second place on Sanderson's own list of universal human traits (Sanderson 2001a, 125). Nevertheless, it must be admitted that this idea, at least in the form in which it is concretely applied by Lévi-Strauss, refuses to function properly. Even the study of Lévi-Strauss's monumental three-volume work *Mythologiques* (Lévi-Strauss 1964-71), in which he tracks the effect of this principle on the myths of the natives of North and South America, leaves the reader with the feeling of amazed admiration rather that of having really been persuaded.

In this area belongs the question about the natural laws that conceal themselves behind the binary oppositions. The question may be formulated thus: What force or what law forms in turn the social grammar? Sanderson maintains, as we have seen, that neither Lévi-Strauss nor any other structuralist has ever designated such a law. This assertion is, as I shall show, false.

This brings me to Sanderson's criticism of Lévi-Strauss's *The Elementary Structures of Kinship* (1969). Sanderson's criticism of this work is, in my opinion, quite wrong. In this book, Lévi-Strauss argues neither in a functionalist manner nor does he reduce the forms of marriage and kinship to the effect of binary oppositions. Causally responsible for the social forms of marriage and kinship that he observes is a law determined by content: the law of reciprocal exchange. This may be formulated in two propositions. The first states that one should receive in return for what one has given (sometimes something of the same value). The second proposition states that one must give something, that one should not, so to say, be self-sufficient. The general form in which this law reveals itself is the prohibition against incest. Positively stated, the rule declares at the same time that men must renounce the women of their own group and give them up to other men. "For the prohibition against incest," writes Lévi-Strauss, "establishes the principle that families (whatever idea a society may have of them) may join only with each other and not each on its own account with itself" (1985, 93).

The forms of the exchange of women that arise on the basis of the law of reciprocal exchange lead to the emergence of solidarity between human groups that are not related by blood. In this way, the generated social solidarity is not the cause but rather the more or less unintended consequence of this structure.

THE MISSING LINK

The structuralist program as it was developed by Lévi-Strauss may be represented as follows (Meleghy 2001b). When social scientists consider the multitude of existing human societies, they are commonly struck to begin with by their diversity. The study of earlier, now perished societies reinforces as a rule this impression. Thus they often arrive at the view that, although here as there, now as then, they are dealing with societies of the same biological species, the forms in which human beings realize their life are fundamentally different. If common characteristics are noticed, they are traced to similar environmental influences or to cultural contacts. In this view, only by studying the individual histories of these societies could one come nearer to an understanding of the particular forms of social organization.

This understanding of social phenomena – today one would call it culturalist or social constructivist – is, according to Lévi-Strauss, fundamentally wrong. By this, he does not mean of course that history is irrelevant to the development of particular forms of social phenomena. Wrong is the view that these diverse forms of social life are completely individually and historically unique phenomena. This idea rests, according to Lévi-Strauss, on an illusion produced by the diversity of these forms.

To accept this view would, according to Lévi-Strauss, mean the capitulation of science before its task of describing and explaining the order in the world. In his view, it is perhaps the most important postulate of the sciences that an order prevails in the world (Lévi-Strauss 1968, 21). And this postulate pertains, not only to physical and biological structures, but also to social phenomena.

In order to discover this order, the social scientist cannot stop with the observation of the diversity of social manifestations. He must direct his attention to deeper levels until he arrives at discrete elements whose composition and arrangement ultimately produce the diversity of social phenomena. He must, argues Lévi-Strauss, "grasp these elements at a level which reaches so deep one can be certain that, in whatever cultural circumstances they may appear, they remain the same (like genes, which are identical elements and capable of appearing in various combinations which then yield the various racial types)" (1967, 310). This delving into the depths, he believes, will reward the social scientist with new knowledge: Where before he saw a chaotic disorder, he will now discover the order of social phenomena.

It is an error, according to Lévi-Strauss, to identify the diversity at the level of social forms with indeterminacy or arbitrariness. However numerous, the observable social types are, in his view, only variants of one definite pattern founded in the pregiven conditions of deeper levels or, as I should prefer to put it, variants within a definite realm of possibilities founded in the pregiven conditions of deeper levels.

Yet with this statement Lévi-Strauss's structuralist program is not yet complete. For, finally, it is a matter of "reintegrating culture into nature and ultimately life into the totality of its physio-chemical conditions" (Lévi-Strauss 1968, 284).

This statement completes the sketch of Lévi-Strauss's structuralist program. Let us now look at one of his empirical theories. The theory that I should now like to discuss may be called the theory of intrafamilial behavior or the theory of the valences of familial relations (Lévi-Strauss 1967, 54ff).

Lévi-Strauss develops this theory with reference to the now very famous article by Radcliffe-Brown, "The Mother's Brother in South Africa" (Radcliffe-Brown 1924). In this article, Radcliffe-Brown reports his observations concerning valences of the relations of sons to the brother of the mother on the one hand and to their fathers on the other. He notes that in the cases in which the relation of sons to their maternal uncle was familiar and amiable, their relation to their fathers was marked by distance and strictness. But the reverse also obtained: If the relation between the mother's brother and her sons was distant and authoritarian, then the relation between the sons and their fathers was amiable and familiar.

Both kinds of behavior form, Lévi-Strauss notes, two pairs of oppositions: If the one relationship is positive (amiable and familiar), then the other is negative (strict and authoritarian), and vice versa. According to Lévi-Strauss, the significance of the relational character of these behaviors can hardly be exaggerated.

Radcliffe-Brown himself reduced these behaviors to the rules of descent in the relevant societies. In matrilineally organized societies, authority lies with the mother's brother (and with other persons in his line of descent), whereas the father is looked upon as a kind of male mother; in patrilineally organized societies, authority lies by contrast with the father (and with other persons in his line of descent), whereas the father's previously mentioned role now falls to the mother's brother.

Lévi-Strauss here observes critically that the two analyzed relations (son-father, nephew-maternal uncle) make up only half of a complete structure of relations; that is, the relations between father and mother (man and woman) and that between brother and sister must also be included in the analysis. Lévi-Strauss bases his investigation of the relations neglected by Radcliffe-Brown especially on a report by Malinowski (1929). Malinowski's report shows that the valences of the relations which Radcliffe-Brown found in societies with matrilineal rules of descent (strict and tense relations between nephew and his maternal uncle and amiable and close relations between father and son) go along with a close and loving relation between man and woman and a strict and tense relation between brother and sister. These relations, according to Lévi-Strauss, are exactly reversed in patrilineally organized societies. The valences observed by Radcliffe-Brown in relations between father and son (formal and tense) and mother's brother and his nephew (informal and amiable) go together with a strict and tense relation between man and woman and a close and loving relation between brother and sister.

The relations between the valences of the described four types can be represented as in Figure 9.1, where a close and amiable relation is symbolized by a "+" and a strict and tense relation by a "−". The figure shows first the symbols for the matrilineal and then those for the patrilineal case:

maternal uncle / nephew   brother / sister
          "−"   "+"   "−"   "+"
        father / son   man / woman
          "+"   "−"   "+"   "−"

Figure 9.1. Lévi-Strauss's Law of Intrafamilial Behavior

The relations between the valences of the four types shown in the figure can, according to Lévi-Strauss, be understood as manifestations of a general law. This law can be formulated thus: "The relation between maternal uncle and nephew is to the relation between brother and sister as the relation between father and son is to the relation between man and woman" (Lévi-Strauss 1967,

57). And to this he adds "that when one relational pair is known, the other can always be inferred from it" (1967, 57).

George Homans (1972), who concentrates on this example in his criticism of structuralism, maintains that this connection does not represent a scientific theory but rather an empirical generalization or, more precisely, several linked discoveries. Such empirical generalizations are, in his view, the most valuable component of our social-scientific knowledge. They are genuine scientific discoveries. What is lacking here, and what according to Homans would make a scientific theory of this system, are general hypotheses from which the system could be logically deduced. A theory, in his opinion, is a deductive system, whereas here the generalizations all lie on the same level: They are equally general or equally specific. Without a deductive theory, Homan adds, nothing can be explained (Homans 1972, 111; Meleghy 2001a, 34).

Here, in my opinion, there is a confusion. For of course Lévi-Strauss's theory is not a scientific explanation but rather an empirical generalization. Yet in other cases (think, for example, of Archimedes's laws of the lever and displacement) we are quite ready to call empirical generalizations laws. By means of such empirical laws, we can explain and predict quite specific events and, proceeding from such laws, we can develop technologies. And such explanations, predictions, and technologies unquestionably have a deductive character. Homans, however, demands that we in turn deduce such empirical generalizations or laws from more general laws. But this is not as a rule demanded of other laws, nor is this demand a matter of course. If we succeed in deducing an empirical generalization from a general law, this is undoubtedly an important scientific achievement and also provides as a result a deeper understanding of the matter in question. What Homans demands here is finally a product of his own reductionist program. As we have seen, however, reductionism is also an important element of Lévi-Strauss's structuralist science.

To draw this discussion to a close, we can at any rate note that Lévi-Strauss, at least in this case, does not stick to his own reductionist plan: The excursion into the depths that he demands (that is, the reduction of the relations observed at the level of culture to their natural, biological foundation) remains unrealized. If the structuralist program is to be advanced, we must attempt to reduce the observed regularities in the area of intrafamilial behaviors to underlying biological principles. In other words, we must seek a biomaterialist explanation. This brings us to the missing link; that is, we have arrived at sociobiology. The question is: Can Lévi-Strauss's law of intrafamilial behaviors, taking into account the modes of organization of the relevant societies, be deduced from general sociobiological principles? I shall pursue this question from only one side of the relation.

An explanatory sketch on the basis of sociobiology could look something like the following. In patrilineally and patrilocally organized societies, women live under the authority and surveillance of men and their kin. In such societies, as Horne (2004) has recently shown, there usually also prevails a sexually restrictive morality. In these circumstances, men can be relatively certain of their fatherhood. Correspondingly, in order to maximize their total fitness, it may be expected that they invest time and effort in their own children and assume control over their conduct. In this situation, tensions between sons and fathers are preprogrammed. In order to maximize his general fitness, the maternal uncle may likewise be expected to invest time and effort in the sons of his sister, if to a lesser degree than their progenitor, corresponding to the uncle's lower kinship coefficients. In this system, the less demanding role of the "male mother" falls to him.

In matrilineally and matrilocally organized societies, men (and their kin) are to a lesser extent in the position to control the behavior of women and (as again Horne has shown) a freer sexual morality usually prevails. In these circumstances, men enjoy less certainty about their biological progeny. The kinship of the maternal uncle to his nephew, however, is certain. Hence, in the interest of his total fitness, the maternal uncle may be expected to assume responsibility for the sons of his sister. The tense and authoritarian relation will now be between the maternal uncle and the nephew. In this situation, the father assumes the more comfortable role of the "male mother," corresponding to the lesser degree of certainty about the biological kinship of his sons.

If this admittedly only cursorily indicated reduction of both relational models of intrafamilial behaviors to the principle of maximization of total fitness is accepted, then both no longer seem to be arbitrary or random, but rather two possible variants or, better, models, of cultural manifestations of an underlying biological principle.

As we have seen, Lévi-Strauss emphasized the necessity of anchoring culture in nature within the framework of his structuralist program; that is, anchoring social forms and their related interpersonal behaviors in underlying biological principles. The proposed reduction of the regularities at the level of intrafamilial behaviors observed by him and earlier by Radcliffe-Brown to biological principles may therefore be understood as a step in the direction of carrying through the structuralist program.

As we have also seen, in the work of Lévi-Strauss discussed by Sanderson, *The Elementary Structures of Kinship* (Lévi-Strauss 1969), Lévi-Strauss reduced the diverse models of marriage, kinship, and particularly cross-cousin marriage, abstracted from observation of social reality, to the law of reciprocal exchange. At work here, according to him, is an unconscious principle of the human mind that reveals itself in structure and in marriage and kinship. It is this principle of the human mind, always and everywhere the same, which brings it about that man, "ancient and modern, primitive and civilized," (Lévi-Strauss 1967, 35) always realizes at bottom (that is, considered from the point of view of structure) the same forms. Reciprocal exchange is for Lévi-Strauss a principle of the human mind, unconsciously acquired over long periods of social life, genetically fixed and inherited. Man's ancestors in fact lived in societies or in groups before they became human beings, that is, cultural beings. They were, in other words, social beings before they were human beings. This is, it seems to me, something quite like a biomaterialist explanation, and it is in essence the same one as proposed by Sanderson's DCT.

Reciprocal exchange or, as this phenomenon is called in the literature of evolutionary theory and sociobiology, reciprocal altruism, is a product of evolution (as Sanderson has pointed out in *The Evolution of Human Sociality*), which in the presence of certain hereditary conditions, like individual identifiability of the other and frequent interaction with him, develops in the service of maximization of total fitness both in various animal species and in man (Sanderson 2001a, 266-67; Axelrod, 1984).

The principle of maximization of total fitness has thus been identified as the missing link within the structuralist program. In both cases discussed, diversity at the level of cultural phenomena can be reduced to this biological principle; or, differently stated, proceeding from this principle the realized models appear as variants within one of the realms of possibility opened by the principle.

DISCUSSION

In order to arrive at the preceding evaluation of structuralism, one should not allow oneself to be detained too long by Lévi-Strauss's binary oppositions. In the foreground of consideration should stand instead his structuralist scientific program. If his work is approached through his analogies to language, one will tend to reject it; if, on the contrary, one chooses the way through his scientific program, one may discover a comrade-in-arms in one's own concerns.

Further, one should not be misled by Lévi-Strauss's claim that he has reduced the structure of marriage and kinship, particularly cross-cousin marriage, to a deeply sociological law, the law of reciprocal exchange; that is, that he has explained the social by the social. Not everything emblazoned with "Durkheim" actually has Durkheim inside.

The rules of marriage that Lévi-Strauss undertakes to explain are in fact moral, that is, social facts in Durkheim's sense; the law of reciprocal exchange, however, describes an (unconscious) tendency of the human mind or psyche. It pertains to a psychological law that has a social phenomenon as its content in the sense that the described tendency of the human mind refers to the behavior of others. The "social" in Durkheim's sense is here reduced to a psychological law which has a social phenomenon in Weber's sense as its content.

We have seen that Lévi-Strauss reduces the structure of marriage and kinship to the law of reciprocal exchange. The prohibition against incest is for him only the negative formulation of this rule. As is well-known, he here assumed that animals commonly reproduce incestuously, within the close kinship group, so that the prohibition against incest or the avoidance of incest is a specifically human trait.

Sanderson sees the relation of marriage rules and the prohibition against incest exactly reversed: "Exogamy rules" are, according to him, "just ... an extension of nuclear family incest regulations" (2001a, 239). The prohibition against incest is in turn only a confirmation, elevated to the status of a rule, of the general or more fundamental psychological mechanism of incest avoidance described by Westermarck which, as Bischof (1985) in particular has shown, is encountered not only among human beings but also among many higher animals. Sanderson then explains the Westermarck mechanism with the fitness diminishing consequences of incest, caused by the negative effects of such propagation in the offspring.

Several theorists have, however, pointed out that these consequences are only temporary. With persistent incest within the close family circle, the disadvantageous recessive gene would disappear after a few generations. The disadvantage of incest for the offspring cannot therefore be the reason for the emergence of the mechanism of incest avoidance. The deeper-lying biological meaning of the incest taboo is rather the same as that of sexuality in general: the long-term advantage of greater variability of the genetic makeup compared with non-sexual reproduction and incestuous propagation (Bischof 1985, 412). Then Lévi-Strauss would, in the end, be right. The deeper reason for exogamy rules would be something like a law of reciprocal exchange, and the prohibition against incest only the negative formulation of this law.

ACKNOWLEDGMENTS

This chapter was translated by Jonathan Uhlaner.

10

A CRITICAL APPRAISAL OF SANDERSON'S DARWINIAN CONFLICT APPROACH TO HUMAN WARFARE

Johan M.G. van der Dennen

INTRODUCTION

Sanderson's *The Evolution of Human Sociality: A Darwinian Conflict Perspective* is a major synthesis of neo-Darwinian, Marxian, and Weberian materialist theories of conflict (though it is not *prima vista* clear why the perspective he presents is called Darwinian, and not, say, Spencerian or Lamarckian or neo-Hobbesian). Since human beings (presumably hominids/hominins included), at least the male half of the species, have been extremely prone to solve their multiple and manifold conflicts with collective, armed, and more or less orchestrated and disciplined violence (i.e., war), it is very important that the theory of war to accompany the vicissitudes of the evolution of human sociality is correct.

In his *opus magnum*, Sanderson presents a highly eclectic collection of theories, an eclecticism which, I shall argue, is, moreover, somewhat biased toward conventional, noncontroversial "mainstream" theorizing (e.g., Ferguson 1984, 1990, who does not present a theory so much as a brief but exhaustive enumeration of reasons why he believes people wage war).

In this contribution, I intend to present some suggestions to improve, if possible, Sanderson's work, especially the theory of war, and to identify some traps and pitfalls which merit some caveats.

Suggestion 1: Sanderson does not make a distinction between raiding-type warfare and combat-type warfare ("ambush" and "line" in Otterbein's 2004 terminology), thereby precluding a long-term "dual input" perspective. He seems to acknowledge Wrangham's (1999) claim of raiding-type warfare as a synapomorphy (or shared derived trait) from the common ancestor of humans and chimpanzees some 7 to 5 million years ago. But the combat-type of warfare (or its nonhuman equivalent), as exemplified by (*the females of!*) some 50 terrestrial species of primates and some other mammals (van der Dennen 1995) may have evolved several million years before the evolution of raiding. This may have had major impacts on the forms of human sociality as well as specific behaviors such as hunting. (See the Appendix for a detailed contrast of raiding- and combat-type warfare.)

Suggestion 2: Sanderson does not make a distinction between "wars of carnage" (genocidal wars), "wars of coercion" (instrumental wars), and "wars of callisthenics" (more or less ritualized wars), as already suggested by Speier (1941) and elaborated by van der Dennen (1995), nor does he distinguish between endemic and instrumental wars as proposed by Mühlmann (1940) and Meyer (1981). Such distinctions may significantly contribute to the sophistication of theorizing on war in human history.

Caveat 1: Furthermore, Sanderson (2001a, 319) has fallen victim to the "great war figures hoax" or mystification, which was exposed long ago by Jongman and myself (Jongman and van der Dennen 1988). It is one of those myths that has acquired the status of "scientific fact" due to uncritical quoting of "authoritative" sources. Jongman and I have shown that these imaginary figures have no factual basis whatsoever.

Caveats 2 and 3: Finally, I will briefly comment on Sanderson's treatment of peaceful peoples and periodicity (Kondratieff waves).

SANDERSON ON WAR

Sanderson briefly discusses the "ecomaterialist" theories of warfare in band-level and tribal societies proposed by Divale and Harris (1976; Harris 1984), which have been severely criticized on both theoretical and empirical grounds; Ferguson's (1984, 1990) "ecomaterialist" theory, which Sanderson deems a very sensible theory of warfare in general (and which is not so much a theory as an enumeration of reasons why Ferguson believes people should wage war); and Shaw and Wong's (1989) "biomaterialist" ethnocentrism-cum-xenophobia theory, in which warfare in foraging societies is supposedly rooted. Sanderson also pays attention to "classical sociobiological theory" in which male competition for (access to) women is the "root cause" of "primitive" warfare. He thereby refers to my work on women and warfare in "primitive" societies all over the world (van der Dennen 1995, 317-31). He notes, for example, "Focusing in particular on the Yanomamö case, Chagnon (1988) argues that this group fights primarily over women and that blood revenge is a major motive for war once it has started.... Obviously the key to mates and reproductive success among Yanomamö men is to gain status by killing other men" (Sanderson 2001a, 322-23).

Actually, the "fighting over women" is not an intentional objective of Yanomamö warfare, as the following quote from Chagnon makes clear:

First, [Yanomamö] intervillage raids are almost never conducted with the explicit intent of capturing women. Their "wars" are not initiated or intended to capture females from enemies, although if they find a woman at a safe distance from the enemy village and dragging her back with them will not cause much additional risk, they may "capture" her. Although abduction of females is common among the Yanomamö, most abductions take place right at home – when visitors from distant villages come in small numbers and bring their wives and daughters with them" (Chagnon 1996, 222).

Furthermore, as I found in my research on war motives (van der Dennen 1995), the majority of "primitive" peoples indiscriminately kill everybody – men, women and children – in their raids, a finding which does *not* support the access-to-women argument.

The whole notion that foraging societies wage wars to abduct women is a modern myth, eagerly parroted from "authoritative" sources (e.g., Pinker 1997, 510; Buss 1999, 304; Ghiglieri 1999, following Cosmides) and a travesty of the truth. Societies, from bands to empires, have been documented to fight for self-defense, land (territory, boundary disputes), material resources and commodities (water wells, mineral deposits, oil), game, livestock (horses, cattle, pigs, camels), plunder and booty, food, women, trophies, captives for sacrifice and/or cannibalism, slaves, revenge, refusal to pay bridewealth, control of trade routes, tribute and taxation, dynastic succession, conquest and imperial aspirations, but also for power, dominance, status, honor, prestige, glory, freedom, autonomy, even for sports and spleen-venting (see Davie 1929; Turney-High 1949; van der Dennen 1995; Gat 2000a, 2000b). To single out *one* motive, women capture, is too simple. This is not meant to deny that the prospect of rape and sexual access to outgroup women may have been a powerful *incentive* of young males to participate in raids.

A biological foundation for human warfare is, according to Sanderson, also strongly suggested by a human-chimpanzee comparison. "There is a stunning similarity between intergroup violence among chimpanzees and human warfare between bands and villages, and it is striking that chimps and humans are the only primates who engage in this particular type of behavior" (Sanderson 2001a, 324). The particular type of behavior Sanderson refers to here is *raiding*, which is totally distinct, in both motivation and phenomenology (morphology, choreography) of behavior, from the other type of warfare: *combat* (or *pitched battle*, or *line*). Sanderson does not make this crucial distinction between the sneaky, ambush-like raiding-type warfare, and the phalanx-like disciplined combat-type warfare. (See Figure 10.1 for the evolutionary implications of this distinction.) Battle-type warfare occurs in many primate species and some other group-territorial mammals, such as social carnivores. Battles result mainly from chance encounters by primate groups, failed raids or surprise attacks and chance encounters in "primitive" peoples, and among standing armies in historical and contemporary warfare in which the armies are too large to operate undetected. Turney-High (1949) already illuminated the "biomechanics" of the line which develops more or less automatically when two groups meet in an agonistic en-

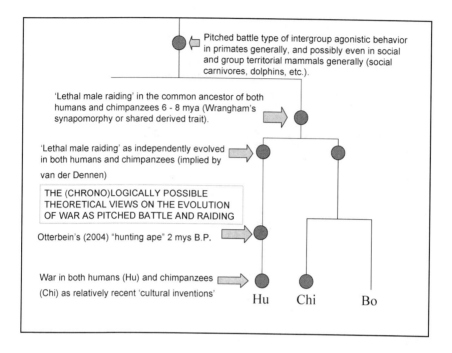

Figure 10.1. (Chrono)logically Possible Views on the Evolution of War

counter and every individual organism strives to have its vulnerable flanks protected by its neighbors. In social carnivores and "female bonded" (or female
philopatric) primate species, female participation in these more noisy than
bloody battles commonly exceeds male participation.

Furthermore, Sanderson seems to conflate warfare and violence in general
in presenting percentages of deaths of adult males as a result of violence in general, outside the context of war. The belligerent and fierce Yanomamö, Huli,
Mae Enga, Dugum Dani, and Murngin are not typical representatives of tribal
societies around the world. In fact, with the possible exception of the hunting-
and-gathering Murngin, all these societies are fairly advanced horticulturalists.

Sanderson's view of state-level warfare does not deviate from the conventional monogenic cultural-invention theory.

CRITICISM OF MATERIALISM

Lately, theorists of (cultural) ecological, ethological, sociobiological, and Marxian perspectives and/or signature have found themselves happily united, *bien
etonnés de se trouver ensemble*, in a common emphasis on "primitive" war as a
strategy to secure scarce and vital or strategic resources, such as land, protein,

women, etc. Simply *cherchez la ressource* and you will find the basic cause, the deeper reason, the ultimate explanation, or the in-the-last-analysis rationale of that type of war.

The roots of the materialist school sprouted in the 1940s when a number of anthropologists reinterpreted Plains Indian, Iroquoian, and Zulu warfare in thoroughly economic terms, i.e., as conscious, deliberate, and violent struggles over material resources. In the case of the Iroquois, for example, it was argued that their belligerence was based on attempts to control the fur trade (Ferguson 1984, 1990). Previously, economic motives were thought to underlie war only in state-level societies, or societies approaching that level (chiefdoms). Generally, material gain was not believed to be an important motivating force in the wars of "primitive" societies, or if it was it was only one of many types of motives. Sport, revenge, or prestige (honor, glory) were thought to be at least as important. Thucydides already reminded us that states fight for "fear, self-interest, and honor" – not always out of reason, economic need, or survival. Hobbes emphasized diffidence and glory. Fear, honor, and glory have virtually disappeared from modern materialist vocabularies.

Materialist studies of "primitive" war have focused mainly on two issues: land and game (or "high-quality" protein). However, as Ferguson (1984, 32) notes, the focus on land and game has created an oversimplified picture of ecological explanations. Whatever significance environmental phenomena have is a result of their interaction with a society of a given form. The salient environmental condition in any case may be something other than a scarce resource. Nevertheless, competition for scarce resources very often is the basis of war. What type of resource may be involved will vary from one war pattern to another, and resources may be scarce due to many processes besides population numbers pressing on absolute supplies, as in cases when demand is affected by trade, contact circumstances, or political and economic differentiation. With higher levels of conflict and political development, actual scarcities of resources may be only one of several factors contributing to war.

The materialist view contrasts with theories that explain war as generated by certain values, social structures, and so forth, in the absence of any material rationale. Such factors do affect the conduct of war and thresholds of violence. But a materialist theory directed at explaining the occurrence of war must hold these factors to be secondary, and not regularly capable of generating and sustaining war patterns in themselves (Ferguson 1984).

All explanations of war are premised on some assumptions about human psychology, although these are usually not made explicit. The motivational assumption of materialism is that nonmaterial goals will not regularly lead to war unless they accompany material objectives or incentives. That is because war itself typically involves major costs. This must be emphasized: War costs lives, health, resources, and effort. So, if the motivational premise is correct, we should expect peace if the probable costs of war are not outweighed by potential benefits. The motivational premise can be expressed in one general proposition: Wars occur when those who make the decision to fight estimate that it is in their material interests to do so (Ferguson 1990). The model can be summarized as follows: (1) infrastructural factors explain why war occurs; (2) structural factors explain the social patterning of war; and (3) superstructural patterns shape the way individuals perceive and act on conditions related to war. But independent of infrastructural and structural patterns conducive to war, superstructural elements have a very limited effect. (This is, *grosso modo*, also Sanderson's view).

Materialism apparently is a powerful paradigm. There is, however, an inherent tendency of this school toward "vulgar" materialism. War, *any* war, whether "primitive" or modern, is waged for the sake of securing material resources: territory, protein, women, pigs, cattle, mineral deposits, oil, etc., and that is all there is to it. Can competition for prestige, power, glory, or even strategic interests be considered material resources? Is the equation of realistic conflict with material conflict a valid one? Not even the contemporary political realists (the Morgenthau school) define interests as only material ones. Security, for example, may be one of such "superordinate" interests.

The focus on material causes leaves little room for consideration of human decision-making, and such concerns are often explicitly disavowed. Such disclaimers notwithstanding, any theory of human behavior must necessarily presuppose a theory of motivation. It must at least incorporate some assumptions about why people behave at all.

The motivational premise of materialism has been questioned in a most caustic criticism by Robarchek (1990). In most materialist approaches the motivational theory is straightforward: Human motivation is maximization of material interests. If such striving results in conflict with others, the material "ends" are its "cause." Both terms of the "material cause" equation, Robarchek argues, are open to serious question. Are material causes, in fact, "material"? And are they "causal"? Can the need for security (which Ferguson lists as "to forestall attacks by others") really be classified as a *material* need?

The basic fallacy of materialism may simply be its conflation of the dimensions material (vs. nonmaterial), rational (vs. nonrational), and realistic (vs. nonrealistic). It implicitly presupposes that only conflicts for material resources are rational and realistic, and, conversely, that rational actors only come into (realistic) conflict over material resources. Security, which Ferguson is eager to categorize as a *material* resource, is actually of quite a different order. It can neither be possessed nor exchanged. Its only similarity with material resources is that it always seems to be in short supply, necessitating a never-ending quest, which by its very nature reduces the "volume" of security for all actors involved (this is the well-known security dilemma) (van der Dennen 1995).

Robarchek also questions the proposition that only material factors are relevant to the explanation of behavior. From there, he says, the ontological assumption is made that only material causes are "real," thereby banishing human intentionality from the realm of science. When the subject is human behavior, materialist explanation must at least acknowledge (even if it does not address) the question of how the posited *material causes* become parts of actors' *motivational schemata*.

A harsh criticism of materialism and related approaches may be that it is ir-refutable or nearly so. One can always invoke a limiting resource, be it land, protein, or something else again, in any conflict. It seems so trivial a pursuit: *Cherchez la ressource.* It also tends to obscure the fact that it is human beings, in certain cultures and with their culture's idiosyncratic notions, cognitions, and constructions of reality, under certain circumstances, in certain political constel-lations, and facing certain deprivations or certain forms of the security dilemma, who perceive and define what is a vital resource and decide whether or not it is worth fighting for: "To put it briefly, people don't fight for resources but for ideas of resources. Some of these ideas are closer to the 'real' importance of these resources in terms of metabolic needs, others are more distant from such realistic assessment. . . . [A] culturalist notion of resources emphasizes the ne-cessity of mental processing of resources or any other objects of human striving" (Meyer 1990a, 232).

For example, in the endemic stage of primitive war cultural ideas and defi-nitions of resources are mainly metaphysical, magico-religious, or animistic notions of power (sometimes residing in heads or other trophies), or restoration of a threatened universe or restoration of the legitimate *status quo ante* (e.g., the Anggor of New Guinea: Huber 1975). What strikes most researchers of "primi-tive" war is the virtually total absence of any "economic" motivation at this stage. Somewhat paradoxically, the literature on primitive war, though brimming with accounts of predatory wars, does not unequivocally support the materialist theory of primitive war causation. Pillaging, cattle raiding, and slave raiding are distinctly "advanced" motives. So might well be territorial acquisition. The most-desired "resources" for "primitive" peoples are the objects in which supernatural or spiritual power resides. Whether one wants to call these material or not is a matter of appreciation and personal taste. The "economic" motives in primitive war have been, and still are, vastly overrated.

POLEMOMYTHOLOGY

Sanderson has fallen victim to the "great war figures hoax." He says, for exam-ple, "Shaw and Wong (1989) summarize evidence collected by Montague show-ing that there have been on the order of 14,500 wars over the past 5,600 years of world history, as well as evidence from Burke (1975) indicating that in the last 3,400 years of history there have been a mere 268 years of peace" (Sanderson 2001a, 319), i.e., peace comprising only 8 percent of the entire history of recorded civilization. These nonsensical figures are often accompanied by the equally ab-surd claim that "the value of the destruction inflicted would pay for a golden belt around the earth 156 kilometers in width and ten meters thick" (RAND Corpora-tion, Internal Publication, 1961, 1).

These figures have been shown, however, to be a hoax or a mystification (Jongman and van der Dennen 1988). It is, again, one of those myths that has acquired the status of scientific fact due to uncritical quoting of "authoritative" sources. Jongman and I have shown that these imaginary figures have no factual basis whatsoever.

Jongman and I discovered, partly by sheer luck, the historical source of these "magical figures": the work of an obscure French philosopher, Odysse Barot, *Lettres sur la philosophie de l'histoire* (Paris, 1864), in which Barot claims to have counted 8,397 treaties between 1496 BCE and 1861 CE (which were later extrapolated to 14,500 *wars* during a period of 5,560 years), and, furthermore, to have found the ratio of 13 years of war to every year of peace (which is the basis for the rather nonsensical figure of only 8 percent of all years being peaceable during the history of civilization). These figures are total fantasy to begin with (Barot nowhere presents any shred of evidence), erroneously interpreted, and tenaciously presented as facts in the pertinent literature, mostly with the addition of the equally "magical" number of 3,640,000,000 people killed in these wars. The war figures hoax was exposed earlier by Haydon (1962) as well as by Singer and Small (1972), but they were unable to explain the arbitrariness of the figures, or to trace the historical source of the grandiose claims.

PEACEFUL PEOPLES

Peaceable preindustrial (foraging, preliterate, "primitive," etc.) societies constitute a nuisance to most theories of warfare and they are, with few exceptions, either denied or "explained away." Contending theories have also tended to severely underestimate the costs of war to the individuals as well as to the communities involved. Materialist theory, as formulated by Ferguson, is one such exception: "[I]n contrast to the Hobbesian view, we should find nonwar, the absence of active fighting, in the absence of challenges to material well-being" (Ferguson 1984). Where the costs of initiating violence outweigh the benefits, war is expected to be absent. There is no theoretical reason to deny the possibility of peaceful societies.

Most peoples seem to prefer peace *when they can afford it,* i.e., when they can solve the internal problem of the "young male fierce warrior syndrome" (especially prevalent when the warrior role is rewarded with social status, honor and prestige, and/or sexual privileges), and the external problem of being "left in peace" by other peoples (van der Dennen 1995). The ecological roots of peace may be as complex as, or even more complex than, the roots of violence and war. There may be as many reasons for peaceability as there are for belligerence: Intercommunity nonviolence may be a response to overwhelming odds; it may be the taming effect of defeat; it may be enforced by colonial or imperial powers; it may be the result of isolation and/or xenophobia; it may be due to a negative cost-benefit balance of war, making peace more opportune under the given circumstances; it may be due to a voluntary decision to abstain from or abandon violence, or to a nonviolent ethic or pacifistic ideology; or some combination of all these factors. As Dentan (1992, 215) reminds us, "Peaceability is not disability, not a cultural essence unrelated to a people's actual circumstances." Thus, warlike people are quite capable of peacefulness, while peaceable peoples are perfectly capable of intergroup violence *under altered circumstances*.

The opportunistic nature of warlikeness and peacefulness is shown by the following example. The Oowekeeno and Haihai belong, together with the Bella Bella, to the Heiltsuk language group of the American northwest coast. The Bella Bella were well skilled in military strategies. The Oowekeeno could easily afford to be peaceful as they were out of the main path of the war canoes, being well protected by the easily defendable Wannock River. The unfortunate Haihais, on the other hand, "had no chance to be peaceable as they were forever embroiled in and afflicted by attack from both the northern tribes and the Bella Bellas, having to defend against predatory expeditions directed toward their resource base and to protect themselves from these warring tribes who wanted to practice on them in preparation for more serious expeditions" (Hilton 1990).

Among the (allegedly) peaceful societies (or rather "highly unwarlike" societies) critically investigated by van der Dennen (1995 et seq.) are the Attikamek (Tête de Boule), Battle Mountain and Hukundika Shoshone, Bella Coola, Central Californians, Columbia Salish, Copper Eskimo (Inuit), Gosiute, Hopi, Kaibab Paiute, Monache, Panamint, Polar Eskimo, Pueblos, Similkameen, Wenatchi, Zuñi, Amueixa (Amueisha), Apinayé, Bara, Cayapa, Cayua, Guato, Guayaki, Island Arawak, Maku, Napo, Puri, Siriono, Taino, Tarahumara, Waorani, Xinguanos, Yahgan, Aradhya, Badaga, Batti, Birhor, Bodo, Buid (Taubuid), Chewong, Dhimal, Gond, Hierro, Kota, Kubu, Ladaki, Lapps, Lepcha, Malapandaram, Mangyan, Mishmi, Paliyan, Punan, Semang/Semai, Tenae, Tikopians, Toala, Toda, Vedda, Yanadi, Barea, Dorobo, Fipa (Wafipa), Hadza, !Kung, Mbuti (Bambuti), Thonga (Bathonga), Arafuras, Aranda (Arunta), Arapesh, Fore, Hagahai, Ifaluk, Moriori, Pesechem, Sio, Tapiro, Timorini, and Wape.

The evidence of a substantial number of peoples without warfare, or with mainly defensive and/or low-level warfare (i.e., seldom exceeding the level of petty feuding or desultory skirmishes) does not support the view of universal human belligerence. It does not support the equally erroneous view of universal peaceability either. Rather, it supports Dentan's (1992), as well as van der Dennen's (1995), view that peace as well as war are the results of enlightened and opportunistic self-interest in the political arena.

KONDRATIEFF WAVES

Attempts have been made to discern macroscopic patterns in the history of war. Efforts to determine whether there is a war-and-peace cycle in the international system have been made since the mid-1930s by several analysts: Sorokin, Quincy Wright, Richardson, Toynbee, Singer and Small, Bouthoul, Ellul, Macfie, Blainey, Levy, Gilpin, Wallerstein, Modelski, Thompson, Goldstein, Sayrs, Mansfield, and others.

The Russian economist Nikolai Kondratieff claimed in the 1920s to have discovered fifty-year waves (or cycles) in prices, production, and consumption in the economies of the major capitalist nations. He argued that these cycles were indicative of rhythms within the international economic system as a whole. His research also suggested that upswings in economic long waves were related to the occurrence of major wars.

A study of global economic cycles and war from 1495 to 1975 by Goldstein (1988) finds a strong and consistent correlation between the severity of war and economic upswings. A psychological explanation for the relationship between war and economic upturns is also frequently made. Indeed, several researchers suggest that economic recoveries are associated with a general mood of *optimism* which is the real cause of war (Cashman 1993, 135-36). Cashman also points out that many economists today do not believe that Kondratieff waves even exist, while other researchers have discovered a picture at odds with Goldstein's theory. Though many of these long-cyclists have discovered 20- to 100-year cycles, many others have failed to do so. Sorokin (1937, 357-60) already discounted cyclical theories of changes in warfare: "The curve just fluctuates, and that is all." An extensive international relations literature using spectral analysis almost invariably finds no evidence for long cycles. Despite disagreements, controversies, and inconsistencies (or contradictions), the theoretical and statistical debates about war cycles are bound to continue. Some will see cycles that others deny (Dougherty and Pfaltzgraff 2001, 313).

CONCLUSION

Students who are interested in the problem "Why war?" generally pose three distinct but interrelated questions: (1) Where does the institution of war come from? Is it a cultural invention? Or is it better understood as a product of evolution? This is the question of the genesis or origin of war. (2) What are the causes of particular wars? This is the question of war causation. (3) Why do warriors and soldiers fight? What is in it for them? This is the question of combat motivation. In terms of evolutionary biology, the first question is an ultimate-level question, while the other two are proximate-level questions. The capitalization on aggression and material motives has had the unfortunate effect of obscuring an important insight of many less recent anthropologists and ethnologists, namely the insight that fear may play a much greater part in the proximate explanation of "primitive war" (which is actually an endless cycle of revenge and counterrevenge, raid and counterraid) and the perpetual security dilemma than aggression or material motives. Whiffen (1915, 61), for instance, writes on the Putomayo River Indians in South America, who lived in a permanent *status belli*: "This state of endless warfare is based not on avarice but on fear. They fight because they are afraid of each other, and see no protection but in the extermination of their neighbors." This insight has not been totally lost, however. Meyer (1977) has also recognized the role of mutual fear (Hobbes's "diffidence") and the perceived threat to each other's security, leading to preemptive strikes. Already Thucydides identified the root cause underlying the Peloponnesian War as fear. In contemporary warfare fear, mutual "apprehension," may also be the most common cause (Taylor 1979).

APPENDIX

Differences Between the Battle (Baboon Pattern) and the Raid (Chimp Pattern)

Feature	Battle	Raid
known as	guerra (real war), combat	guerrilla (little war)
motivation	fight/flight-like	predation-like
precipitated by	approximate balance of power	imbalance of power
occurrence in animals	very common in social carnivores and primates	confined to panids and hominids
sex of the belligerents	females and males (much less so in humans)	exclusively male
occurrence in "primitive" peoples	relatively uncommon among foraging peoples (if present often ritualized)	predominant and most lethal among foraging peoples
occurrence in modern warfare	very common in modern warfare (but apt to be less common in future)	relatively uncommon in contemporary warfare (but apt to be more common in future)
appearance	parallel lines/phalanxes	ambush/dawn attack/raid
characterized by	clamor/bluff/intimidation	stealth/secrecy
explained by	biomechanical principles	tactical requirements (?)
tactics	impact of mass and speed, encirclement, feigned retreat	hit and run, torching, indiscriminate killing
underlying psychology	psychology of the soldier (discipline)	psychology of the warrior (frenzy)
weakness and vulnerability	line too short (envelopment), line too long (penetration)	logistics, retreat
historical theorists	Thucydides, Vegetius	Sun Tzu
conditioned by	chance encounters, failed raid, failed surprise attack	surprise attack as default
ritualization?	ritualization (game-like war) possible	no ritualization possible, *guerre à l'outrance*
reconciliation?	reconciliation possible in principle	no reconciliation, incessant cycles of retaliation and revenge raiding
metaphysical aspects	divine ordeal, expiatory combat	magico-religious magnet
lethality (casualties)	relatively low but may result in routing and massacre	relatively low but rapidly accumulating

11

THE RISE OF MODERN SCIENCE AND TECHNOLOGY

A Test Case of Sanderson's Evolutionary Model of Human Society

C. R. Hallpike

THE MIND AND NATURE

Sanderson's model of society is strongly materialistic and made up of four basic subunits or structures:

- The *biostructure*: that is, our nature as biological organisms, and their needs
- The *ecostructure*: comprising ecological, technological, and economic structures in particular
- The *structure*: social institutions of all kinds
- And finally, the *superstructure*: the primary forms of mental life, including religion, philosophy, and science, in particular

"The flow of causation," he says, "is primarily from the biostructure to the ecostructure, then from the ecostructure to the structure, and finally from the structure to the superstructure" (Sanderson 2001a, 150). The biostructure and the ecostructure have this causal priority because they concern vital needs, so that the superstructure of ideas, which includes religion, philosophy, and science, has the least causal impact on the social structure, and in any case the objective requirements of the natural world cannot be altered by our mental constructs, which he refers to as "the priority of nature over mind" (Sanderson 2001a, 143).

It is obvious that nature cannot be altered by our mental constructs, but also entirely irrelevant, since it is possible for false or unprovable ideas not only to survive indefinitely, but to be an important basis of human action. Primitive humans are, in a sense, just as practical as we are, in the sense that they want health and prosperity. But they have a very different idea about how to *be* practical because they view the world from the perspective of what Piaget and other developmental psychologists refer to as preoperational thought, which makes no clear distinction between natural and social laws:

> Until the age of 7–8 there does not exist for the child a single purely mechanical law of nature. If clouds move swiftly when the wind is blowing, this is not only because of a necessary connection between the movement of the wind and that of the clouds; it is also and primarily because the clouds "must" hurry along to bring us rain, or night, and so on (Piaget 1952, 429).

In *The Foundations of Primitive Thought* (Hallpike 1979) I have shown in great detail that preoperational thought is quite capable of surviving into adulthood in the cognitively undemanding milieu of primitive, nonliterate society, and indeed it left many traces in ancient theories of nature, such as Aristotle's theory of motion. Since the social and natural worlds are not clearly distinguished, causal explanations are based on how people behave. People act for a purpose, and because of their inner, essential nature, so preoperational thinkers suppose that the movement of things such as clouds and streams is a sign of life and purpose, expressing the force and vitality inside them. The preoperational idea of causes, therefore, is a universe of independent substances that behave as they do because of their essential natures, not as the result of relations between objects. The shadow, for example, is not understood as the result of a beam of light from a light-source that is obstructed by an object, and thereby casts a projection of the object onto a flat surface, but as something that emerges from inside the person or object that casts it, and that may have magical properties, while darkness and light are themselves quite different things.

More advanced thinking about the physical world became possible when human cognitive abilities were stimulated by specific social conditions, especially in China, India, and Greece, in the first millennium BCE. During this period, social instability had produced a sense of confusion and despair, and increasingly sophisticated debate among members of the educated class about a range of social, ethical, and religious issues developed the abstract intellectual skills of formal operational, philosophical thinking. So for the first time there appeared rational, unified, general theories about the state and the cosmos, which was thought to be governed by fundamental principles of order – *logos, tao,* or *brahman.* Unless the Greeks, in particular, had been convinced of the basic order and rationality of the universe, they would never have begun the serious investigations of nature that they did, or persevered in the face of enormous difficulties. But, of course, the study of natural philosophy, among the very small minority who were interested in it, was not intended to be useful since it had no practical application.

The result was a fusion of highly sophisticated philosophical and mathematical thinking with assumptions about the physical world that were imbued with many of the preoperational ideas of traditional folk culture. In Aristotle's system, what things do is explained by their essence: Celestial bodies, made of ether and set in motion by the Unmoved Mover, naturally move in circles, whereas fire, air, earth, and water naturally move in straight lines; air and fire move upwards, earth and water downwards. Aristotle denied the possibility of the void, which included the vacuum, among other reasons because there would be no up or down, or any center or periphery, whereas he held that the earth is at the center of the cosmos, which is why heavy bodies fall towards it. Nature, for Aristotle, does nothing without a purpose, and the earth is itself an organism in which everything is struggling towards perfection. Just as man is the perfect animal, so gold is the perfect metal, into which base metals are trying to develop.

Aristotle's theories of motion and the elements, and his general teleological model were all, as we now know, entirely wrong, but they were also extremely fruitful. What really matters in evolution is not how immediately useful or correct something may be, but its future possibilities, its evolutionary potential, which the Darwinian emphasis on selection ignores. If Greek astronomers had not accepted the doctrine that celestial bodies are perfect and therefore must move in circular orbits they could never have devised their geometrical model of the solar system at all. Astrology and religion were essential foundations of astronomy, and Copernicus himself argued that since God is perfect he must have chosen circular orbits for the planets, and the anomalies of their motion could only be resolved if they orbit around the sun and not the earth. Again, the four-element theory and the transmutation of metals was an essential basis for alchemy, which in turn was necessary for the eventual development of chemistry. The Greeks also held the primitive belief that the eye emits visual rays in the form of a cone; this was, of course, nonsense, but, since the function of the lens was unknown, this false belief was the basis on which Euclid could lay the foundations of geometrical optics.

Sanderson says that "the natural world – the empirical evidence – does indeed act as a very powerful constraint on the beliefs of scientists" (2001a, 36), and "it is competition and conflict that are critical to scientific advance because only they give science a self-correcting mechanism"(2001a, 37). But what actually *counts* as empirical evidence, and how is it to be used? Nature does not simply impose itself upon us through our senses, but has to be interrogated, and its answers are often ambiguous. This was especially true in antiquity because scientific method itself was undeveloped, especially the need for experiment. Even the measurement of physical properties like moist and dry and hot and cold was a problem, since Aristotle held that they were qualities that could not be quantified. It was only in the seventeenth century, when scientists had become much better at integrating evidence and theory by experiment and measurement, that the vigorous scientific competition which Sanderson assumes as the norm finally became possible. Experiment is a cultural, not a natural phenomenon. If, then, nature cannot impose itself on the mind, do our biological needs stimulate new technology?

TECHNOLOGY AND INVENTION

Once we get beyond such obvious adaptations as using leaves as shelter from the rain, or cutting down a tree for a bridge across a stream, inventions and discoveries cannot simply be *responses* to material needs because they require intellectual creativity. What people would like if only they knew about it can be of no help in actually discovering it, especially since the early stages of some human endeavors are often distinctly unpromising from the practical, materialistic point of view. Good examples are the origins of metals, because in their native state they are far more suited to ornamental than to practical uses; as R.J. Forbes has said, "Metal made its first impression as a fascinating luxury, from which evolved a need" (1971, 10). Technology is not, then, a set of responses to human needs, *but a set of discoveries about the uses of things*, which may then become needs.

Our biological needs do not therefore exert a constant pressure to invent, and in the ancient world there was a strong tendency for technology to stagnate. "Technical progress, economic growth, productivity, even efficiency have not been significant goals since the beginning of time. So long as an acceptable lifestyle could be maintained, other values held the stage" (Finley 1973, 147). As the complexity of technology increases, innovation becomes increasingly dependent on the social and cultural milieu, and on two factors in particular. The first is experimentation on nature, motivated by theory, and this will go beyond anything required by practical technology. It involves, in other words, an interaction between theoretical and craft knowledge.

In antiquity there was a profound gulf between brain-work and manual labor, between theoretical and practical knowledge. Manual labor was despised, and craft knowledge could only be acquired by years of practical, hands-on experience in the workshop, and in this sort of apprenticeship book learning would have been irrelevant. The knowledge of literate high culture, however, especially philosophy, acquired from books, was speculative, self-consciously intellectual, and concerned with the general nature of things rather than with practical detail. Natural philosophy was not intended to be useful and had very little connection with technology, which developed almost entirely at the craft level.

The second factor is cost, because any advanced form of technology is expensive, and technology cannot build itself. It requires investment, and decisions about what to invest in will be taken by a very small minority, notably rulers and rich men, and their decisions will reflect their own interests and values. Rulers favored military technology and entertaining gadgets. For example,

the Ptolemies founded and financed the Museum at Alexandria, for two centuries the main western centre of scientific research and invention. Great things emerged from the Museum, in military technology and in ingenious mechanical toys. But no one, not even the Ptolemies themselves, who would have profited directly and handsomely, thought to turn the energy and inventiveness of a Ctesibius to agricultural and industrial technology. The contrast with the Royal society in England is inescapable (Finley 1973, 148).

Landowners had no need to patronize technology, and while rich men were another potential source of investment, in the ancient civilizations generally the status of merchants was rather low. Wealth was legitimated by participation in state structures, and the pillars of the state were the king, the priesthood or some equivalent body, the landowning nobility that normally had military functions as well, the army, and provincial governors and other senior officials. Merchants were outsiders in relation to the state, and their wealth was individual, private profit which had no social function at all and was spent for purely personal gratification. Making profits by trade was often regarded as contemptible, especially by comparison with glorious military exploits, and also as dishonest. In the Roman Empire, for example, while businessmen obviously wanted to become rich, if they were successful they typically invested their wealth in landed estates or public benefactions rather than in their businesses. While *we* can imagine waterwheels driving banks of potters' wheels, or powering blast-furnaces and triphammers in iron foundries, although technically feasible they would have been very expensive to develop, and the Romans did not invest capital in that way.

Modern technology only developed in Western Europe because only there did the necessary social and intellectual conditions accumulate in the course of the Middle Ages and the Renaissance. These were: the availability of Greek natural philosophy, especially Aristotle, and science such as astronomy, optics, and statics, that provided an advanced theoretical starting point; a unique urban environment, free from the constraints of feudalism, in which craftsmen had unusually high social status, where a close intellectual association was possible between educated men, such as physicians, engineers, architects and alchemists, and artisans such as goldsmiths, printers, painters, clock- and instrument-makers, lens-grinders, and so on, in an experimental milieu, and a milieu in which profits could be made from clocks, navigational instruments, telescopes, vacuum-pumps, etc.; where there was a fair degree of mathematical knowledge among the artisan class as well as the educated and a growing familiarity with quantification and measurement in society generally; and, notably, a prosperous and vigorous capitalist society where the urban merchant class had high status, and commerce was largely unrestricted by arbitrary government controls and taxation. I would like to illustrate some of these points by looking at the origins of steam power and electricity, because these are excellent examples of how scientific theory, craft skills, and capitalist enterprise combined to produce two of the essential foundations of industrial civilization, but which could never have developed from ordinary technology by itself.

STEAM POWER

The expansive power of steam had been known to Hero of Alexandria in constructing temple gadgetry and automata for entertainment, but the technology of that day was unable to harness it effectively. The only practical route to the use of steam was by using atmospheric pressure and the vacuum instead. By the beginning of the seventeenth century the problem of the vacuum was being discussed again in an Aristotelian context, and Galileo knew that the vacuum created by a suction pump could not raise a column of water higher than about 30 feet. But he rejected the idea that the weight of the atmosphere could be the explanation, although he had discovered it, and believed that it was due to the tensile strength of the water giving way at this point. It was Torricelli who correctly understood the significance of atmospheric weight – for the ancients air, of course, naturally moved *upwards* in relation to water. He took a glass tube 4 feet long and closed at one end. This he filled with mercury, applied his finger to the open end, and inverted it in a basin of mercury. The mercury in the tube sank at once to 2½ feet above the basin, leaving 1½ feet apparently empty. Torricelli deduced that it was the pressure of the atmosphere that maintained the level of mercury, but this was even more conclusively shown by Pascal, who heard of Torricelli's work. He took a tube and tied a bag of mercury to the end, then sank the tube into a deep vessel of water with the mouth of the tube above the surface. He showed that the deeper the bag of mercury was sunk in the water, the more mercury flowed up the tube, so establishing that pressure increases with depth. He then gave his brother-in-law the task of carrying one of Torricelli's barometers up a neighboring mountain who found, as Pascal had predicted, that the higher up the mountain he went the lower the mercury sank in the tube. These experiments conclusively verified that pressure increases in depth in any fluid (denied by Hero of Alexandria), and that the level of mercury is produced by the atmospheric pressure. One is struck by how technically simple the experiments were to perform, how readily men of the seventeenth century resorted to experiments to settle theoretical questions, and how none of these experiments would have been performed unless there had been a theoretical reason for doing so.

Independently, Otto von Guericke, Burgomaster of Magdeburg, wanted to test Descartes's revival of Aristotle's theory that a vacuum is impossible against Hero's findings that it is possible, and therefore constructed an air-pump. At Ratisbon in 1654 he set up a vertical cylinder 20" in diameter in which a well-fitting piston was suspended by a rope passing over a pulley. Connecting the air pump to the cylinder he pumped out the air below the piston, causing it to descend in spite of the joint efforts of 50 men to hold it up. He followed this with a demonstration in front of the Emperor Maximilian at Magdeburg in 1657 in which 2 iron hemispheres were placed together and from which he again pumped out the air. Teams of 8 horses attached to each hemisphere were unable to pull them apart. This demonstration became the talk of Europe, and the reality and power of atmospheric pressure became a well-known fact.

The air pump, however, was not a practical way of using atmospheric pressure, and various experiments were made to create a vacuum with gunpowder and alcohol, but one of these experimenters, Denis Papin, had invented a pressure-cooker and was well aware that steam creates a vacuum when it condenses. He also spent some time in England and collaborated with Robert Hooke of the Royal Society. In 1690 he made a model engine consisting of a tube 2½" in diameter inside which was a piston and rod. A little water was then placed in the bottom of the cylinder and heated, thus driving the piston up to the top of the tube, where it was held in position by a catch. As the steam condensed, atmospheric pressure then forced the piston down again. None of this work, of course, would ever have been carried out by ordinary craftsmen because it had no apparent practical application.

The first practical use of steam in an engine was by Thomas Newcomen, an ironmonger and blacksmith, but who came from an educated background; and it is clear that he was also familiar with Papin's work in London, which had been published in the *Transactions* of the Royal Society. The Newcomen engine only required low pressure steam, which was easily achieved with the technology of the day and did not need to produce rotary motion because the engines were intended for pumping water from coal and tin mines, the first being set up at Dudley in 1712. The size and power of these engines rapidly increased and they became of fundamental importance in expanding the coal industry.

James Watt was the mathematical instrument maker to the University of Glasgow. This was an institution, as Gresham College had been in sixteenth- and seventeenth-century London, that brought practical skills such as engineering into close contact with scientific theory. Watt, who was given a model of a Newcomen engine to repair, became intrigued with steam power and discussed many of the problems, notably the crucial question of latent heat, with the great professor of chemistry Joseph Black. As a result of his research he made a series of fundamental improvements to the design of the Newcomen engine, because greater efficiency meant lower costs, and went into partnership with Matthew Boulton, a factory owner and entrepreneur of Birmingham, to sell his improved engines. A great advantage of the steam engine over the waterwheel was that it could be located anywhere, and once it had been improved by Watt it could not only produce much more power than waterwheels, but could do so more cheaply. Studies of steam engines then fed back into pure science, notably in the form of thermodynamics.

During the eighteenth century small textile mills had already been developed using waterwheels to drive new types of machinery. These machines, unlike mine pumps, needed rotary motion to drive them. Once Watt had devised a means of converting the linear motion of the steam engine into rotary motion, there were similar industrial opportunities for Watt's engine as there had been for Newcomen's in mining. Very large numbers of these machines powered by steam could now be concentrated into the great factories of the industrial revolution, with all the social consequences that followed. The development of high pressure steam by Trevithick then allowed the steam engine to become portable, on railway locomotives and ships. Only steam power, moreover, could generate enough electricity for modern industry, and it is to the discovery of electricity that we can now turn.

MAGNETISM AND ELECTRICITY

Knowledge of magnetism and electricity in the ancient world was largely a blank: Nature gives us few clues that they even exist, and in any case the two seem very different. Lightning is the most obvious example of electricity, but in antiquity was regarded as a form of fire; the torpedo fish was known to cause numbness to humans as well as to kill small fish, but the nature of this power was unknown, as, of course, was the electrical basis of nervous stimuli and muscular activity in the body. Magnetism was originally discovered through the ability of magnetite to attract iron, and the power of amber, when rubbed, to attract chaff was assumed to be similar, although amber actually attracts by static electricity. Neither of these cases of attraction, however, seems related to lightning or torpedo fish.

The only practical route to the discovery of electricity therefore lay through the study of attraction, but while philosophers theorized about its nature remarkably few experiments with magnetite or amber seem to have been carried out, although these would have been extremely easy. While it was known that pieces of iron can be magnetized, no Greek or Roman seems even to have realized that a piece of magnetite has two poles so that like poles repel each other and opposite poles attract, let alone that a freely suspended piece of magnetite or one floating on a piece of wood will point in a north-south direction. This discovery seems to have been made by the Chinese in the use of the divination board. This was a map of the heavens at the center of which was a spoon-shaped object made out of magnetite to imitate The Great Bear, or Big Dipper. This could freely rotate, and the tail of the spoon was used to show the southerly direction and correctly orient the divining board. It was also used in the orientation of buildings according to the mystic art of geomancy, but the predominance of river and canal traffic in China delayed its use by seafarers until the eleventh century, and it seems to have reached Europe by the end of the twelfth century.

It was first supposed that the needle pointed to a magnetic mountain, but Peter Peregrinus (*Epistola de magnete*, 1269) realized that the lodestone, as it was known at the time, had two poles and was oriented in relation to the earth as a whole. He fashioned a lodestone into a sphere and showed that a needle followed the meridians of this model globe; he also knew that like poles repel whereas unlike poles attract one another. But the most significant investigation of the magnet after Peregrinus was by the physician William Gilbert, who was familiar with his work, and was the first man to carry out a really thorough piece of experimental research in the modern manner, the *De Magnete* published in 1600. He systematically investigated the magnetic properties not only of the lodestone and amber, but of a range of other metals and materials such as glass, sulphur, and resin, using a specially devised instrument, the versorium, a long steel needle balanced on a point, to measure the different amounts of attraction involved. He distinguished between those magnetic substances that attracted without rubbing, such as magnetite, and those electrics, such as amber, that did require it, arguing that magnetic substances were of the element earth, while electrics were of the element water.

Gilbert's belief that the earth is a giant magnet, and that gravity is a form of magnetism was taken up by Kepler, but when the universally curious von Guericke wanted to investigate the earth's attraction he disagreed with Gilbert's magnetic theory and decided to test the alternative possibility of electrics. He therefore made a model globe primarily of sulphur, which he mounted in a frame so that it could be rotated. When rubbed he found that the globe not only produced a strong attraction but sparks as well, a new phenomenon that for the first time clearly distinguished electricity from magnetism. Electrical machines attracted a great deal of attention, and increasingly elaborate ones began to be made in many parts of Europe. (One of the striking features of European science in these centuries was the extraordinary variety of apparatus of all kinds that was applied to scientific problems, and sold widely on the market.)

It was believed that electricity had two forms – the vitreous from rubbing glass, gems, and crystal, and the resinous from rubbing amber, paper, and hardwood. Benjamin Franklin proved experimentally that this was not so, and that friction either caused an excess of electricity, a positive charge, or a deficiency, a negative charge. He also demonstrated in a famous experiment with a kite in a thunderstorm that lightning is a form of electricity. During the eighteenth century it was discovered that the charge from electrical machines could be stored in capacitors, such as the Leyden jar. These could deliver powerful shocks and their effects on the body, especially muscular contraction, stimulated a whole new field of research in animal motion.

Since Aristotle the subtle spirits responsible for this had been associated with the ether, and the idea of the ether as an elastic, subtle fluid that was the prime cause of all motion had been given new currency by Newton. The properties of electricity that were being discovered seemed to fit those of the supposed ether very well, and in 1772 John Walsh showed that the upper and lower surfaces of the torpedo fish had opposite electric charges, like the Leyden jar. The anatomist Galvani, in his experiments with electricity on frog muscles, concluded that the muscles were a unique source of movement by generating electricity within themselves. In the course of this work he fixed a brass hook through a frog's legs and attached it to an iron rail. This also produced a jerk, which Galvani explained as the action of the inherent muscular force, animal electricity. This created a sensation when published in 1791, but while Galvani was ultimately proved correct in his belief that cells produce an electric charge, Professor Volta believed that the legs twitched because of an exterior stimulus coming from the brass hook and the iron rail, "metallic electricity," generated by the contact of different metals in a conducting fluid. So he constructed a "pile" of silver and zinc plates between pads of cloth soaked in brine and for the first time produced an electric current. He communicated his results in 1800 by letter to Sir Joseph Banks, President of the Royal Society, and when William Nicholson and Anthony Carlisle read this letter they immediately constructed their own pile of 36 silver half-crowns and zinc discs. They noted a drop of water bubbling on one of the terminals and realized its cause because it was already known that water is composed of oxygen and hydrogen. So they were soon able to produce, for the first time, oxygen and hydrogen by passing an electric current through water (electrolysis). Sir Humphrey Davy then installed a huge Voltaic battery in the cellar of the Royal Institution and used this for decomposing a wide range of chemical compounds into their elements, which laid the foundations of a new chemical industry.

Now that a supply of current electricity was available, it at last opened the way for fundamental experiments on the relations between electricity and magnetism, which had been impossible with static electricity. The Danish physicist Oersted discovered in 1820 that the needle of a compass would deviate whenever a current flowed in a wire adjacent to it, thus demonstrating that magnetism and electricity were somehow related. Stimulated by this, Faraday in 1821 showed that a wire carrying a current would rotate in a magnetic field, and in 1831 produced an electric current by rotating a copper disc between the poles of a magnet, thus discovering the electric motor and the dynamo. When generated in vast quantities by steam power the evolutionary potential of electricity was obviously enormous, and as we know, produced fundamental changes in our society.

CONCLUSIONS

These facts about the origins of steam power and electricity entirely contradict Sanderson's model of the causal flow from the ecostructure to the structure, and from the structure to the superstructure. This is because that is a linear model, whereas, in fact, the relations between technology, social institutions, and thought are essentially nonlinear and dialectical. The human mind is not at the end of the causal chain, but central to all these so-called "structures," which constantly interact with one another through the agency of individuals, so that technology has not had a causally privileged role throughout history, and its advances have been increasingly dependent on modes of thought and social organization.

Sanderson has not given this determining role to technology and the ecostructure on the basis of any serious evidence, but on a priori, philosophical grounds, because of the importance of materialism for Darwinian theory, which he believes is "the most successful theoretical concept ever developed in the entire history of human thought" (Sanderson 2001a, 332). A more sober assessment would be that atomic theory, genetics, and probability theory, to name just a few, have been much more important than natural selection.[1]

Whatever the merits of Darwinism in explaining biological evolution, when applied to social and cultural evolution it becomes seriously misleading. It is based on atomistic, competitive individualism, so the obvious fact that institutions and structures have a logic of their own, regardless of the motivations of individuals, is deeply repugnant, since the whole explanatory task is to reduce all aspects of society and culture to individual motives. But these tell us nothing, for example, about the traditional gulf between scholars and craftsmen, or the status of merchants, in premodern society. My account of the origins of steam power and electricity was also directed at a more general failing of natural selection when applied to human society, which is that it takes no theoretical interest in the origins of things, but treats them simply as the result of variation. Survival is all that matters, and depends on being adaptive, materially useful in some way. There are, however, no prizes for guessing that people will prefer electric light to candles: the question is how electricity got there in the first place. The origins of things are therefore absolutely fundamental, because only when something has come into existence can it be selected at all, and when some invention or institution survives, what is really important is not how many of them there are, or how long they last, but their *effects* on society and what they make possible. The reciprocating steam engine had a much shorter life than the waterwheel, but its evolutionary potential for society was vastly greater. The idea of evolutionary potential is part of a wider conception of social evolution that thinks in terms of *construction* rather than selection, and by construction I mean in particular the *accumulation of necessary conditions* for further evolution, such as the social and intellectual milieu that was necessary for modern science and technology to develop.

NOTE

1. Neither Darwin nor Wallace was even the first to think of natural selection; rather, it was Patrick Matthew in a book published in 1831. A disciple of Adam Smith, and an expert on fruit trees, Matthew gave a concise and complete account of the theory which, he said, "came intuitively as a self-evident fact, almost without the effort of concentrated thought" (Dempster 1983, 46), and which Darwin later conceded had anticipated his own theory of natural selection in every detail.

Part III

EVOLUTIONARY THEORY IN SOCIOLOGY

Diverse Applications

12

ÉMILE DURKHEIM VERSUS EDWARD WESTERMARCK

An Uneven Match

J. P. Roos

RIVAL FOUNDERS

The complicated relationship between Durkheim and Westermarck began to interest me when I happened to read Durkheim's (1896) long article on incest to see what he said about Westermarck's theory and found that Westermarck is mentioned only in a short dismissive footnote. This was odd, because Westermarck and Durkheim were contemporaries and competitors in the establishment of sociology. For many years, Westermarck was by far the better known of the two. Westermarck was appointed docent in sociology in 1896 at the University of Helsinki. He became the first lecturer of sociology in England in the University of London (London School of Economics) in 1904 (the Sociology Department of LSE celebrated its centenary in 2004 thanks to Westermarck's course) and professor in 1907 on the strength of his doctoral thesis, published almost simultaneously with Durkheim's first major works (Westermarck 1891). Durkheim published his Ph.D. thesis *Division du travail social*, in 1893 (Westermarck's thesis was published two years earlier), and *Les règles de la méthode sociologique* in 1895, or the same year that Westermarck's *The History of Human Marriage* appeared in French. Durkheim became full professor in sociology at the Sorbonne in 1906, one year earlier than Westermarck achieved that rank.

One important difference between Westermarck and Durkheim was that the latter was an empire builder who gathered followers, fought for academic power, and tried to annihilate his enemies and competitors, whereas Westermarck lived many years in isolation in Morocco and shared his time between England, Finland, and Morocco. In Finland he had some prominent followers but in England only a few direct students. For instance, Bronislaw Malinowski was his student but went on to become more of a follower of Durkheim.

In addition to his books, Durkheim produced a continual flow of reviews and comments and practically filled the *Année sociologique* himself. As to Westermarck, his ability to work was even more impressive. He lived to almost 80 and continued to work until the end, participating in debates in the 1930s concerning his own work. In fact, Westermarck lived to see the rise of the "new anthropology," which eclipsed the comparative method, and he even reacted to this change by developing a joint approach wherein both intensive case studies and the broad comparative perspective could be combined (see Westermarck 1927; Lagerborg 1953, 19-20).

Westermarck's "comparative method" based on extensive reading of secondary sources is nowadays considered obsolete, being based on armchair research, containing innumerable and disparate facts taken out of context, and seemingly devoid of any theory. The criticism about "armchair research" is mistaken, as Westermarck did do extensive field research starting in the 1890s, including learning Arabic and spending much more time with his informants than was usual among ethnographers at that time. It is also a mistake to say that Westermarck's books were devoid of theory and that the collections of facts were completely disparate. As Westermarck himself notes, he took great care to group his evidence in contextually relevant categories and not jump haphazardly from one piece of information to another. And he was very critical of "case studies" where the results were based on only one tribe or place of study and generalized from there (Westermarck 1922a, 21), as often happens in sociology.

The main reason for the eclipse of Westermarck must be that he was a Darwinian and based his theories on natural selection and empirical assumptions about human nature. The three major names in his first book on the history of human marriage were Darwin, Spencer, and Wallace. If you do not understand Darwinism, then the book becomes an incoherent collection of materials. Westermarck was an early evolutionary psychologist who was interested in the psychological explanations of human nature and especially in the role of emotions in sociology. In this he followed on the footsteps of Adam Smith, although Westermarck's main inspiration came from early anthropology.

Durkheim, on the other hand, was the foremost representative of a more autonomous theoretical sociology, but he did engage in empirical research, which was theoretically directed and conceptual. One of his most famous dictums is the requirement that the social should be explained only by the social. This is not as restrictive as we now understand, because for Durkheim biologically determined social behaviors were also social facts.

Durkheim referred to Westermarck in footnotes or only indirectly. One reason was certainly the typically French way of leaving direct competitors unmentioned. In his book on the methods of social science (Durkheim, 1895b), Westermarck is only referred to indirectly, but at least one chapter is a straightforward critique of Westermarck. According to Durkheim, he wrote his critique before reading Westermarck, but this appears to be untrue: The critique is clearly directed against what Westermarck had written. Westermarck reciprocated in his new edition of *The History of Human Marriage*, where in the opening chapter he mentions the absurd school of thought that wants to explain social facts by social facts, but he does not mention Durkheim in this connection (Westermarck 1922a; and see below).

A good example of this is Durkheim's long article on incest in the first issue of *L'Année sociologique* (1896). There is one footnote (p. 72) in which Durkheim says that for the sake of completeness, Westermarck must also be mentioned, although his idea is completely impossible. There are two exceptions to this rule of silence. One is the long critique by Durkheim of Westermarck's book on the origins of human marriage (which was translated into French only four years after its publication in English), where Durkheim tries to demolish the thesis that human marriage has existed as long as humans (see Durkheim 1895a). The second exception is a similar critique of the first volume of *The Origin and Development of the Moral Ideas* in *L'Année sociologique* (in 1907). Both can be explained by the fact that, at the time, Durkheim was internationally much less known than Westermarck and could thus use an attack on Westermarck to build his own reputation.

Rolf Lagerborg (1953, 17), a friend and relative of Westermarck's who also had close contacts with Durkheim, informs us that the review was directly inspired by the bitterness felt by Durkheim that Westermarck's book received enormous acclaim and completely eclipsed his own approach. Westermarck was not the only one treated in this way: Max Weber is mentioned only a few times by Durkheim. But in Westermarck's case their major themes were close to each other, and Durkheim had been planning to write books both on the family and on the development of morals.

DURKHEIM'S CRITIQUE OF THE HISTORY OF HUMAN MARRIAGE

Durkheim's long critique of Westermarck, "Origine du mariage dans l'espèce humaine d'après Westermarck" (1895a), is in many ways very interesting and contains much that mainstream sociology still considers valid today. He begins with a very positive evaluation of the data collection and the extensive use of observations, which compare favorably with the typical French approach to sociological research. However, there are problems connected with the method of Westermarck (by method, Durkheim means the disciplinary orientation and the logic with which he draws his conclusions, not method in the current sense).

The first criticism is that Westermarck says that "social" is defined as something that cannot be explained otherwise, i.e., that other explanations should be tried first. Also the use of Darwinism without hesitation and almost without criticism is noted. Durkheim criticizes Westermarck for posing "as an evident axiom that our psychic constitution and even our animal nature, that is, that part of us which depends immediately on organic conditions, is also the main source of social life" (i.e., the present starting point of evolutionary psychology).

According to Durkheim, the use of Darwinism means that one bases science on a simple hypothesis, which is not a reliable approach. Neither is it certain that those qualities which humans have now, and which exist in primitive societies, have always existed; they may be absent during periods we know nothing about; they may have disappeared and reappeared through other causes. As an argument for this, Durkheim notes that bees have a highly developed social organization and birds are very faithful in marriage like humans, whereas many mammals have much less developed social institutions than humans do (this is taken from Westermarck, not Durkheim's original knowledge). Only causal chains that are well established can assure good sociological explanations, Durkheim affirms.

Another counterargument is that there is an enormous diversity of social forms so that the kinds of explanations used by Westermarck (maternal instincts, sexual desire, instinctive horror of incest) can never account for all the different forms and institutions. For example the Roman family or the German tribes may have the same maternal love, but their family forms are completely different, and in the Roman family the mother was not even legally a parent of her children. The Iroquois children do not have official paternity, but paternal love nevertheless exists. Durkheim protests strongly against the assumed unchanging basic ingredients of the nature of the human family, when its forms are so enormously varying and almost everything is possible. Thus Durkheim typically speaks of very different things than Westermarck: of rules instead of emotions.

This leads to the second important difference, the use of concepts. Westermarck treats his concepts loosely, Durkheim complains. He defines "family" simply as the unit of male and female that exists longer than just for reproduction and the birth of children. That is, the family is a (not exclusively human) arrangement which is necessary to take care of the children until they can become independent (Westermarck 1891, 19-20). This is a Darwinian definition in that it defines the survival condition for the offspring. Westermarck clearly and pointedly rejects juridical or rule-based definitions. Rules can never be the basis of social institutions (Westermarck 1891, 22), but emotions can. Again, we see how the essential difference between Durkheim and Westermarck is that for the former anything social must be based on an explicit rule or law, never just on a simple, trivial emotion. Thus for instance marriage (which is the precondition of the family) is marriage only if it is confirmed by a legal institution; being someone's relative must be determined by legal relationships. ("There is marriage when there is reglementation, mutual recognition of rights, and duties with sanctions," Durkheim (1895a, 80) says.) Durkheim claims that Westermarck imputes legal rules where he can only show anecdotes. It is interesting that, for Durkheim, the concept of family used by Westermarck is wholly ideological. In present usage we should say that Westermarck's approach is naturalistic whereas Durkheim's approach is, if not ideological, then at least idealist and rule-based.

ORIGINAL PROMISCUITY

In Durkheim's time, the view that the original situation of the human family was one of promiscuity was a novel idea. It had been posed by several authors (Morgan, Lubbock, and others; see Westermarck 1891, Chapter IV) and it was assumed that the family as an institution must have developed later and therefore, before such civilized regulation was established, human beings must have had free and unrestricted sex. Prior to the promiscuity hypothesis, the general assumption had been that the family was a fundamental form which had existed since time immemorial (the "biblical" family concept). For Durkheim, then, Westermarck's theory of the origins of the family was a return to the classic, but mistaken, view of the permanence of the family. In fact, Westermarck goes further and posits a type of family organization for the apelike ancestors of humans. He also sees the mother-child bond, not the heterosexual union, as constitutive of the family (Westermarck 1891). Against both the promiscuity hypothesis and Westermarck, Durkheim posits an immensely varying family that can have been at one time extremely polygamous, at times patriarchal, at times matriarchal, and that only lately has developed into the more permanent and unified family form typical of European societies. Durkheim is familiar with the Darwinian argument to the extent that he points out that, as family forms depend on environmental conditions, it is quite possible that there have been *"conditions d'existence"* that have required completely different family forms. To him it is purely conjectural to claim that the original form would be the bonds of the nuclear family.

Durkheim also says that even if it were true (which he disputes) that the observations of anthropologists show that in all existing primitive societies the family form of one man and one or more women and children is observed, this is not a proof because there can have been many more primitive societies where this was not true. Westermarck can thus never prove his claim. From an evolutionary point of view this is not a tenable proposition.

Durkheim accepts the critique of Westermarck against the original promiscuity hypothesis, but he does not believe marriage was an original state of human societies. Instead, the original state was that of *sexual anomie*, lack of all rules, where many different kinds of unions existed – monogamy, polygamy, free unions, etc. Durkheim notes that it is quite possible that this situation would not have led to any free love on a continual basis, but the essential thing was that *there were no sanctions against free love or for more permanent unions.* He also claims that Westermarck has not even considered the possibility of sexual anomie, which is a serious shortcoming (and the result of his unsatisfactory concepts of family and marriage).

According to Durkheim, there are two fundamentally separate sexual unions: a free union and legal marriage. These two are completely different and cannot be treated as one, as Westermarck does. As Durkheim says, in complete seriousness, "Lovers who are together for their entire lives are not for that reason married" (1895a, 80). So, even if it were true that there is a certain permanence of the couple, which is more accentuated when we get to humans, the interesting question for Durkheim is how this union becomes regulated, based on rules, where violators are punished. Only this interests sociology, because only this is a social institution.

Another example cited by Durkheim is that even if one could show that most people have had monogamous families, there is an enormous difference between a situation where people could have been polygamous, if they had wanted, and the present situation where they cannot. Nor does the universal prevalence of jealousy prove anything. And why should jealousy exist when we know that men are naturally polygamous and always interested in the wife of the neighbor, asks Durkheim. "In one word, sexual egoism, however much force we assume it has, cannot have been the source of marital rights, as little as economic egoism can have been the origin of property" (Durkheim 1895a, 84, my translation).

Durkheim concludes that Westermarck is correct in that there have never been group marriages or general promiscuity, but the information collected by Westermarck shows without any doubt that there has not been marriage in Durkheim's sense. This is also shown by the fact that the concept of kinship varies enormously. According to Durkheim, it is unclear whether fathers have understood that they are fathers to their children. Children may use the same names for fathers and other kin and even the word referring to mother and father can have been identical. (In this Durkheim is clearly wrong: The assumption of fatherhood is not restricted to civilized humans; see Hrdy 1999.) So, according to Durkheim, Morgan's research shows the existence of large family collectivities that had no clear nucleus but a lot of homogeneous strata. By contrast, a matriarchal family form where the father's position is undefined and kinship connected to the mother is a highly developed family form, which must have been preceded by many others.

Westermarck is thus accused of bypassing the difference between primitive family forms and the present-day family in the "great European societies" and the huge development from the first to the second.

DURKHEIM AND WESTERMARCK ON THE ORIGIN OF THE INCEST TABOO

Durkheim's "La prohibition de l'inceste et ses origines" (1896) poses the challenge of explaining how a totally superstitious and irrational prejudice can explain a fundamental aspect of contemporary morality. To know the reason for the universal prohibition of incest we must go to the root of it. This root is the law of exogamy, which is defined as the prohibition of marriage to members of one's own clan. A clan is defined by people who have the same totem. (Although there may be several clans with the same totem, notes Durkheim. In this case, it is the totem that is essential.) Thus rules concerning the totem are at the root of incest prohibitions. This is in all simplicity the logic of Durkheim's explanation. The material on which this conclusion is based comes mainly from Durkheim's armchair studies of Australian aboriginals (published as *Les formes élémentaires de la vie réligieuse* in 1912*)*, but also from American Indians. In the new edition of *The History of Human Marriage*, Westermarck showed that the totem explanation did not hold water even in Australia (see below).

This text, some 70 pages long, thus claims to present the origin of the incest taboo, the *law of exogamy*. As to the origin of exogamy Durkheim has no real explanation, except to say that it is just based on religious prejudice. Nevertheless, he notes that the reasons cannot be based on any Darwinian principles. (In this text, there is, as previously mentioned, only one footnote (note 5, p. 72) referring to Westermarck: "To be complete, let us mention a hypothesis of Westermarck: abhorrence of incest is instinctive, and this instinct is the consequence of cohabitation. This suppresses sexual desire. . . . But it cannot be applied to exogamy, because members of the same totem do not live together and even live often in different areas. We shall see in what follows that this explanation is no more valid for more recent forms of incest.")

Westermarck replied to this article in the fifth edition of his *The History of Human Marriage* (1922b, 183-85, 198) by connecting Durkheim's arguments to those of his authority, Sir James Frazer, and showing that Frazer himself disproves Durkheim's theory. Totemism and exogamy have no necessary connection but may be completely separate. There are several examples of exogamy without totemism (Westermarck 1922b, 184). The explanation that shedding of (menstrual) blood is the main reason why marriage would be forbidden for people of the same totem is not relevant at all: All kinds of blood shedding are quite possible, such as circumcision. (In this text, Westermarck disposes of some other criticisms too: For instance Durkheim's criticism that instinctual aversion should apply to spouses, not only children, siblings, and parents; Westermarck 1922b, 198.)

I shall not cover all of Durkheim's rather rambling article. I just want to stress that, read with hindsight, it is obsolete and has only a historical interest, at least compared to Westermarck. It also shows that Durkheim did not understand the principles of evolution. For instance, on p. 45 Durkheim gives us the following reasoning: Exogamy is the first form of the prohibition of incest in history. It cannot have existed before, because otherwise there could not have been such prohibitions in more primitive societies. In Durkheim's own words, "All repression of incest presupposes family relations which the society recognizes and organizes. Society cannot prevent the relatives from getting together unless it attributes a social character to this union; otherwise it would not be interested" (my translation).

Here we have a nice case of circular reasoning: Only socially defined family relations can be forbidden, incest prohibition is social, and therefore Westermarck is wrong. The "naïve" ideas of Westermarck about a much earlier (even nonhuman) origin of incest prohibitions are by definition out of the question. Durkheim is fascinated by complex clan rules in which children will have different totems from parents and thus different prohibitions from those of the parents. Yet these complex rules must have a common cause: This is what he sets out to investigate from religious rules. In fact, this is one of his reasons for studying incest: How is it possible that the "absurd prejudices" of primitive people may have anything to do with our contemporary morals. But again, as with marriage, rules are essential. Without rules there is no society.

For Durkheim, one cannot prevent irregular unions between relatives by forbidding them to marry. The refusal of incest is rather based on duty; there is an impersonal imperative which prevents us from having sexual relations with our relatives. Incest destroys the family by subverting the rules: If a man wants to make love to his sister, she is no longer his sister (Durkheim 1896, 93)! Later, some additional counterarguments appear. Durkheim mentions the idea that a long period of togetherness dilutes sexual sentiments, but claims that this cannot be the cause of incest prohibitions because the same is true between spouses (Durkheim 1896, 95; see Westermarck's 1922b reply to this).

No, the causes of incest prohibition, for which Durkheim now can give different rational moral explanations, have their origin in the superstitions that led to exogamy. And these superstitions led to our seeking sexual partners, instead of in close relatives, from groups outside the primitive clan, where we are all related. While the original superstitions disappear, the actual prohibition remains.

According to Westermarck, the universal refusal of incest is not the result of the social construction of a norm, but of an evolutionary adaptation that is not unique to humans. Evolutionary rules are based on "algorithms" where the choice is made semiautomatically and based on observation or experience. The rule is: Do not have sexual relations with someone with whom you have grown up since a very young age (human beings who have been in close contact with each other since the early childhood of at least one member of a pair are not interested in sexual intercourse).

Similar rules work for recognizing parenthood (both by parents and by children) or being a close relative. Additionally, it is important to note that incest aversion is not a simple lack of sexual interest, but an active aversion, even with regard to thinking about such actions. This active aversion, the function of which is to prevent genetic damage, is the root cause (ultimate cause) of incest taboos (Westermarck 1891, 1922b, 192-98).

Note a very important corollary of this: In the cultural theories of exogamy, the problem is that the rules are very ancient. There is no written evidence and the original reason for the rule has since disappeared. Thus we can never know for sure the original reason, and the only possibility is to speculate about it. Westermarck's theory, by contrast, supposes that the rule is constantly reproduced, because the original reason still exists. Westermarck's thesis can be empirically proven or disproven: To disprove it, an investigator only needs to show that being reared together has no effect on sexual desire. A second means of disproving the Westermarck effect is to show that there is no actual genetic disadvantage in incestuous sex. There is now much empirical research showing the significance of the Westermarck effect (regarding apes, childhood marriages, and kibbutzim [e.g., Wolf 1995; Shepher 1972], and most recently an elegant demonstration of the sibling effect [Lieberman, Tooby, and Cosmides 2007]).

DURKHEIM'S CRITIQUE OF THE ORIGIN AND DEVELOPMENT OF THE MORAL IDEAS

As his last comment on Westermarck, Durkheim wrote an extensive critique of the first volume of Westermarck's *The Origin and Development of the Moral Ideas* (Durkheim 1907). To begin with, Durkheim notes with satisfaction that Westermarck follows the same approach as he does, i.e., the comparative approach, to study the genesis of morals. He is also satisfied that Westermarck has referred explicitly to him in the book. But, after this positive note, a very critical review follows, starting from the (for Durkheim) absolutely false idea that human evolution should be the basis of a study of moral ideas. In countering Westermarck's contention that moral ideas come from the universal and permanent aspects of human nature, Durkheim argues that the causes of moral ideas are essentially social. Durkheim notes that to prove his claims Westermarck seeks confirmation from very different societies, but instead one should concentrate on facts which are more precise and specific. These specific facts are the rules concerning moral conduct. For Durkheim, if there are no rules or sanctions, there is no morality. The fact that Westermarck concentrates on moral sentiments means that he is not really dealing with morality at all. And Westermarck's attempt to describe original moral states is impossible, Durkheim argues, because the original states cannot be observed.

Because guilt can be attributed to collectivities, the individual agent theory of morality does not work. Westermarck passes too quickly to shared feelings of morality from individual feelings. This is what is central for Durkheim and he agrees with Westermarck about the end result, but not about the cause. In particular, Durkheim complains, Westermarck does not devote any thoughts to the question of the very wide range of sanctions despite having developed a theory of moral sanctions.

Durkheim also complains that Westermarck is not able to explain the fact that people in many societies often direct retribution towards the innocent. There is some truth in this complaint, the problem being that Westermarck did not adequately distinguish between punishment and vengeance. To avenge a misdeed, one does not have to choose the actual guilty person; any member of the same group will do (actually, the effect is then greater).

WESTERMARCK REPLIES TO DURKHEIM

Westermarck did not take Durkheim seriously at first (he only referred to his critiques indirectly) and later avoided mentioning him. In his memoirs (Westermarck 1927), he does not refer explicitly to Durkheim, but mentions a French author who had criticized him of reverting to the biblical beliefs concerning Adam and Eve. In 1921, Westermarck formulated in a letter his main point against Durkheim: "Thus Professor Durkheim, in his book on the totemic system in Australia with the significant title *Les formes élémentaires de la vie re- ligieuse*, confidently asserts that his system contains 'all the great ideas and all the principal rival attitudes which are at the bottom even of most advanced reli- gions'; he then proceeds to a discussion of religion in general, in the belief that if you have carefully studied the religion of one people only, you are better able to lay down the main principles of religious life than if you follow the compara- tive method of a Tylor or a Frazer. It almost seems as though some kind of so- ciological intuition were to take the place of comparative induction" (see Lager- borg 1953).

Westermarck reacted strongly to the point made by Durkheim that Darwin's theory of evolution is only a hypothesis on which one cannot base claims. He retorted that if Durkheim does not believe in the evolution of humans from lower animals, then he must support the thesis of divine creation, which is com- pletely unscientific.

Note that while Durkheim is against generalizing from one hypothesis, Westermarck criticizes Durkheim for generalizing from a single case. It seems to me that generalization based on a testable hypothesis is certainly closer to a "good method."

Another essential difference between Durkheim and Westermarck is obvi- ous: Westermarck, on the basis of evolutionary theory, assumed that humans had evolved a common, universal human nature that formed the basis of the development of moral sentiments. Here he was inspired also by David Hume and Adam Smith. By contrast, Durkheim believed that there exists a panoply of different moral rules and no such thing as a common human nature. This was also the view of Rolf Lagerborg, Westermarck's Finnish student. For him it was clear that Durkheim was right in the end: The division between mind and body is essentially the division between biological and sociological aspects of human life. Social institutions cannot and should not be explained by simple psycho- logical facts, such as instincts "Thus, it is the task of sociology to examine the social origin of all higher conscious life. Social facts, such as moral phenomena, can least of all be explained solely from biological and psychological points of view" (Lagerborg 1953, 22). Lagerborg here gives voice to what became the dominant paradigm in the social sciences from the 1930s on, as Westermarck lost and Durkheim and his followers won the battle over sociology.

CONCLUSION

My original intention in this paper was to see what distinguishes Westermarck and Durkheim with regard to the family and the question of incest and how their arguments relate to what we know today. If one looks at what theses Durkheim defended and what Westermarck defended, it appears evident that the former's views are now more or less false. Durkheim was wrong in his idea that sociology is mainly about rules and sanctions, not habits and practices, so that the origin of marriage must be exclusively discussed as a problem of explicit rules. He was mistaken in rejecting Darwin's theory of evolution as a mere hypothesis, in which he did not believe. He was also mistaken in seeing the prohibition of incest as a social institution based on superstition that has nothing to do with natural selection. (Unfortunately, this is still a popular misconception among social scientists.)

Collective consciousness was for Durkheim a social fact. For him, it was simply impossible to connect individual psychological processes to the collective actions of a group. As noted by Bergesen (2004, 398), Durkheim strongly believed that all basic cognitive categories (space, number, cause, substance, personality, sociality) are developed only via learning and social interaction (but see Pyysiäinen 2005 for a claim that Durkheim did try to connect the individual and collective level).

Durkheim used an analogy drawn from chemistry in defense of collective consciousness: Bronze derives its characteristics from being bronze, not from the individual characteristics of its components, copper, tin, or lead. This is typical of the way Durkheim used the natural sciences and completely contrary to the way Westermarck used them, never as analogies but concretely. One claim which was clearly intended against Westermarck (among others; no names are mentioned): "That the subject-matter of the social life cannot be explained by purely psychological factors, i.e., by states of individual conscience, seems to us perfectly evident" [Durkheim 1895b, 83]).

Westermarck, on the other hand, seems to have gotten most of his fundamental claims right. He was also an extremely meticulous researcher who really checked his facts, who had gone through all the relevant literature, and who compared all the known information. His problem was that his books were seen mainly as compilations of disparate facts lacking an overarching theory – or nothing that could be understood as a theory from a sociological point of view. This misunderstanding is based on the invisibility of Darwin's theory of evolution as the theoretical foundation of Westermarck's books. The same critique could be directed against Darwin himself!

The main reason for Westermarck's eclipse was his evolutionary, Darwinian approach to sociology and anthropology, and most specifically his views about human nature. Although he has not been reproached as an "evil" social Darwinist (because he did not make any direct generalization from a Darwinian theory of evolution to a theory of social evolution), he has been seen as someone who was an anthropologist or a psychologist, but certainly not a sociologist. And, as part of our legacy from Durkheim, psychological explanations have been seen for a long time as an easy avoidance of real explanations.

Many of Westermarck's facts may be nowadays obsolete or wrong. Indeed, it would be an interesting research project to see how much or how little this would be the case. Nevertheless, Westermarck's main conclusions regarding human family formation, incest aversion, the importance of emotions in family life and moral behavior, etc., still stand, and are even being reinforced by the modern synthesis of evolution and the social sciences, developing rapidly, if still more or less unnoticed by the mainstream of sociology.

ACKNOWLEDGMENTS

This article originated as a small comment comparing the incest theories of Westermarck and Durkheim. I thank especially Anna Rotkirch and Heikki Sarmaja for extensive comments, but also Martin Kohli, Claude Fischler, and Stephen Sanderson.

13

WHAT IS "BABY FEVER"?

Contrasting Evolutionary Explanations of Proceptive Behavior

Anna Rotkirch

The truth is, I've had a strong desire to make a baby ever since I turned 18. I still remember how I walked around with my five baby dolls as a child!

Actress Nicole Kidman, mother of two adopted children, who longed to give birth in 2005. (Ala-Risku 2005)

It's hard to become a father because everything turns around the mother for a long time. But men also have a biological clock and baby fever.

Nicke Lignell, Finnish actor and father of five children in 2003. (Hallsten 2005)

Some may be motivated by romantic love, or a desire to carry on the family line, or a primeval urge to perpetuate the species.

The London Financial Times, June 24-25, 2006, W1-2.

INTRODUCTION

There exists a strong lay perception that desiring children is something "natural," "normal," and universal. In its more urgent forms, this desire is often referred to through metaphors of *baby fever* or the *biological clock*. The biological clock refers to the right time to have children, usually the first child.[1] It may concern the right age to begin childbearing, a kind of physical and psychological maturation – "I'm 25 and my biological clock is ticking" – or more directly a necessity to get pregnant before it is too late, i.e., before the woman reaches menopause. Baby fever denotes a wish to have children of one's own and especially to touch, smell, and carry infants. It may be induced or aggravated by seeing other people's children. Women who do not wish to have more children may laughingly say, "I shouldn't take her into my arms, it's too dangerous." Women talk more about baby fever, although men also experience it, as the second quotation above indicates. Potential grandparents may also say they have baby fever. Thus baby fever denotes a strong feeling, which may be against the speaker's rational considerations, while the biological clock relates more to the proper beginning of childbearing in the lifespan. I will here use these expressions as synonyms.

What does evolutionary theory say about wanting children? Contrary to lay perceptions, evolutionary theorists show that fertility decisions are not simply age-related but a complex mixture of environmental, contextual, and genetic factors (Kaplan and Lancaster 2003). Today's state of affairs appears quite fragmented (for a review, see Borgerhoff Mulder 1998). The opposite arguments partly follow the differences between evolutionary psychology and sociobiology, or what Sanderson (2001a, 128-30) calls Darwinian psychology and Darwinian social science. Darwinian psychologists readily question any evolved and direct wish for children, whereas sociobiologists sometimes appear ready to claim that desiring children is adaptive before empirical research has been undertaken.

In the 1980s, Warren B. Miller (1986, 1992) presented his concept of "proception," behavior that favors childbearing and is the opposite of contraception. Proceptive behavior includes everything from rational long-term planning to getting pregnant "by mistake." I suggest that baby fever has a special place in this continuum of proceptive behavior. By "baby fever" I mean a conscious wish for children that is connected with persistent, bodily emotion and recurring, spontaneous thoughts.

Many authors suggest that the main biological basis for childbearing is related to the pleasures of having sex and of parenting (Miller 1986, 268; Morgan and King 2001). While agreeing with them, I here look for a more specific cognitive trait, which may also arise outside a sexual relationship and without a person's already being a parent. Neither is baby fever necessarily connected to a general attachment to all babies.

My guess is that baby fever is an emotion, the function of which is to guide the behavior of the person experiencing it and her or his environment, especially in the form of testing or persuading sexual partners. Anecdotal evidence from contemporary low-fertility societies suggests that children in the near environment trigger baby fever. It also appears to "rise" when there is a conscious wish to have a child of one's own but there is some obstacle in the way – when the financial or social situation, one's partner or the lack of a partner, the adoption agencies, fertility treatments, or one's body refuse to cooperate in granting that wish. It may serve as the "irrational" part that pushes the woman to make a complicated decision. Although baby fever is not an illness, it may develop into pathological conditions such as depression or false pregnancies.

Whether the emotional and behavioral patterns I here call baby fever do have a genetic basis lies outside the scope of this theoretical paper. Instead, I will first briefly discuss the most usual kinds of evolutionary theorizing about fertility, i.e., adaptations for reducing and postponing fertility. I will then present four major schools of thought during the last century that propose theories concerning a conscious desire for children, from Edward Westermarck's early evolutionary sociology through women's studies to evolutionary psychology and behavioral genetics.

ADAPTATIONS DECREASING FERTILITY LEVELS

As a rule, existing research has focused on adaptations that *reduce* fertility. This is related to the long-standing demographic challenge of explaining declining fertility. Anthropological demography has shown that in all known societies, the number of children is regulated, usually so as to decrease the number of pregnancies and infants. This happens by systematic infanticide as in early modern Japan (Skinner 2004), the use of foundling homes and wet-nurses in Europe, or with the aid of modern contraceptives and induced abortions (Hrdy 1999).

There is a bewildering multitude of explanations of cognitive and emotional traits affecting fertility decisions. While most of them appear to presume evolved adaptations regulating fertility decisions, only a few try to define such evolved predispositions. Furthermore, different disciplines vary in their emphasis on explanatory levels – do we look at evolved behavior varying among populations, neighborhoods, households, or individuals?[2]

Population Level Explanations

Sanderson's *The Evolution of Human Sociality* features a chapter on human reproductive behavior and one subchapter devoted to fertility decline. It discusses fertility on the population level as it may be related to economic conditions, female empowerment, and infant mortality. Sanderson finds on the basis of regression analyses of cross-national data that infant mortality is the variable with the most empirical support: "Infant mortality was the best predictor . . . and clearly best in predicting actual fertility *change*." The economic value of children's labor or a "simple increase in material wealth or the standard of living" are, by contrast, weak predictors (Sanderson 2001a, 173-74). Sanderson's view suggests an evolved strategy of choice between the so-called *r* (quantity) and *K* modes of reproductive behavior in humans: In poor conditions with high infant mortality, people have more births, whereas in better conditions with low infant mortality they have fewer. The strategy requires adaptations facilitating cognitive assessment of infant mortality in ways that can rapidly (during a few generations) spread through whole populations.

It is unclear to me whether this explanation applies to other levels, such as different social classes within a society. The tendency for the poorest to have the most children fits with their greater risk of infant mortality, but in the Scandinavian countries for both the wealthiest and the poorest to have 3+ children does not (e.g., Duvander and Andersson 2003). Neither does Sanderson's explanation explain change in low-fertility societies. For instance, Russian fertility levels sharply declined in the 1990s, while infant mortality increased somewhat.

Household Level Explanations

Other explanations focus on household composition and wealth. For instance, evolutionary psychology posits an adaptation for scheduling female reproduction within the family: As long as the mother has small children in need of care, her older daughters will not have children themselves (Flinn 1989; Barrett, Dunbar, and Lycett 2002, 137-70). This posits the existence of an "anti-baby fever medicament" distributed by the mother of the household. However, in Northern Europe today such constellations are rare, due to the low number of both children and their age differences in most households.

Group Level Explanations

Some scholars look for between-group differentials in fertility. For instance, Kevin MacDonald (1999) shows how marginalized ethnic communities, in his case the Ashkenazi Jews, adjust their reproductive strategies from high to low fertility depending on the economic situation of the household. The supposed adaptation would "respond to cues of scarcity by delaying or lowering reproduction" (MacDonald 1999, 227). He supports the so-called fertility opportunity hypothesis developed by Virginia Abernethy. According to it, "a perception that economic opportunity is expanding, so that relatively many children could probably be successfully raised to maturity, is associated with early marriage and larger family size" (Abernethy 1999, 119).

The fertility opportunity explanation is more contextual than the "simple material well-being" Sanderson (2001a) discarded as an explanation of fertility decline. It could work for some families or groups only, not necessarily whole populations. However, the fertility opportunity hypothesis appears to contradict most other explanations, which suggest that expectations of increased wealth limits fertility instead of increasing it.

Social Status and Personality Level Explanations

Finally, a growing body of research explains variations in individual fertility by linking them to *social status* in general, and more specifically to status and IQ: "The proposal is that the evolved desire to increase or maintain one's social status may conflict with the desire to have large numbers of children and therefore influence fertility decisions" (MacDonald 1999, 227). This argument is frequent in general economic reasoning. It also appears in behavioral ecology, which finds intercorrelations between spousal and parental relations, sexual behavior, and IQ (Belsky, Steinberg, and Draper 1991). Haaga (2001, 58) states that the cognitive adaptation involved may be a relatively simple "if . . . then" logic. People may follow a simple cue related to status competition: "Whom might my children surpass? What do I see my potential rivals providing for their children?" In a similar vein, Hill and Reeve (2005) explain low fertility as the outcome of snowballing resource games. Their mathematical model indicates that fertility should become lower if wealth is inherited and there is increased competition for resources. In their view, this explains "why fertility correlates negatively with wealth both within and between populations" (2004, 401; cf. Mace 1998.)

Thus most explanations of fertility decisions indicate the existence of "biological guillotines" rather than biological clocks. The cognitive and emotional triggers involved appear to say: Do not have children if you cannot take care of them, if they do not fit into your household's division of work, if your friends do not have children, or if you are bright and ambitious. Additionally, societies and household types with high fertility levels are usually associated with high infant mortality, low parental investment, lower number of desired than actual children, etc. – that is, they do not bear any indications of strong baby fevers.

POSSIBLE ADAPTATIONS FOR WANTING CHILDREN

It is undoubtedly true that having a child at the wrong moment often has disastrous consequences. However, from the gene's point of view having no child at all has even more disastrous consequences. Although so many triggers aim at limiting the number of children, one may turn the question upside down and ask: Why do people in contemporary wealthy, competitive societies have any children at all (Morgan and King 2001)? Why have fertility levels nowhere fallen to zero, or even close to 0.5?

Explanations for the emotional incentives in childbearing decisions have varied widely during the last century. I present here four different versions of why "baby fever" and other related types of wishing for a child have arisen, and to whom. These versions take us from the hypothesis of a primitive instinct to the constructionist rejection of any instinct, the evolutionary psychological byproduct explanation, and then back to a hypothesis of some, albeit feeble and context-dependent, procreative instinct.

Version 1: A Childbearing Instinct

In his *The History of Human Marriage*, a classic nineteenth-century bestseller that deserves to be rediscovered (Roos, Chapter 12 this volume; Sanderson

2007a), Edward Westermarck (1894, 379) briefly discusses people's wish to have children. He approaches it as part of Darwinian sexual selection. Fertility assessment is an important component of men's and women's mate choice, he writes, even if not the most appealing one: "We have hitherto dealt only with the poetry of sexual selection – love; now something is to be said of its prose – dry calculation. And we may conveniently begin with man's appreciation of woman's fertility, as this has some of the characteristics of an instinct." Westermarck (1894, 376) immediately continues with a clear statement: "Desire for offspring is universal in mankind. Abortion, indeed, is practiced now and then, and infanticide frequently takes place among many savage peoples; but these facts do not disprove the general rule."

After reviewing anthropological evidence from cultures all over the world, Westermarck (1894, 379) concludes that the desire for children has various causes. First, he repeats, "there is in man an instinct for reproduction . . . [and] with this instinct a feeling of parental pride is associated." Men value female fertility in their wives and in the women of their community, sometimes to the extent that slaves or younger men were allowed to inseminate the wives of infertile or deceased husbands. Some societies value children even if the woman has no husband, Westermarck also notes. However, the socioeconomic support provided by children is most important: "No doubt children are most eagerly longed for by savage men because they are of use to him in his lifetime" (1894, 380).

Finally, Westermarck (1894, 381) sees the desire for offspring as "less intense" in modern societies. This is because children's rearing and education are more expensive, religious motives are weaker, women are not viewed only as mothers, and "marriage is something more than an institution for procreation of legitimate offspring." However, we should not think that fertility has no bearing on contemporary marriages. Westermarck notices the "remarkable" fact that in Switzerland marriages without children end in divorce twice as often as other marriages.[3]

Westermarck thus finds evidence of a universal desire for children, even in the Europe of his day, which was passing through the first phase of fertility decline. This universal desire is motivated first and foremost by the economic support provided by children. There are also "some characteristics of an instinct" in the way males value fertile women, that is, the universal desire is at least partly rooted in evolved psychological adaptations. They appear related to male sexual choice (fertile women as more attractive) but also to the feeling of parental pride.

Interestingly, Westermarck and the sources he uses emphasized a male or gender-neutral desire for children. There are no examples of women longing for babies and no talk of "maternal instincts," only of how stigmatizing barrenness or accusations of infertility are to women. This may of course be influenced by a male-centered bias in data collection that ignored female folklore. The whole issue is also discussed as "sexual selection influenced by calculation," not direct emotional ties to potential children. Either Westermarck's material lacked depictions of "baby fever," or he ignored them.

Seeing childbearing as an instinct was common for the early social sciences. Westermarck quotes T. H. Marshall, who viewed the "desire for progeny" as a frequent and strong phenomenon, "to all appearances apart from the sense of personal ambition, and separate from any demands of religion or requirements of support in old age, as to give the impression that it was the primitive faculty of philoprogenitiveness, acting so insensibly, naturally, as to have the character more of a plain instinct than of a human feeling" (quoted in Westermarck 1894, 379). Marshall thus appears more perplexed by this "primitive faculty" and is more eager to draw a line between "plain instinct" and "human feeling" than Westermarck.

Many lay comments today continue to talk about an "instinct" or "innate desire" to have children. They are often connected with the explanation of species survival – "a primeval urge to perpetuate the species" as a *London Financial Times* article put it (Tomkin 2006).[4] It is therefore important to remember that Westermarck, a forerunner of today's evolutionary psychology, did not advance explanations on a species level. He explained the desire for childbearing with material, social, and (male individual) emotional mechanisms.

Version 2: The Socially Constructed Clock

While lay people today continue to talk about instincts, the term gradually disappeared from the vocabulary of the social sciences after World War II. The second wave of the women's movement and, a bit later, the emerging academic field of Women's Studies criticized abstract mythologies connected to motherhood and especially presumptions about any universal and automatic maternal instinct.

As social constructionism became dominant in Western social sciences in the 1980s, a view emerged whereby the "biological clock" was seen as a purely social phenomenon. The lay perception of an innate desire for children was rejected. As one Women's Studies textbook puts it: "This [maternal] 'instinct' is characterized by two desires: to have children, and to care for them. . . . However, it has become increasingly clear that this 'instinct' is a socially constructed myth" (Nicolson 1997, 383). Feminist scholars have also stressed the fact that many people never desire children and many pregnancies are unwanted. For instance, a recent survey of fertility intentions in 28 EU-member and acceding member countries showed that, while every third woman had fewer children than she would ideally like to have, as many as 10-15 percent had more children than they would have wanted (European Foundation for the Improvement of Living and Working Conditions 2004, 55-56). This is an important point, but of course totally compatible with the evolutionary explanations for avoiding reproduction that I presented in the beginning of this article.

Nevertheless, surveys on childbearing intentions usually find only a small percentage of voluntarily childless people. Most men and women everywhere say they would like to have at least one child. This desire is ignored or explained by social pressure and "discourse" in constructionism and postmodernism. A bit surprisingly, quite a similar view is found among evolutionary psychologists.

Version 3: A By-product of Evolved Psychology

Evolutionary psychologists and other theorists often provide two complementary explanations for why humans have children: "sex suffices" and "caring takes care of it." All adaptations promoting heterosexual intercourse (sexual desire, romantic love, the conjugal bond, etc.) can be considered sufficient for procreation. Then, once the child is born, adaptations for caring and attaching suffice. There is no direct wish to have children. According to the leading evolutionary psychologist Steven Pinker (2006, 139),

> sociobiology is [often] refuted by the many things people do that don't help to spread their genes, such as adopting children or using contraception. In this case the confusion is between the motive of genes to replicate themselves (which does exist) and the motive of people to spread their genes (which doesn't). Genes affect their goal of replication via the sub-goal of wiring people with certain goals of their own, but replication per se need not be among those sub-sub-goals: it's sufficient for people to seek sex and nurture their children.

In this view, the question is why we want so much more sex than reproduction demands – as Jared Diamond (1997) asks, why is sex fun? – not whether sexual desire and romantic attachment are enough from the point of view of reproduction.

The most influential monograph on evolutionary theory and mothering (Hrdy 1999) does not discuss an evolved desire to have offspring. Hrdy's main aim is to emphasize the complicated chain of successive elements that trigger attachment and care after the woman has already become pregnant or the child is born. She also discusses how some species rehearse parenting skills in previous life stages: Babies universally attract primates, and female primates in particular are often used as "allomothers" (Hrdy 1999, 161-64; cf. Nicole Kidman's baby dolls in the introductory quotes). Additionally, Hrdy suggests that contemporary child spacing patterns, where the ideal is three or more children with large birth intervals, may be close to female reproductive behavior in prehistoric times. Otherwise the book does not mention a desire for children. Likewise, the topic is practically absent from Anne Campbell's (2003) excellent book on women's evolutionary psychology.

Thus the constructionist critique of maternal instincts would be partly true: There is no instinct to have children. While mating and caring is part of human nature, the urge to have children would be mostly a social construction. If childless people suffer, it is because they have witnessed how enjoyable parenthood may be; if parents long for more children, it is because they want to repeat previously rewarding experiences.

One frequent explanation for fertility transitions sees the biological clock as a typical meme. When to start and stop childbearing would be based on imitation as fertility patterns spread from elite groups throughout the population (Boyd and Richerson 1995; Hill and Reeve 2004, 398).

For several years, I used this argument in my teaching, precisely because it contradicted lay perceptions of what is and is not "biological." The biological clock is actually social, unrelated to any direct adaptations, I claimed. Caring for the children of relatives and friends, seeing other people's children and the status connected to this, may indeed constitute the main way of transmitting "baby fever."

However, on an emotional and motivational level, the desire to have a baby does not appear to equal desiring other things. As one Finnish woman expressed it in an e-mail discussion on baby fever, "It is seldom the case that somebody has hated cars all his life and then suddenly feels he can't live without getting one." Neither does the longing for a child equal the desire to have sex or an urge to care for children: One may well experience one without the others. Unwanted and tiresome pregnancies may be followed by strong maternal affection, while other mothers appear to enjoy pregnancy but not actual child care. The desire to have a baby also appears emotionally distinct from the reserve and anxiety often connected with actual pregnancies (Hrdy 1999, 166). How can this be explained, and do evolved traits play any role in this?

Version 4: A Weak but Expanding Instinct?

In contrast to the standard evolutionary psychology argument, some authors stress that reproduction is too all-important to rely on one route only (sex leads to children, which triggers caring behavior from their parents and other kin). While I have not found any text dealing directly with the question of a possible baby fever adaptation, several authors presume there exists something of the sort.[5] In the last decade, such "proceptive" behavior has been discussed especially among sociobiologically oriented demographers and population researchers. For instance, Paul Turke (1989, 66) speculates that there exists "a conscious desire to conceive children" but that it is relatively weak compared to the desire for intercourse and for economic success. Developing Turke's idea, Kevin MacDonald (1999, 228) sketches a conflict between two universal human motivational systems:

> I suppose that the default mechanism is to adopt a high-fertility, early-marriage strategy (Turke 1989). However, in the event that people perceive that such a strategy will result in poverty while delaying marriage and having fewer children would result in relative economic ease and an increase or maintenance of one's social status, there is a shift to a later-marriage, low-fertility strategy.[6]

Economists and biologists have used modeling to show that, especially when wealth inheritance and accumulation is accounted for, very low birth numbers appear to enhance fitness (Rogers 1994; Hill and Reeve 2005). As in much economic theory on fertility, they presume the existence of desires to have children – thus Rogers defines "reproductive motivations" as the desire for sex *and chil-*

dren – but do not elaborate the issue or define how such motivations would have evolved.

Some venture further. Bock (1999) thinks that the dual satisfaction to be derived from sexual intercourse – sex as pleasure and sex as leading to procreation – is still at play. "We can hypothesize that this consistency and predictability [because frequent sex leads to frequent conceptions] is an essential prerequisite for facultative adjustment of the timing of reproductive events and varied investment in children" (Bock 1999, 213-14). Bock also finds (1999, 214)

> strong empirical evidence that the demand for children is an endogenous characteristic of humans in the high level of adoption and fostering seen in many societies, and more importantly perhaps, in the multi-billion-dollar fertility treatment industry in industrialized countries. If breaking the jointness of demand resulted in a very low demand for children but a high demand for sex it is hard to imagine large numbers of people incurring the great expense and time investment in fertility treatments.

In a similar vein, Udry (1996, 329) suggests we could "avoid the terminology [of maternal instinct] but hypothesize that there may be a biological basis for motivating behavior that leads to childbearing." Udry's most interesting discussion notes that today's situation of more and more women remaining childless is the first to favor potential hereditary motivations: "In a society where women have no control over fertility, variation in childbearing hardly reflects biological predispositions. In modern societies, such predispositions can become very important" (1996, 329).

Behavioral geneticists have confirmed Udry's prediction. Using a Danish twin sample, Kohler, Rodgers, and Christensen (1999) found evidence of an increasing heritability of childbearing patterns (see also Rodgers, Hughes, Kohler, Christensen, Doughty, Rowe, and Miller 2001). They studied monozygotic and dyzygotic twins from age cohorts from two different periods, 1853-64 and 1870-1910. Before the first onset of the so-called demographic transition in the late 1870s, the heritability of childbearing patterns was very low and the effect of shared environment notable. However, in the early phase of the transition to lower numbers of births, the amount of genetic influence *increased for women*. The pattern is even clearer for more recent reproductive age women: "Females born after 1953 are characterized by relatively strong genetic effects on fertility which become even stronger with later birth cohorts" (Kohler, Rodgers, and Christensen 1999, 279). In the youngest birth cohorts, the effect of shared environment practically vanishes. Interestingly, the relative impact of genetically mediated proceptive behavior is clearly gendered: Environmental influences remained important for men from all age cohorts. Perhaps women are indeed more frequently and deeply affected by baby fever.

The genetic influence found in the Danish study was not diminished when education was controlled. Neither was it related to biological fecundability: The time for first *attempt* to get pregnant correlated with genetic relatedness, regardless of the outcome of that attempt. Heritability thus appears to vary with both gender and age cohort, and is especially related to female reproductive control: "Genetic influences on fertility are most relevant when the number of children results from a deliberate and conscious decision, and when social norms and economic conditions allow a relatively broad range of life-course alternatives" (Kohler, Rodgers, and Christensen 1999, 254).

CONCLUSIONS

I have reviewed existing theoretical support for the existence of an evolved desire to have children, a hypothetical "baby fever adaptation." Evolutionary theory has produced many explanations for the phenomenon commonly called the "biological clock" or "baby fever," which presumably ticks or rises semimechanically, at a certain age, and especially among women. The fields of demography and population studies, behavioral ecology, economic and modeling theories, and behavioral genetics have contributed their own explanatory frameworks.

There appears to be no consensus yet on how baby fever is transmitted. Some explanations complement each other while others are incompatible. Several cognitive predispositions are aimed at limiting childbearing. Human fertility decisions are highly sensitive to environmental cues, among them levels of infant mortality (in high fertility regimes) and resources needed to invest in offspring (in low fertility regimes). Behavior aimed at avoiding childbirth, from spontaneous abortions and infanticide to contraception, are legion, making the "biological guillotine" stronger than any baby feverish biological clock.

Explanations for proceptive adaptations usually assume unconscious causes that are then reinforced by social customs. Few consider any direct, reflective wish for children. However, there is fresh evidence from behavioral genetics in support of genetically mediated behavior that is growing in importance for contemporary women. The heritability of childbearing decisions has been shown to increase as the number of children falls (Kohler et al. 1999). This fits the prediction by Udry (1996), who noted that in a society of wide female reproductive choice any genetic disposition to desire children would be selected for.

Thus the environment and social norms played a larger role for fertility decisions in the nineteenth century than in contemporary developed countries. This may be the reason why Westermarck (1894) related desire for children primarily to male sexual selection and not to maternal emotions, and why he removed his views on a childbearing instinct from the revised *The History of Human Marriage*. Otherwise, Westermarck's arguments hold well today, especially his point that the frequency of abortion and infanticide does not disprove the general desire for children, as social constructionism has claimed. Indeed, theorizing about childbearing has come full circle in a century: We can again be open to the possibility of evolved desires for children. It is not a question of any hard-wired "instincts," but of evolved cognitive predispositions that are context-sensitive and may be of growing importance for some generations of women.

More and different types of empirical data are needed to proceed from here. As Haaga (2001, 58) puts it, "We need much more direct evidence on the 'psychological proximate determinants' of fertility preferences, including aspirations for one's children, perceptions of status, and the avenues of social change. What are the cues that convince large numbers of people that the rules of their society are changing?" Future research has a fascinating task in clarifying the contextual and emotional ingredients of fertility behavior, including what "baby fever" is really all about.

ACKNOWLEDGMENTS

I thank Marko Hamilo, Rosemary Hopcroft, Markku Javanainen, Markus Jokela, Janne Kivivuori, Hanna Kokko, J. P. Roos, J. P. Takala, Stephen Sanderson, and Heikki Sarmaja for comments and suggestions on earlier drafts of this paper. It is part of the research study "Fertility Patterns and Family Forms," Academy of Finland, project number 208186.

NOTES

1. I here ignore other uses of the "biological clock," e.g., as a metaphor for our sense of day and night.

2. An integrative framework is provided by evolutionary demography's life course perspective (e.g., Low 1991; Kaplan and Lancaster 2003), but it does not completely solve the question of how to assess the impact of cognitive triggers on various levels.

3. Interestingly, in the fifth edition of *The History of Human Marriage*, published in 1922, Westermarck omitted the words "universal" and "instinct" with regard to child-bearing, and the discussion of a desire for children is reduced to one page (Westermarck 1922b, 31-32).

4. From a neo-Darwinian point of view, species-level explanations are faulty. Behavior that favors genetic interest may well lead to community or species destruction.

5. Obviously, much demographic research concerns "fertility demand" and measures explicitly stated desires and reasons affecting childbearing decisions. Researchers assume and find a general desire for children, but do not explain its existence theoretically. Miller (1992) found evidence of personality traits and developmental experiences in childhood that affected fertility intentions.

6. Note that Turke is credited for having had the same assumption, not for having provided any empirical evidence.

14

CLASS MOBILITY, ENVIRONMENT, AND GENES

A Darwinian Conflict Analysis

Frank Salter

The conventional view in sociology is that social mobility is due to the cultural transmission down the generations of acquired characteristics, both material and cultural. According to this view, people are vessels of equal capacity into which different quantities of resources and culture are poured, resulting in the perpetuation of class differences. This conventional view, which I shall term the environmental hypothesis, fails to explain social mobility into and out of the professional class, because empirical findings are inconsistent with it. They point to a role for individual ability and indicate that much ability develops in a manner insensitive to class environment.

An alternative hypothesis, the hereditarian or genetic one, emphasizes that the specialized knowledge and working skills that distinguish the middle class are developed from biological capabilities that are unevenly distributed across the population. This hypothesis downplays economic and social privilege and instead focuses on individual differences. The hereditarian hypothesis has the advantage over strict environmentalism of acknowledging innate differences in ability and of according with society-wide patterns of class mobility.

After reviewing the evidence for environmental and hereditarian theories, this chapter offers a synthesis of these theories to generate strategies that individuals could in principle adopt to boost the class status of their children and grandchildren. The basic idea is that regression to the mean might be counteracted by culturally transmitted mate choice strategies in which people choose mates with one or more elevated middle-class competencies and thus an above-average chance of bearing the genes for these competencies. These families would still show regression to the mean but would reduce its impact by choosing mates of higher ability.

DARWINIAN CONFLICT THEORY AS A BASIS FOR RENOVATING CLASS ANALYSIS

Darwinian conflict theory, named by Sanderson (2001a), provides an integrative framework for conducting sociology. Operating within the accumulated empirical sociological tradition, it incorporates knowledge of human nature. It treats individual competition as fundamental to the human condition, based on evolutionary theory. It incorporates modern neo-Darwinian theories such as inclusive fitness, parental investment, sexual selection, and reciprocal altruism. Broadly, Darwinian conflict theory opens avenues for incorporating behavioral biology. It is this bridge-building that makes Sanderson's enterprise so promising, quite apart from his substantive empirical and theoretical contributions (1999a; Sanderson and Dubrow 2000). One of those contributions is the finding that proxies for fitness payoffs often complement and underpin the material and psychological payoffs deployed in conventional sociological theory. For example, Sanderson's treatment of stratification and class mobility (1999a, 270-85; 2001a, 287-307) indicates that class mobility is based on the motivation to acquire status and resources.

Sanderson's work contains much that is useful for studying status and class processes. For example, it is relevant to know that the motivations of status and resource striving are cross-cultural universals that evolved in the Paleolithic. That idea is likely to be fleshed out by ethnographic data on contemporary hunter-gatherers. Sanderson's critique of social constructivism also is noteworthy, especially when he notes that this approach is usually idealistic and posits that social behavior is largely unconstrained by the realities of human nature or other externalities. That idea can be tested by studying experimental lifestyles and novel systems of social organization. In general, Sanderson shows ways to link macro and micro and proximate and ultimate processes. He opens the way for deploying data on species universals as well as individual and group differences.

There are also weaknesses in Darwinian conflict theory for present purposes, though these are not intrinsic to the theory. Sanderson's approach is yet to be applied systematically to relative class mobility. It lacks a specific theory or hypothesis of the phenomenon. On the methodological side the approach also overemphasizes archival sources and underemphasizes observation. However, sociology has a rich tradition of observational methods on which to draw, for example Erving Goffman's (1959) urban anthropology. The transdisciplinary ambitions of Darwinian conflict theory dictate inclusion of harder behavioral-ethnographic observation methods found in ethology and behavioral ecology (Cashdan 1993; Salter 1996), the genetic assay methods found in population studies, and the methods used in behavioral endocrinology and behavior genetics. There might be some logistical constraints on doing this—often multidisciplinary research groups will be needed and funding agencies made familiar with novel research designs—but there are no obstacles of principle. Sanderson's broad theoretical approach is compelling: He shows that sociological theory lacks a modern evolutionary dimension and thus is incomplete not only by omitting the ultimate level of explanation but by forgoing the heuristic potential of biology and Darwinian theory in particular.

ENVIRONMENTAL HYPOTHESES ON CLASS MOBILITY

Social competence undoubtedly increases status in all societies at all stages of evolutionary development, though different cultures and economies give rein to ability in different measure. Hunter-gatherer and other egalitarian societies are active levelers that redistribute wealth and limit political ambition. With the advent of agriculture, population and social complexity increased and stratification emerged. Competence remained one means to getting ahead, but in preindustrial societies *hereditary rank* conferred the largest social and economic opportunities. With economic privilege came ontogenetic advantages in nutrition, housing, and clothing.

With growing economic complexity *inherited wealth* became a separate means for privileging kin. In mercantile societies capital accumulation by families joined hereditary rank as a powerful cause of differential class opportunities. In addition to passing on resources, parents and grandparents could also boost their descendants' competitiveness by investing in their nutrition, health, and education. Before state-sponsored welfare and universal education, these investments could give children significant advantages in vigor, longevity, and skills. In addition these developmental advantages would have increased their general intelligence and hence competitiveness (e.g., Lynn 1990).

The privileges of aristocratic descent and wealth had secondary advantages of various *status markers*. In societies with an established upper-class rank, some class mobility can be gained by the appearance of nobility or wealth, including accent, bearing, manners, and surname. In ethnically stratified societies ethnicity can also provide a status boost. There are often economic and social benefits for individuals who pass as members of the dominant ethnic group in colonial, slave, and postslave societies (Roediger 1999). The effects of such markers have been in decline across Western societies for many decades as accreditation and professionalization have increased the role of merit and antidiscrimination sentiment and laws have stiffened.

Environmental hypotheses for class mobility in modern societies include various forms of privilege but also refer to greater competitiveness due to individual *performance*, though this superiority is held to be acquired, not genetically inherited. The environmental causes of enhanced performance include Protestant Christianity (Weber 1958), role models and mentors, family socialization into class-specific attitudes and culture, health and nutrition, and high-

quality education. The unifying environmentalist hypothesis is that socioeconomic status is the major determinant of social mobility (e.g., Schiff and Lewontin 1986).

There is much evidence consistent with environmental hypotheses in modern societies. In the United States, 40-60 percent of income differences persist
between generations (Mazumder 2002). A main cause is posited to be poor
credit-worthiness leading to poor education. Analysis of *Forbes* lists shows that
great wealth is concentrated in families—descendants of recent or distant for-
tune-makers (Hacker 1997, 94). Another study found that British "service" class
children tend to retain their class status because their parents impart less "cultural capital" and material resources (Savage and Egerton 1997). These data
confirm the conventional social science opinion that class mobility and inertia
are driven by class itself, embodied in material and cultural privilege: Class re-
produces itself.

The most sophisticated environmentalist hypothesis for class mobility
comes from Gary Becker in his book *A Treatise on the Family* (1981). In places
Becker discusses the conditions that produce superior children, meaning those
who as adults enjoy high earnings. He argues that the quantity and quality of
children are inversely related. The core idea is that bearing few children and
investing more in each on education and health might improve their likelihood
of surviving and reproducing (1981, 137). This model of competition in subsistence conditions is then applied to modern societies.

Throughout his analysis, Becker emphasizes acquired characteristics. For
example, he discusses the relationship between fertility and parental investment
among Jews and blacks. He notes an inverse relationship between income and
fertility and suggests that this is caused by Jews investing more in each child to
achieve higher future earnings, whereas blacks have many more children and
invest less in each because of the low wage outcome to be expected. "Blacks
have invested less in training because rates of return on investments in education, health, and other training have been lower for blacks than for whites"
(1981, 152). Here Becker no longer relies on survivability as the payoff, but on
wages or social status.

Another section of Becker's book dealing with social mobility is Chapter 6,
"Family Background and the Opportunities of Children." Here Becker seems to
be embracing biological and sociological interactionism: "The well-being of
children is determined by these expenditures, the reputation and contacts of the
family, their genetic inheritance, and the values and skills absorbed through
membership in a particular family culture. Children from successful families are
more likely to be successful themselves by virtue of the additional time spent on
them and also their superior endowments of culture and genes" (1981, 179).
This chapter discusses the "inheritability" of parents' social standing (class), but
at this point the discussion neglects genetic factors: "Inheritability can be increased by supervising the upbringing, training, and occupational, marital, and
other choices of children to ensure that their behavior is suited to the social

standing of their parents, grandparents, uncles, aunts, and other relatives" (Becker 1981, 184).

Becker models intergenerational social mobility under various conditions. He takes the family to be a long-lived multigenerational lineage. His model is based on an ideal family that maximizes a utility function spanning two generations. He assumes that the inheritability of parental characteristics is largely due to parental investment, such as education and enculturation. Endowments are not passed on genetically but by parental investment. In traditional societies families can keep up their reputation by indoctrinating children to emulate their parents. But in open societies such as the United States, children are less like parents because they are not trained to be so.

Becker does not consider the effect of such acquired qualities on the individual's attractiveness in the marriage market, and thus on the genetic quality of mates chosen and the genetic quality of offspring. Neither does he consider the increase in efficiency of parental investment produced by higher quality offspring. In discussing the rate of return from investing in human capital in the form of children, Becker assumes that the return on investment (children's future income due to being fed, clothed, housed, and educated) will decline on further investment once the basics of human capital are secured. However in the econometric spirit it is not difficult to surmise that return on investment in children of higher ability will decline more slowly than in normal children.

Finally, Becker reviews the data on social mobility in relation to parental investment. Longitudinal data gathered up to the late 1970s across several Western societies found that a 10 percent increase in father's income resulted in a 2 percent increase in sons' earnings (1981, 263). Standardization of the data raises that estimate to perhaps 4 percent, still a substantial regression to the mean and a blow to the hypothesis that parental investment is the main cause of children's future earnings. In the United States, "Almost all earnings advantages and disadvantages of ancestors are wiped out in three generations" (1981, 272). Becker concludes that this shows that inheritability of endowments and capital is not large.

Despite some evidence (and elegant equations) consistent with environmentalist theories, the contradictory evidence is so strong that it disqualifies those theories as complete explanations of social mobility. Analysis of the same *Forbes* lists of wealthy individuals discussed earlier shows that only 3 of the wealthiest 30 Americans in 1918 had descendants among the wealthiest 400 in 1996 (Hacker 1997, 94). Social mobility in industrial states is in the range of 30 to 40 percent per annum (Erikson and Goldthorpe 1993, Tables 6.3, 9.4, and 10.5). Longitudinal studies of mobility show that class differences are much less self-perpetuating in modern market economies than proposed by simple environmental theory. While family background has an effect, the income earned by British and U.S. siblings from the same families is largely dependent on ability, especially work attitudes and intelligence as measured by IQ tests (Bond and Saunders 1999; Jencks 1972; Murray 1997; Saunders 1997; 2002). In Britain lower-class children reach the same level as middle-class children of the same

IQ (Nettle 2003). IQ scores are the single most powerful predictor of class mobility in industrial societies, and they are only slightly influenced by class. Measures of environmental factors on IQ in modern societies show that between-family differences in environment account for as much as 35 percent of the variance in status in early childhood. However, by late adolescence the environmental impact drops to nearly zero. Large-scale studies of the effects of compensatory education also show diminishing returns, with only slight improvements in IQ remaining by the teenage years. Concluding one such study, Wolfe (1982, 213) states that "childhood cognitive development plays a minor role in the intergenerational transmission of wealth, and . . . programs to supplement family incomes would not have much effect on children's IQ scores." The genetic contribution to social mobility is indicated by the study of cross-class adoptions. When children born to lower-class parents are adopted into middle-class families, their average IQ scores rise but by the teenage years resemble those of their biological parents more than those of their adoptive parents (Lynn 1994; Waldman, Weinberg, and Scarr 1994). These results undermine the hypothesis that class differences are the only or even the main effect on ability and class mobility (Jensen 1998, Chapter 9). Genetic variation cannot be ignored, though as we shall see, the hereditarian hypothesis might also be incomplete.

BIOLOGICAL HYPOTHESES CONCERNING CLASS MOBILITY

Biological hypotheses have mainly dealt with differences in intelligence. I shall begin with Cyril Burt's (1961) classic analysis of IQ and class. Burt was a psychologist yet his analysis dealt with genetics. It is therefore instructive to summarize his argument from the perspective of two leading geneticists, Luigi Cavalli-Sforza and Walter Bodmer (1971, 795-96). The study was based on London school children and their parents. It found a high correlation between class and IQ. The range of differences – the IQ difference between the highest and lowest classes – was 55, or almost four standard deviations. Regression to the mean was marked. Children's IQ fell between that of the biological parents and population means, consistent with genetic causation. The most straightforward explanation is that IQ differences are largely genetic in origin, and IQ differences are a major determinant of class differences.

Cavalli-Sforza and Bodmer continue summarizing Burt to the effect that, due to regression to the mean, maintaining the interclass IQ distribution shown in Table 1 requires at least 22 percent class mobility in each generation. Observed UK intergenerational mobility in the 1960s was about 30 percent, broadly confirming this expectation. Burt's model of social mobility based on his hereditarian hypothesis is:

$S = 0.35I + 0.27M + 0.16H + 0.15E$, where
S = social mobility
I = intelligence
M = motivation
H = home background
E = educational achievement

Burt's analysis has been confirmed by subsequent research. For example, Gottfredson (1997, 80) concludes that "IQ is probably more strongly related to key educational, occupational, economic, and social outcomes in a person's life than is any other single, measurable trait." The heritability of IQ – the fraction of differences due to genetic differences – has been measured by many independent tests in Western societies. In children the heritability is 0.4-0.5, in adolescents 0.6-0.7, and in mature adults it approaches 0.8 (Jensen 1998, 181). Thus environmental effects are strongest in children.

Further research confirming Burt's thesis was conducted in Britain in the 1990s. Bond and Saunders (1999) used data from the National Child Development Study, which allowed them to track 4,298 British males from childhood to age 33. IQ and motivation were three times more influential than class background (including parental support) in predicting adult earnings. This is consistent with the analysis conducted by Herrnstein and Murray (1994), who found that IQ correlates with class. Herrnstein and Murray also noted that marriage partners assort by class, and thus by IQ, though the causes of this assortment are not made clear.

Nielsen (2006) tested a sample of U.S. adolescents' verbal IQs, grade point averages, and college plans for genetic and environmental influences. The study used a behavioral genetic design, collecting data on six types of sibling pairs:

Table 14.1 Intelligence by Occupational Class (based on Burt 1961)

Occupational Class	Percent of Population	IQ (means and sd's) of Parents	IQ (means and sd's) of Offspring
I. Higher Professional	0.3	139.7, ±4.7	120.8, ±12.5
II. Lower Professional	3.1	130.6, ±6.7	114.7, ±11.2
III. Clerical	12.2	115.9, ±9.3	107.8, ±13.6
IV. Skilled Manual	25.8	108.2, ±9.9	104.6, ±14.3
V. Semiskilled Manual	32.5	97.8, ±9.9	98.9, ±13.8
VI. Unskilled Manual	26.1	84.9, ±10.9	92.6, ±13.8

identical and nonidentical twins, full siblings, half siblings, cousins, and biologically unrelated (i.e., foster or step) siblings. Results showed a large genetic effect that explained 74 percent of the variance in verbal IQ, 66 percent of grade point average, and 80 percent of planned college degrees. Shared environment had a small effect, and unshared environment a substantial effect, though necessarily considerably smaller than the genetic effect.

Kanazawa and Kovar (2004) went beyond IQ in the biology of class, though speculatively. They argued that any heritable trait that helps men attain higher status (e.g., intelligence, aggression, social skills) will tend to covary with female traits valued by males in choosing mates (e.g., beauty, social skills, intelligence).

There are weaknesses in the hereditarian hypothesis for class mobility. Much of this research emphasizes just one variable, IQ. Some personality characteristics are also likely to be important, such as conscientiousness. This and other personality traits have heritabilities in the range of 0.4 to 0.5 (Bouchard 1997). Another weakness of the theory is that it does not attempt to identify local peculiarities of social mobility or the idiosyncratic strategies that might explain them. This is surprising because general intelligence should increase the ability to plan and execute solutions to the novel adaptive problems presented by modern societies, such as regression to the mean. Yet in general, hereditarian-minded theorists pass over cultural agency and human problem solving. For example, no role is posited for accumulated tradition. A reason for this might be that most of this work has been done by psychologists and microeconomists. With exceptions, anthropology, sociology, behavioral ecology, and ethology are poorly represented among scientists who accept that class-raising competencies have robust heritabilities. This disciplinary alignment seems arbitrary.

Comparing environmental and hereditarian approaches, the former are often naïve about innate differences and often reject them with an ideological fervor. Biological approaches are interactionist, incorporate some environmental factors, and are more successful at explaining macropatterns of social mobility. However, they are themselves naïve about sociological variables.

STRATEGIES FOR CLIMBING THE CLASS STRUCTURE AND STAYING THERE

Is there anything individuals can do to increase their children's and grandchildren's social mobility? An answer might be revealed by reverse-engineered (hypothetical) families whose members were of high average ability and that managed to stave off regression of those abilities to the population mean. The first step would be to discover what distinguishes such families.

Such lineages would not be explicable by the heritability theory reviewed above because their ability would regress slowly to the mean. They would also defeat simple environmentalist theory, because privilege and resources have limited effect on high-heritability traits. Their behavior would probably have cultural as well as biological causes bound up in a tradition that shapes mate choice.

Evolutionary ideas about class might provide some guidance. Van den Berghe (1979) has argued that marriage and reproduction are governed by human nature and culturally derived rules. The demographic transition was due to parents increasing their investment in fewer children as a strategy to increase offspring competitiveness and thus individual fitness. Low (2000, 2002) observes that this strategy has reduced fitness compared to lower-class strategies of more children and less per capita investment in them. These theories introduce the concept of strategizing but do not develop it.

The idea of conscious strategizing is better developed in the work of Boyd and Richerson (1985) and MacDonald (1983, 1995). The notion of "cultural group strategies" is a version of gene-culture coevolution that recognizes the agency of conscious human strategizing. The theory has so far been applied at the level of local populations such as tribes and medieval European societies. The core idea is that a tribe inherits or invents culturally transmitted rules that shape behavior. Free-riding is controlled through monitoring and punishment. The resulting rule-governed behavior increases the competitiveness of the group.

Another culture-based evolutionary theory is social technology theory (STT), developed since the late nineteenth century by scholars such as E. A. Ross (1896: "social control"), Eibl-Eibesfeldt (1970, 1982), Reynolds (1973), Tiger and Fox (1971), Caton (1983), and Salter (1995). The idea is that human behavior, both innate and acquired, can be manipulated using techniques that are invented using general intelligence. These "social technologies" can be learned and thus culturally transmitted. STT allows for transformative social change via social construction without changing human nature, though the latter does limit what can be constructed. Human universals constrain social technologies in ways general to the species.

Cultural group strategy theory and social technology theory both incorporate environment and biology, including culture and strategic abilities. Both theories point to the ability of humans to invent, adopt, and pass on strategies in the form of traditions that shape behavior of various kinds, including mate choice. Their evolutionary and competitive elements qualify them as Darwinian conflict theories. These theories are also promising guides for researching family strategies.

Preliminary observations of behavior associated with social mobility are consistent with cultural evolutionary theory. Middle-class families begin childbearing later than working-class families and have fewer extramarital births. Middle-class parents make greater efforts to guide their children's behavior, especially in the areas of educational achievement and work performance, but also with respect to choice of friends and mates, choice of cultural experiences, and use of alcohol and other drugs. Some elements of middle-class behavior can be characterized as "snobbishness" or exclusiveness.

The data do not exist with which to determine whether these middle-class behaviors succeed in steering children toward mates with competitive characteristics. It is possible that there is some effect but that this is hidden in the society-wide data. Producing such data will require research focused on this specific issue.

Identification of class-specific mate-choice criteria must begin with the description of species-typical criteria. The neo-Darwinian analysis of mate choice posits a "gene shopping" function in which individuals are attracted to potential mates on the basis of phenotypic characteristics that correlate with genetic quality. Other criteria relate to fecundity and nurturing potential. Criteria include beauty (an honest signal of health and "good genes" for immunity to parasites), average traits (evidence of broad adaptiveness), youth (an honest signal of fecundity), male status/wealth (an honest signal of resources and/or resource holding potential), and social skills (evidence of networking ability and child care potential). Prior to modernization marriages were arranged by parents in most societies. Parental choice of children's mates is typically based on a broader set of criteria, including resources, the social standing of the mate's family, and the two families' compatibility. It would seem that greater scope for deliberate choice of mates exists within the tradition of arranged marriages than within modern Western societies that emphasize individual choice. A partial substitute for parental choice in modern societies would be any tradition that increased parental influence on the choice of mates, whether through advice or indoctrination during upbringing.

I want to end with some hypotheses of mate-choice criteria and family culture that could increase the competitiveness of offspring, based on the foregoing discussion. These are intended to guide field research of socially mobile behavior.

Competence. I have already noted assortative mating by educational attainment, which will have some effect of slowing regression to the mean. A socially mobile lineage might go further by encouraging children to choose spouses with genealogical evidence of distinction in activities related to resource acquisition. Typical mate-choice behavior can constrain choices that would boost children's social mobility. Although there is assortative mating for educational attainment, males and females appear to favor pairings in which the male is better qualified (and older and taller). This conforms to mobility maximization by females but not males. Families that prepared their sons for marriages with highly competent women would improve their class prospects (but only if the result was not nil family size).

Trivers-Willard effect. According to this hypothesis, the sex ratio of high-status families is relatively high because sons have higher status, thus a better chance of reproducing than sons of low-status families (Trivers and Willard 1973). Joined to the fact that males have higher potential individual fitness than females, this would be a strategy for elevating inclusive fitness. But would it improve class mobility? At first sight this should only be true if males are more mobile than females, a premise that is untested. However, favoring the production of sons or daughters would increase mobility if it increased their attractiveness for high-ability mates. How that might operate is an open question. The answer will need to account for the widely observed trend of hypergyny, in which higher-status males marry lower-status females.

Family size. In modern societies family size and class are inversely related (Vining 1986). (However see Hopcroft 2006a for contrary data. The same data indicate that intelligence is inversely related to fertility.) Low fertility allows parents to invest more in children, not only materially but in time spent in close contact, with payoffs due to closer attachments ("family warmth" below). If these were the only factors to consider, social mobility of offspring would be increased by choosing spouses likely to seek low fertility. However, below-replacement fertility of the bearers of a strategy will render the strategy evolutionarily unsustainable.

Evolutionary stability and fertility. If a lineage's high status is to be sustained down the generations it must reproduce itself. Reproduction below the replacement rate of 2.1 children, maintained for several generations, dramatically reduces the fitness of the lineage relative to the population. Delayed reproduction has the same effect (Low, Simon, and Anderson 2002). If such a pattern were adopted by most families of high social mobility, then over time there would be a decline in the frequency of genes for high economic ability in the overall population (Lynn 1996). One effect would be to reduce mate choice options. Another would be to weed out socially mobile lineages. A long-term strategy must necessarily achieve replacement fertility.

Monogamy. Intact families generally are wealthier than those with one parent. Investment in children and familial warmth will be maximized in monogamous marriages with high confidence of paternity. Paternal and paternal-grandparental investment are increased by paternity confidence, whether consciously via the reputation of the mother or subconsciously via similarity between father and offspring (Burch and Gallup 2000; Euler and Wietzel 1996). It follows that investing in stable marriages will increase social mobility. This would be partly achieved by selecting spouses who come from stable families, since the tendency to marry appears to be partly genetic in origin (66 percent in men, 72 percent in women—Johnson, McGue, Krueger, and Bouchard 2004, 290).

Endogamy-exogamy. Endogamy would be a strategy for slowing the regression to the mean of valued abilities when the actor's ethnic group shows high average economic performance. Exogamy is indicated in cases where it would result in regression to a higher mean. However, exogamy would be counterindicated if it reduced marital stability and significantly reduced parents' genetic similarity (kinship coefficient) with offspring. The parent-child genetic kinship coefficient is reduced in matings between populations (Hamilton 1975, 144). Harpending (2002) argues that parental kinship in endogamous matings is F_{ST} greater than for exogamous pairs, where F_{ST} is the genetic variation between the populations involved. Intermarriage among related ethnic groups only slightly lowers parental kinship, but on a global basis parental kinship in endogamous families typically will be 25 to 50 percent higher than that in exogamous families (Salter 2002, 137-38n4).

Family warmth. A family tradition cannot get started if children do not take up their parents' values. Even a tradition of rebelliousness requires that that characteristic be passed on with fidelity, genetically or culturally. The building of parental bonds through close positive contacts and solicitation can be expected to intensify children's identification with the parents and pride in the family, its accomplishments, and its traditions. Warm parental relationships increase children's desire to please the parents and thus "allows children to take advantage of adults' greater experience and cognitive competence" (MacDonald 1992, 767). There would appear to be some room for environmental boosting of children's perception of warmth despite some twin study data indicating a significant genetic contribution to a child's perception of parental support (over 40 percent; Hur and Bouchard 1995). This genetic contribution indicates that class mobility would be raised by individuals choosing mates who perceive their parents to have provided support. This could be one way to increase parental influence on mate choice without instituting a formal practice such as parental mate choice.

Nepotism. Investment in offspring and other kin increases family warmth and is a precondition for the training needed to transmit traditions within a family. Social mobility will be improved by adopting family routines that help bond members, for example eating meals together and sharing positive experiences. Evidence that such strategies could have some effect is that about 20 percent of the variance in prosocial behaviors is explained by within-family environment. However, the same studies indicate that genetic differences contribute between 40 and 50 percent of the variance in altruism, empathy, and nurturance (Rushton 2004), again pointing to mate choice as an important influence on offspring's social mobility. Notice that these mechanisms are linked. Parental investment is affected by fertility, and indoctrination of parental values in children is affected by family warmth. Transmission of genetic and cultural traits is affected by genetic similarity, which in turn is affected by degree of endogamy. This increases the importance of each factor, though none has such a high impact that it is indispensable.

Choosing a constellation of tactics and fitting them into an overall strategy would be performed by domain-general intelligence. A scientifically informed strategy could be guided by biosocial science and particular theories such as the new "life history" theory that integrates genetic and environmental influences on the organism's adaptiveness from conception to death (e.g., Figueredo, Vasquez, Brumbach, Schneider, Sefcek, Tal, Hill, Wenner, and Jacobs 2006). Those tactics include "gene shopping" by selecting capable mates with other desired phenotypes and shaping children's personalities and beliefs through environmental means. Transmitting that strategy to the next generation would be accomplished through cultural as well as genetic reproduction, thus blending environmentalist and hereditarian approaches.

CONCLUSION

This paper examined environmentalist and hereditarian theories of social mobility and found that neither fully explains the available evidence. Environmentalist theories fail to explain the overall pattern of regression to the mean, while hereditarian theories fail to explain some local peculiarities and the cultural strategies behind them. A complete theory is not proposed here, but it is argued that such a theory will be a type of Darwinian conflict theory. A Darwinian conflict sociological account of the mate choice strategies imbedded in family traditions should conceptualize families as lineages that produce individuals who enter the wider society where they compete with other individuals for resources. Individual qualities are a major factor determining the outcome of this competition, and families largely produce these qualities. The theory should explain society-wide trends in social mobility but also account for possible exceptions. Of special interest is the hypothetical family lineage that manages to maintain an elevated level of competence and thus wealth down several generations, resisting full regression to the mean. If these lineages are found, a good theory should explain their behavior. In the hypothesis offered here, such families would resist regression of gene-based competencies due to culturally based (learned) strategies embedded in traditions whose main effect is to steer mate choice.

15

THE TWO TRANSITIONS IN THE EVOLUTION OF HUMAN SOCIALITY

W. G. Runciman

I

As is well known, the origin of human sociality lies far in the past which we share with other primate species. Nonrandom interaction based on individual knowledge – as opposed, that is, to mere gregariousness – has been part of our biological inheritance for many millions of years. But after the evolution among the great apes of patrilocal kin-bonding and the divergence of humans and chimpanzees from their last common ancestor, our postarboreal, bipedal, savanna-roaming ancestors began to form stronger social attachments within smaller units in what can begin to be called family structures. It appears to be agreed among palaeoanthropologists that about 2 million years ago encephalization and group size started to accelerate together, and a significant enhancement of stone technology then becomes discernible in the archaeological record. By about 300,000 years ago it is plausible to suppose that the energetic costs of our ancestors' larger brains were not only changing their life histories but making possible, coupled with anatomical changes which included the shape of the thorax and the vertebral canal, the beginnings of language. It is still a matter of debate when "fully modern behavior" first appears in the archaeological record (Klein 2000, 17). But there is no disagreement about the importance for the evolution of human sociality of the dispersal of modern humans out of Africa. Whenever exactly it began, it both required and reinforced a capacity to hold together groups whose members could communicate effectively with one another to the point of the progressive evolution of distinctive cultures on a scale unmatched by any other of the now extinct hominid species. By the time of the well-attested cultural efflorescence of the Upper Paleolithic in Europe, cumulative cultural evolution had been going on for several tens of thousands of years.

It is not that cultural evolution is unique to humans. The capacity for transmission of information affecting phenotype by imitation and learning is present not only in our closest genetic relatives, the chimpanzees, but in other species as well (Avital and Jablonka 2000), and the culture of the Neanderthals, who shared parts of Europe with our ancestors until some 30,000 years ago, is a topic of lively archaeological and palaeoanthropological discussion. But long before the appearance of agriculture, human beings were living in social groups whose members were as familiar as ourselves with art, ritual, gossip, and conventions in Hume's sense of that last term – that is, informal but explicit agreements governing certain mutually acknowledged aspects of reciprocal conduct. The distinctive human capacity for rapid as well as cumulative cultural evolution (Boyd and Richerson 1996) and the concomitant evolution of the capacity for language generated an increasing diversity of lifestyles. In-group cooperation sustained by "altruistic" punishment (Boyd, Gintis, Bowles, and Richerson 2003) went hand-in-hand with self-conscious differentiation from out-groups with their own taboos, totems, dialects (Nettle and Dunbar 1997), myths, techniques, celebrations, symbolic markers, and bodily decorations. Behavior patterns which were the phenotypic effects of information transmitted interpersonally from mind to mind came increasingly to modify and supplement evoked responses to environmental changes acting on innate dispositions and capacities inherited genetically by children from parents. Although the idea that culture evolves through a process of heritable variation and competitive selection of information analogous but not reducible to natural selection is still resisted by die-hard behavioral ecologists on the one side and die-hard cultural anthropologists on the other, the objections most commonly made consist of attributing to theorists of cultural evolution views which they do not in fact hold (Runciman 2005). The many obvious disanalogies between natural and cultural selection are not in dispute. But to deny that there is a process of heritable variation and competitive selection at work which is continuous with natural selection is by now not so much skeptical as perverse.

It is true that we do not know what the units of cultural transmission are in the way that we know what the units of genetic transmission are. For that reason, many sociologists (to say nothing of anthropologists and historians) are resistant to the use of the word "meme" to stand for the items or bundles of information affecting phenotype that are transmitted from mind to mind by imitation and learning. But it can be so used, whatever those items or bundles of information actually are, without any preemptive implication that the analogy between memes and genes is closer than it is. Part of the difficulty is that Richard Dawkins, when he coined the term, assumed that cultural inheritance must, like genetic inheritance, be a process of particulate and not blended reproduction. But memes do not have to be discrete particles, and they can be actively modified by the receiving mind both during and after the adolescence of their individual carriers. They are whatever complexes of information are constitutive of whatever beliefs, attitudes, representations, strategies, and norms do in fact affect phenotypic behavior. They are by definition adaptive to the extent that they have a higher probability of reproduction and diffusion than their competitors whether or not they are also adaptive at the biological level (Richerson and Boyd 2005, Chapter 5). If only as a matter of convenience, therefore, the word is worth incorporating into the standard terminology of comparative sociology in order not to have to choose between a cumbrous periphrasis and an imprecise preexisting usage when discussing a universal process of fundamental importance to the history of the human species.

Once our ancestors were past the transition from nature to culture, successive generations were born and brought up in a world now full of memes. The growing child in a hunting and foraging band acquired by imitation and learning a large store of information which modified what would otherwise have been behavior no different from that of the members of a chimpanzee troop dominated by an alpha male. Then as now, there continued to be constraints imposed on the possible range of cultural behavior patterns by the biological inheritance of the species. Nowhere in the archaeological, ethnographic, or historical record is there a culture in which Hamilton's Rule is stood on its head and a norm of unconditional altruism towards out-groups combined with a norm of consistent noncooperation with close genetic kin. The ethnocentrism inherited from our primate ancestors makes it difficult to disagree with E. O. Wilson (1978, 119) that our brains appear to be programmed to partition other people into friends and enemies in the same sort of way that birds are programmed to navigate by the polar constellations. But cultural selection facilitated cooperative relationships going beyond a small number of close genetic kin and short-term reciprocators. Once past performance could be recalled, coalitions formed between partners deliberately chosen, punishment for defection or fake signaling cheaply carried out through the medium of speech, and unreciprocated altruism rewarded by overtly accorded prestige, the monitoring of band members by one another could both sustain a norm of sharing which would-be free-riders would otherwise ignore and curb the ambitions of would-be alpha males.

Although the ethnographic evidence for the lifestyles of present-day hunters and foragers cannot be used to reconstruct directly those of our Paleolithic ancestors, a present-day anthropologist transported back into their world would have no difficulty in recognizing and interpreting forms of sociality of a similar kind. It can hardly be doubted that they talked about their relations to one another, to their physical environment, to the animals and birds that shared that environment with them, to their ancestors, and to the unseen agencies presumptively responsible for bringing themselves and their world into being. We can say with confidence that long before the Upper Paleolithic efflorescence in Europe, they had long-distance trading relationships in symbolically valued objects; division and specialization of labor; part-cooperative, part-antagonistic relations with other bands on which they drew for marriage partners; and organized communal activities involving members of wider groupings outside of their own immediate bands. If we suppose the hypothetical present-day anthropologist doing fieldwork among them to be accompanied by a present-day primatologist, the primatologist might be equally quick to point out the resemblances between their behavior and that of the chimpanzees in the rain forests – playing, fighting, manipulating, retaliating, grieving, befriending, and handing down culturally inherited behavior patterns to their offspring. But even a primatologist ready to go as far as, or further than, Darwin himself in attributing to other species psychological dispositions and capacities like our own would be bound to concede that the difference in forms of sociality was one not merely of degree but of kind.

II

Seen from today, however, and from a world familiar with governments, armies, bureaucracies, law-courts, markets, banks, businesses, churches, temples, and schools, it is obvious just how much was missing from the forms of sociality which characterized the groups in which our ancestors lived until some 10,000 to 12,000 years before the present. Theirs was a world wholly lacking institutional roles – roles, that is, not merely in a precultural sense (like attacker and defender), or a cultural sense (like mentor and disciple), but in the sense of positions in a multidimensional social space whose incumbents are required to act consistently and predictably in consequence of the rule-governed practices which define them. Person A now behaves towards Person B in a certain way not simply because of information which A has acquired by imitation or learning but because of information encoded in the practices which make A a landlord and B a tenant, or A a priest and B a parishioner, or A a general and B a soldier. The mere existence of rules which prescribe how the two of them are to relate to one another does not, of course, guarantee that they will do so. But once the practices which define the roles are underwritten by formal inducements and sanctions, the incumbents of those roles have no choice but to conform to them unless one party or the other opts out of the relationship altogether. They have to have acquired by imitation or learning the information which enables them to *be* a landlord and tenant, or priest and parishioner, or general and soldier. But unless their roles include, as it might be, membership of a legislative assembly at a time of constitutional choice, neither can rewrite the information encoded in the practices which make their institutional roles what they are.

The new and unprecedented forms of sociality which followed the transition from culture to society evolved thereafter through heritable variation and competitive selection in the same way as the forms of sociality which followed the transition from nature to culture. But practices are no more a special kind of meme than memes are a special kind of gene. Where mutations of memes are generated through reinterpretation within the individual receiver's mind, mutations of practices require renegotiation between the incumbents of complementary roles. Selective pressure comes to bear not only on the extended phenotypic effects of the attitudes and beliefs which we bring to the performance of our institutional roles but on the extended phenotypic effects of the differences in economic, ideological, and institutional power which attach to them. Furthermore, the phenomenon of social mobility now arrives on the sociological agenda for the first time. Not only can we occupy and perform more than one role at a time in the society of which we are members, but we can move out of one role into another to which there may attach significantly more or less economic, ideological, or political power. Coevolving memes and practices now reciprocally influence each other's probability of reproduction and diffusion relative to that of their competitors. The memes in our heads cannot directly modify the practices defining our own and other people's roles. But they can modify the acceptability to us of the modes of production, persuasion, and coercion constituted by the totality of roles of the society to which we belong and thereby, under some conditions, diminish or even destroy the adaptiveness of the practices defining them.

This second transition in the evolution of human sociality is of such obvious importance that it might have been expected to have received more direct and detailed attention in the sociological literature than it has. There are, I suggest, four reasons why it has not.

The first is terminological. As pointed out by Brown (1991, 40), anthropologists have long been prone both to contrast "cultural" and "social" jointly with "biological" and to treat "*a* culture" and "*a* society" as synonymous. But in addition, sociologists and other behavioral scientists regularly use the term *sociocultural* with its inbuilt implication that cultural and social evolution are inseparable. Even the psychologist Donald T. Campbell, who was one of the first to appreciate the implications of natural selection being only one among other special cases of a more general evolutionary theory, consistently did so in his writings (Campbell 1965, 1975).

Second, the historical evidence for the transition from culture to society is, in default of literary or epigraphic material, entirely archaeological, and the inferences about forms of sociality which can be drawn by archaeologists are notoriously problematic. All roles presuppose a vernacular terminology in which they are designated. The evolution of distinctive modes of production, persuasion, and coercion requires there to be words by which the relations between their constitutive roles can be specified: A and B cannot act toward each other as landlord and tenant, priest and parishioner, or general and soldier unless they can talk to each other in a way which makes it clear that they are doing so as such. In the ethnographic record, there are many vernacular terms applied to recognized leaders which merely denote possession of a set of personal attributes (courage, generosity, oratorical skill, knowledge of ancestral traditions or craft techniques, etc.) which influence the behavior of others toward those who possess them without any inducements or sanctions attaching to the position whereby someone else without the same personal attributes could succeed to it in accordance with a formal procedure. But among the Cree of Northern Quebec, for example, the *uuchimaau* is the head of an extended kinship group who controls a hunting ground and the animals on it and will be replaced if he fails to manage the resources for which he is formally responsible (Scott 1991). The difficulty which archaeologists face is that where they find the remains of a house which is substantially larger than those surrounding it, or a circle of storage pits, or what might have been a military fortification or palisade, or a grave in which an unusual number of valuable objects have been buried with the corpse, or a precisely delineated open space, or the ground plan of what might have been a palace or a temple or a granary, how are they to tell whether these are extended phenotypic effects of culturally or of socially selected information? In due course, the inference to institutionalized forms of sociality becomes unmistakable. But the process of transition has by then to be taken as given.

Third, the transition from culture to society is cross-cut by others with which archaeologists and anthropologists are preoccupied for good reasons of their own. Monumental nondomestic architecture, urbanization, domestication of plants and animals, irrigation, literacy, large-scale trading networks, and the preservation and storage of surplus foodstuffs all mark significant turning points in human evolution, but the forms of sociality associated with them vary widely from case to case. Sedentism and the spatial aggregation of year-round habitations can take place without the concomitant emergence of institutional roles. In a group of adjacent houses of the kind conventionally denoted a "hamlet," some households may accumulate substantially more material objects than others and pass them on to a subsequent generation without thereby constituting an economic class; some household heads may enjoy higher esteem and preferential access to mates without thereby constituting a status elite; and some coalitions of household heads may dominate their neighbors by the exercise or threat of force without thereby constituting a permanent political faction, let alone a government. On the other hand, inequalities in material resources can lead to debtor-creditor relationships and the institutionalization of economic exploitation; inequalities in prestige can lead to the institutionalization of a hierarchy of ranks and hereditary status differentiation; and inequalities in coercive capacity can lead to master-slave relationships and the institutionalization of hereditary deprivation of freedom. Once under way, social, like cultural, evolution can be rapid as well as cumulative. But each case then follows a unique path-dependent sequence of its own.

Fourth, there is a longstanding tendency in the ethnographic and archaeological literature to see early forms of social organization as stages along a continuum from bands to tribes to chiefdoms to states. Linear models of evolution are now rightly out of favor. But there is still a temptation to treat as paradigmatic cases societies in which economic, ideological, and political power come to be concentrated in a topmost "chiefly" role (Earle 1991). Admittedly, this is what often happens. But institutional roles can also come into being because of a perceived requirement to control would-be self-aggrandizers in an environment where common-pool resources need to be shared, or to arrive at consensual decisions on behalf of the community in the face of external threat. Furthermore, explicit provisions may be put in place to prevent the incumbents from occupying their roles for too long or designating arbitrarily chosen successors. Monitors of hunting or fishing grounds can be appointed to serve in rotation, new war-leaders can be elected at the conclusion of their predecessors' campaigns, and holders of ritual offices can be chosen by divination or lot. Roles like these can be occupied by separate incumbents whose power is not only limited in extent but explicitly restricted to separate dimensions of rank. They do not have to be stepping-stones along the path to social stratification and monopoly of dominant positions by self-perpetuating elites. But the line between culture and society has been crossed, all the same.

As in cultural evolution, the origin of an innovation which turns out to have far-reaching effects in social evolution does not by itself account for its adaptiveness, even if, in a phrase of Herbert A. Simon's (1990, 2), it contains "large components of conscious invention." The adaptiveness of mutant practices, as of mutant memes, depends on the selective pressure brought to bear by the environment on their phenotypic effects, not on the plans and purposes of their inventors. Somebody, in the course of the transition from culture to society, must have been the first person to hire the labor of others in return for a wage and thus become the first capitalist employer, just as in the course of the transition from nature to culture somebody must have been the first person to claim to be able to foretell the future by interpreting other people's dreams. But no one such episode guarantees that oneiromancy will reach fixation in the culture, or wage labor in the society, where the episode took place. In the many different parts of the world where transitions from culture to society have taken place independently of each other, there may have been many earlier occasions when the institutionalization of economic, ideological, or political roles appeared to be under way only for the practices defining them to fail to be reproduced. On the other hand, there are environmental conditions in which selective pressure is bound to favor the evolution of institutional roles, of which the most obvious is the concentration of a growing population within a bounded residential space. Preinstitutional forms of sociality adequate to hold together a hunting and foraging band cannot preserve a system of overlapping relationships among thousands of individuals who have direct contact with, and knowledge of the behavior of perhaps a hundred or at most two hundred of the others. To supplement relations of interpersonal influence with relations of institutional power does not of itself ensure the ongoing stability of the modes of production, persuasion, and coercion which evolve in consequence: The archaeological record includes much evidence of organizational collapse of the kind clearly discernible among, for example, the short-lived chiefdoms of prehistoric southeastern North America (Bogucki 1999, 317-20). But they could not exist at all without accepted practices defining recognized institutional roles.

III

A well-studied example from which these themes can be clearly illustrated is the evolution of the *polis* in Archaic Greece. Although it involved a reinstitutionalization of social roles following the collapse of the forms of sociality centered on the Mycenaean palaces rather than a first-time transition from culture to society, it has the advantage that there is both literary and epigraphic evidence for the vernacular terms which designate the roles constitutive of the modes of production, persuasion, and coercion of the hundreds of different *poleis* which emerged alongside the best-known (Athens, Sparta, and Corinth). The "World of Odysseus" (Finley 1956) may or may not reflect the culture and society of Greece as it actually was at any specific period. But Homer's vocabulary captures the nature of the transition from relations of interpersonal influence to relations of institutional power in a way that cannot be done where the evidence is restricted to material remains. The *Odyssey* contains a substantial number of words which, even if their meaning cannot be as precisely inferred as participant observation would make possible, unmistakably depict forms of sociality which are incipiently but not fully institutionalized in the economic, ideological, and political dimensions of social space alike.

Production and consumption were centered on households (*oikoi*) of which the larger and wealthier were headed by "best men" (*aristoi*). But it would be misleading to call them an "aristocracy." Sons inherited from fathers, but they had to maintain their position by their proven ability to win booty, to support and reward their retainers (*therapontes*), and to exchange high-value prestige-goods with "guest-friends" (*xenoi*) like themselves. There was division and specialization of labor, but the work was performed either by servants of the household (*drēstēres*), including captive men and women performing domestic talks (*dmōes*), or by craftsmen (*dēmioergoi*), including bards and minstrels, who might move from one *oikos* to another of their own volition. There were prestations, but no taxes; barter, but no markets; beggars, but no paupers; hirelings (*thetes*), but no gang-slaves. The *aristoi* might acknowledge one of themselves as *basileus* (not, in this context, to be translated as "king"), but they did not hold their land from him or owe him dues or services except by personal obligation.

Similarly, there are no institutional roles to which there attaches formal control of the means of persuasion. Relations with gods, and sacrifices to them, are conducted by household heads on behalf of their families and followers, not chiefs or high priests ideologically empowered by the community as such. There are burial sites at which heroes are venerated, but no temples, no monastic foundations, and no professional prophets or seers whose reputation rests on public position as opposed to individual performance. Although genealogies are taken seriously, and there is one explicit reference in the *Odyssey* to "good blood" (IV.611), there is no hierarchy of noble roles into which sons automatically enter on their fathers' deaths. Elders may be venerated for their wisdom, but a wise man (*istōr*) is a private individual, not a member of an age-set with institutional power over the young. The poor may be stigmatized for their poverty, but they are not a caste. On the contrary, they may, like Eumaeus the swineherd, be of good birth but reduced to their present condition through capture or kidnap. There is no discrimination on the grounds of either nationality or race.

Lethal violence, both external and internal, is endemic. But there are no armies: Soldiers are the followers of leaders to whom they are attached by kinship or personal loyalty (*philia*, not always best translated as "friendship"). Decisions which may involve life or death are taken following discussion in a meeting convened for the purpose, but those attending have no formal power to impose a decision. There is no mode of coercion in which deviants are apprehended by police and tried in law-courts. The taking of vengeance is culturally prescribed in the name of personal and family honor, but there is no tariff of blood-guilt. There are ties of mutual obligation between *aristoi* living in different places, but no formal alliances.

How and why economic, ideological, and political institutions evolved in Greece out of the post-Mycenaean "Dark Ages" has been a matter of scholarly debate ever since the opening chapter of Thucydides, whose emphasis on synoecism, defense against marauders, and the capacity to generate an economic surplus (*periousia chrēmatōn*) remains as pertinent as ever. But whatever the relative importance of these and of ecology, demography, trade, arable farming, metallurgy, temple-building, infantry tactics, citizen assemblies, law-making, and chattel slavery, what is striking in the present context is both the extent and the speed of variation once social selection was under way. Institutional roles proliferated throughout the whole of Greece, and the practices defining them generated differences which extended all the way from Sparta, with its joint hereditary kings, its ephors, its subjugated Helots, its property-owning women, its full-time warriors with their military barracks and messes, its secret police, and its disenfranchisement of "tremblers" (*tresantes*) to Athens with its council and popular assembly, its public officials, its autonomous smallholders and artisans, its elected generals, its magistrates chosen by lot, its taxation by liturgy, its housebound women, its wage-earning naval oarsmen, its slave-worked silver mines, and its advocates and jurymen in the law-courts – to say nothing of societies classified as *ethn* rather than *poleis*, like Thessaly with its cavalry, its elected monarchs (*tagoi*), its federal tetrarchs, and its subordinate cultivators (*penestai*). There are councillors (*prytaneis*), generals (*polemarchoi, stratēgoi*), and magistrates (*archontes, cosmoi*), and the word *dēmos*, which in Homer stands simply for the general body of the people, now stands for an assembly of enfranchised adult males with formal political power. Just how the modes of production, persuasion, and coercion of the societies of what we now call "Classical" Greece should be categorized is a question which does not need to be addressed here. What is indisputable is that the transition to fully institutionalized forms of sociality is by then complete and the vernacular terminology clearly reflects it. In a world of practices as well as memes, people behave toward one another as they do because of what, institutionally speaking, they are, not only because of the personal attributes they possess.

From then on, accordingly, coevolution of memes and practices through heritable variation and competitive selection supplemented coevolution of memes and genes. As elsewhere before and since, whenever the transition has happened, the interaction between the two can work in either direction: Mutations and combinations of the memes making up dominant beliefs and attitudes can either enhance or diminish the adaptiveness of the practices coevolving with them, just as mutations and combinations of the practices making up dominant economic, ideological, and political roles can either enhance or diminish the adaptiveness of those memes. That, you could say, is the stuff of which human history is made. But in the case of Greece, meme-practice coevolution took a course which, in hindsight, is both ironic and paradoxical. In certain of the societies of the Greek-speaking world, the new institutional environment favored the cultural selection of memes which have been passed down successive generations in still recognizable forms until the present day. But the practices which made that institutional environment what it was turned out to be an evolutionary dead-end. As I have argued elsewhere (Runciman 1990), the *polis* had little chance of long-term survival for reasons inherent in the combination of practices which had, for a time, been locally adaptive. When democratic government evolved in Europe and elsewhere in its modern forms, it was a democracy quite different from that of the ancient Athenians who have sometimes been misleadingly invoked as a precedent. Although some of the memes in the heads of Plato and Aristotle are in our heads too, the practices defining the roles constitutive of the institutions of the society within which those memes were transmitted from mind to mind have been driven irrecoverably extinct.

16

HUMAN SOCIALITY, COMMUNICATION, AND MEDIA

An Evolutionary Perspective

Peter M. Hejl

Sociological theories very often underestimate the role communication and media play in most social phenomena. This holds even for proposals that focus in various ways on the *social construction of reality*, on the *production of shared meaning*, or on *sociality,* Stephen Sanderson's foci in his impressive book, *The Evolution of Human Sociality*. Sanderson criticizes the widespread sociological ignorance of evolutionary theory. While I agree with his basic critique and with much of what he proposes, communication and media are absent from his theoretical framework. This shortcoming appears to reflect certain decisions and assumptions he makes at a basic conceptual level. In this contribution I argue in contrast that the evolution of sociality depends on communication, and that communication depends on media. My purpose is to place communication in the context of an evolutionary perspective on human society, while commenting on some of the more problematic aspects of Sanderson's arguments. My general goal is of course not a critique of Sanderson's work but a contribution to a richer understanding of human sociality.

I begin by pointing out some general problematic aspects of *The Evolution of Human Sociality*. I then argue that human sociality not only includes human communication, but depends on it. In the third part of this chapter, I draw attention to the sometimes forgotten fact that communication depends, in turn, on media. Finally, using some new research data, I argue that media are not just carriers of communication but that each medium has its own effects: Choice of medium makes a difference.

PROBLEMS WITH *THE EVOLUTION OF HUMAN SOCIALITY*: CONTINUING DUALISM – "NATURE-NURTURE" IN THE FORM OF "MATERIALISM-CULTURALISM"

Conceptually, Sanderson remains within the dualist tradition. In the context of the old controversy between collectivists (Durkheim, Parsons, Luhmann, but also Marxism and social constructivism) and individualists (Tarde, psychological reductionism, rational choice theories, etc.), he joins methodological (or even theoretical) individualism. While I share his position that explanations of social facts have to be linked ultimately to individuals and to human nature, I would argue that such a conviction is compatible with *different* and *more complex* lines of reasoning. What we can learn from the now more than a century-old discussion of the individual/society divide in sociology is that its basic problem is the way it is conceptualized. Past discussions of the relation between the level of "individuals" and that of "society" treated this relation too often as an either-or option, hence as a traditional dualism rather than as a relation of interacting levels defined in the context of an explanatory purpose. It is this "ontological dualism" that I find in *The Evolution of Human Sociality*, with its central oppositions of "individual/society" and "materialism/idealism." Both are conceptual parallels to "naturalism/culturalism" or "universalism/relativism."

All of these dualisms fit into the scheme we inherited from Manichaeism. Its basic form is probably the "mind-matter" opposition, as in the theological and political distinction Augustine made between the "city of God" and the "city of man." From an evolutionary perspective, much more interesting is the position of an outsider like Julien de la Mettrie, who explained in his 1745 *Histoire naturelle de l'âme*, that thinking and hence the soul are "nothing else" but results of the organization of the brain (1974, 174-77). His important insight was that there is no processing of perceived events, ideas, or artifacts without the [evolved, as we would say today] biological organs that *do* this processing, i.e., our perceptual apparatus including our brain. At the same time, this processing is not independent of earlier (or just perceived) events, ideas, or artifacts (as, for example, social constructivists and defenders of an absolute "freedom of will" seem to believe).

No individual actor has the capacity to control all the dynamics of his or her social and cultural environment. Hence, sociological explanations need to include not only the individual and the sociocultural environmental levels, but their interactions as well. The advantage of evolutionary theory is that it allows for testable hypotheses about the behavior of both levels, plus their interactional products, and hence for the accumulatation of relevant knowledge.[1]

To speak of *interactions* between these levels emphasizes that their relation is not a one-way dependency, not the simple cause-and-effect relationship too often assumed in the sociological debate. "Nature" (or "individuals") and "culture" (or "society") *change their ontological status* when seen from this dual-level perspective. Instead of being taken as two separate ontological realms

linked by *linear* causality, they become observer-dependent phenomenal domains coupled in their dynamics through the *recursive* causality of coevolution.

There Is More to Evolutionary Theory than Fitness-Maximizing Sociobiology

The Evolution of Human Sociality is based largely on fitness-maximizing
sociobiology. Sanderson's approach has clear advantages over the highly
restricted conception of human nature used in the social sciences. But the price
he pays for his position is sociobiology's emphasis on the individual and its
sometimes problematic adoption of rational choice theory.

We owe to sociobiology numerous insights still too often ignored in the social sciences and the humanities. However, recognizing both immediate and
potential benefits that the social sciences can draw from sociobiology does not
mean ignoring its shortcomings. The higher above the level of the individual one
moves, the weaker inclusive fitness sociobiology becomes. Sociobiologists typically move from individuals to biological families to populations, rather than to
the societies studied by sociologists. In fact, the social units of sociobiology
above the family level are the rather small bands in which our ancestors presumably lived in prehistoric times. Nevertheless despite the adaptation of our
ancestors to these small units, they managed to form, during the last 10,000-
12,000 years, societies of millions and even, in two cases, more than a billion
members. Certainly sociobiology conceives of humans as social, but its concept
of sociality is not complex enough. We humans are ultrasocial in the sense that
we live in societies where kin-related dispositions still work, but where the percentage of interactions with kin is very small. Yet we are doing thus far extremely well, as the worldwide increasing population demonstrates (Campbell
1983; Dunbar 1996; Richerson, Boyd, and Henrich 2002).

By adopting the inclusive fitness model of sociobiology, Sanderson is also
borrowing its rational "economic man" assumption. Both field observations and
experiments in different societies or social contexts show that humans are to a
substantial degree "irrational" with respect to the predictions of economic rationality and of fitness maximization: Their sense of fairness goes beyond economic rationality; they even accept costs for altruistic punishment and expect
their partners to act as altruistic punishers. Moreover, humans have the adap-
tively important capacity to choose between cooperation and competition or to
"mix" these, economically speaking, "rational" and "irrational" types of behavior (Fehr, Fischbacher, and Gächter 2002; Henrich, Boyd, Bowles, Camerer,
Gintis, McElreath, and Fehr 2001; Guzmán, Rodríguez-Sickert, and Rowthorn
2007). Clearly such behavioral traits are linked to the need (if we are to have
large-scale societies) to ensure cooperation between biologically unrelated partners.

Costs of Constructing an Explanation of Human Sociality Without an Explicit Discussion of Communication

If one opts, as Sanderson does, for a more or less materialist position (in the sense that ideational phenomena become epiphenomena), then there is little apparent need to be interested in communication. The assumption that behavior is rational (i.e., maximizing something) has the same effect. Together, in Sanderson's work, materialism plus "rational man" form the basic structure of a behavioral program supposedly shared by all humans. In this wired-in program, biological reproduction is the basic goal that is then optimized through rational behavior. Interests in economic resources, beauty, prestige, or power are proximate means to achieve the ultimate goal. Actors, seen this way, should never refuse the supreme goal of reproductive success, as do monks or numerous contemporaries who refrain from reproduction for various reasons.

In such a context, communication is often conceived as a use or exchange of signals, comparable to how mobile robots use perceived shape to decide, in terms of the algorithms embedded in their software, how to move so as to avoid obstacles. Though often misleadingly described as "autonomous" or "intelligent," the processing of such signals certainly cannot alter the "worldview" of the robots such that they develop an ideology or decide to destroy themselves, unlike human beings (Eibl-Eibesfeldt and Salter 1998).

Returning to our own species, communication in this conceptually restrained context is of relatively little importance at both the individual and group levels, given that the social units considered are families and rather small bands.

- As human behavior, in Sanderson's system, is mainly seen as determined by our evolutionary past, the processing of observations and the generation and reception/interpretation of messages does not become a focus of theoretical interest. Thus, even when Sanderson does discuss the process of communication, he omits the term itself. For example, in his discussion of Dawkins's meme concept, he quotes Dawkins's description of memes propagating themselves "by leaping from brain to brain" (Sanderson 2001a, 153). From a sociological perspective, of course, the question is how this might happen and what other social factors influence the outcome?

- Although Sanderson treats the struggle for economic resources, power, status, etc., in detail, *communication and therefore media as analytically separate evolving resources are absent.*

Thus, Sanderson analyzes the evolution of human sociality without an explicit discussion of the evolution of communication as an essential part of the changes that led to modern humans. It is to this deficit that I will now turn.

Human Sociality Depends on Communication

The "out-of-Africa" hypothesis tells us that our Environment of Evolutionary Adaptedness (EEA) included the savannas of southeast Africa and, later on, the much harsher conditions of the various ice ages during the Pleistocene (at least for those of our ancestors who migrated to the north of the globe (Boyd and Silk 2003). Although these physical conditions were important, it was the social environment of the groups our ancestors formed that, if we accept the arguments of the proponents of the social intelligence hypothesis (Byrne and Whiten 1988), had an even greater influence. A substantial portion of the problems our ancestors had to solve continually were those presented by living in these groups.

Aiello and Dunbar (1993) argue, on both theoretical and empirical grounds, that a relatively stable relation exists between brain size and group size. This is because *our brain is the organ responsible for the complex social interactions that occur in social groups.* According to their calculations, evolutionarily relevant societies consisted of approximately 100–150 members. Quite often, groups were much smaller. The term "biological societies" refers to societies of this size, characterized by rather broadly shared knowledge and a slow rate of change (if we ignore modifications due to the short life expectancy of our ancestors).

The growth in size of our ancestral biological societies would have required a sequential growth in cognitive capacity. Brain size would therefore have been a limiting factor in the growth of groups of early humans. Aiello and Dunbar argue that in this situation, more efficient means of communication would have evolved. Thus, as group size increased so did brain size and cognitive capacity, as well as the ability to produce and distinguish among sounds and to use them for more efficient communication. Communication would have permitted the manipulation and even exploitation of other group members.

If we look at the evolution of language in the context of the Aiello and Dunbar argument, the function of "communication" becomes clear: Communication serves the coordination of behavior both on the emotional and on the knowledge transmission level. To be more precise: Communication serves the coordination of behavior by the use of signs. Understood this way, communication is at the very core of human sociality.

As human language evolved, it complemented the older means of nonverbal communication. All species transmit information genetically, but our species added a second means, that of language and culture. As evolutionary culture theorists (Boyd and Richerson 1985; Dawkins 1976; Durham 1991) have pointed out, this second level adds a horizontal component of knowledge distribution to the more exclusive and restricted vertical dimension of parent-offspring transmission.

The transition from a hunter-gatherer existence characterized by the collection of dispersed resources to that of the locally fixed production of resources had vast social and economic consequences: We moved from sociality to *ultra-sociality*. Within the brief span of a few thousand years many of our ancestors came to live in larger societies and then in complex states, as we do today. In these built, often urban environments, we earned our livelihoods through cooperative work, managing the storage and distribution of resources between the harvests. Labor organization included the coordination of large numbers of citizens and was based on complex knowledge, which had to be developed, then transmitted both horizontally (among members of the same generation) and vertically (to future generations). These societies were in principle governed through specific institutions and at times even by written law (as is beautifully illustrated by the Code of Hammurabi).

These achievements would have been impossible without efficient communication. However, the biological basis for this efficiency *could of course not evolve as an adaptation to the needs of the transition itself*. It must have been present, at least potentially, even *prior to* the growth in population, the development of cities, the division of labor, and hierarchical social relations. Therefore, my claim is that *human sociality includes capacities for efficient communication unequaled by other species.*

Communication Depends on and Is Influenced by Media

If we understand communication as "coordination of behavior by the use of signs," it is clear that language is not the only means (medium) of communication. Prior or at least parallel to language and its precursors, a whole repertoire of nonverbal media had evolved: *visual* medialike gestures, facial or bodily expressions of intentions or emotions. In addition, there are *olfactory* and to a certain degree even *gustatory* ways to communicate, especially in the context of sexual relations. Often, when we touch someone, it is to express sympathy or compassion so that we are communicating in *tactile* mode. When people communicate in an everyday context, or when politicians meet and greet, there is much body contact. Even hierarchical relations are often expressed in terms of "who touches whom" or through physical distance, allowing politicians to demonstrate that they are "just folks" by touching not only babies but humble citizens (and potential voters). Finally, the *acoustical* channel still exists and it expresses emotional states that are quite likely older than language itself. All these media have a genetic basis, although their use is shaped by the surrounding culture. Given this genetic basis, nonverbal communication as well as language can be called "natural media."

However "natural" the "natural media" may be, we still have to learn to use them. Nevertheless, we can use them to communicate without the aid of any instruments, any physical substratum, or any sophisticated devices or pieces of technology. These *primary* or "natural" media are supplemented by "cultural" or "artificial" media when *secondary* and *tertiary* media appear.

Secondary media may have developed with the need for knowledge storage, retrieval, or geographic transfer. Secondary media allow for the "objectivization" of knowledge. This term refers to the representation of knowledge by objects outside human memory. Such representations would in fact serve as "signs" or "symbols." The early tokens or clay figurines that preceded cuneiform writing in the Middle East represent the transition between the perception of our three-dimensional world and the two-dimensional notation of writing systems (Schmandt-Besserat 1978). But writing and reading remained for many centuries a costly technique. Hence, the representation, especially of holy texts, through series of illustrations, e.g., mural paintings and the stained glass windows of churches, which lasted well after the invention of printing in the fifteenth century. Printing was the technical innovation that was the beginning of modern mass communication and the literacy of those who were to constitute the mass public.

A new type of medium began during the late 1830s, the invention of the telegraph by Morse. This new medium was followed by other inventions, for example, the telephone in 1861 (Reiss) and 1876 (Bell), the phonograph in 1877 (Edison), film in 1894 (Lumière), wireless telegraph and radio beginning in 1895 (Popow, Marconi), television in 1897 (Braun's cathode ray tube) and 1925 (first transmissions by Jenkins) (Faulstich 1996-2004). These tertiary media all required not only that the producer of a message use technical equipment for its production and transmission, but that the potential recipients also make use of technology. As human society has grown increasingly ultrasocial, it has grown increasingly dependent on technology for communication.

The development of human culture would not have been possible without increasingly efficient communication. With societal growth, the coordination of the behavior of the members of these "societies of strangers" (Vowinckel 1995) became critical both for individual existence and that of society as a whole. The very basis of any coordination of behavior is a mutual cognitive adaptation. It allows participants to interpret communicative acts in a similar way, at least to a certain extent.[2] The basis of this coordinating behavior is of course genetic. It is complemented through the processes of imitation and teaching that characterize social interaction from early socialization of children to an age at which cognitive change unfortunately means mainly "forgetting." All these processes take place in cultural contexts and depend on communication. If I want to imitate the prestigious or successful members of my social group, I have to know – and this means I have to learn through communication – who satisfies these criteria. The same holds, of course, for teaching. The interesting point here is that *communication is required to trigger the mutual adaptation* that allows and enforces cooperation between actors who have the alternative of noncooperation permanently in mind. At the same time, the (always relative) cognitive "standardization" resulting from socialization processes in a given culture is an *important condition for successful communication.*

Let us now look briefly at the relation between the societal level and that of the individual.

Of course, *societies* can be seen as "nothing but" networks of interacting individuals, whose "interactions" seem to be very often directly oriented toward sexual reproduction. This is what sociobiologists refer to when they speak of "populations." If, however, we look at the processes involved, we find that considering human societies as nothing but "populations" is clearly simplistic. Not only are interactions both within and among societies highly variable, but any given society is characterized by a body of knowledge. This knowledge is composed of the more or less ordered concepts a given society has developed to refer to itself and to its physical and social environment. As a result, the members of a given society have access to cognitive concepts that facilitate their social interactions and their interactions with their environments. This knowledge goes with technical competencies that include tools and tool-related skills. There are as well behavioral "programs" and moral standards adapted to such mental and behavioral ensembles. In fact, they constitute worldviews differing from one cultural context to another, but nevertheless showing numerous universal or near-universal aspects (Brown 1991; Hejl 2001). Following a variety of different structuring criteria, this knowledge is socially distributed among the individuals and subsystems of which larger social systems are composed.

From an evolutionary point of view, societies provide better chances of reproductive success than does solitary, nonsocial life. However, the advantages of social life can only be realized if cooperation and competition among individuals and subgroups are balanced so that competition does not result in exploitation. A rapidly growing body of empirical literature shows that humans possess a complex of evolved behavioral dispositions (e.g., cheater detection, altruistic punishment, or commitment to groups) that lead to the development of explicit norms permitting a certain level of cooperation. Moreover, the division of activities requires complementary specializations to satisfy various basic requirements of life, as was emphasized by the founding fathers of sociology's organismic tradition (e.g., H. Spencer, A. Schäffle, É. Durkheim). Increasing societal complexity is necessarily paralleled by an increase in the extent and the complexity of communication. Societal complexity would include, for example, the movement of functions formerly performed by families to external institutions (e.g., education, health care, justice). Distributed knowledge and its management, the organization of cooperation and of political decision-making, all of these communication-based activities did not have to be invented from scratch with the advent of ultrasociality. They all have an evolutionary basis and therefore are an integral part of human sociality.[3]

Returning to human *individuals*, we have to assume that they are, at any point in their lives, the product both of a phylogeny common to all humans and of a unique ontogeny reflecting environment-genome interaction.[4] This holds for cognitive-emotional processes as well. As a result, our cognitive and emotional situation is well characterized by Barkow's (1992) formula "Beneath New Culture Is Old Psychology"; any "information" or "entertainment" offered by the media has to be processed by this "old psychology."

This leads to consequences that illustrate how the inevitable interaction between the individual and the social level is based on communication and hence on the use of media, how the evolution and mastery of media are essential for an

understanding of sociality and the functioning of society, all of which support
the thesis that "Media Make a Difference." Let us look at some evidence and
arguments.

1. In a famous article published in 1963, Goody and Watt discussed the
cognitive and social consequences of the transition to *writing*. Their main point
was that writing and reading are so different from normal communication that
they necessarily have had a profound impact on our thinking about time and
objectivity. The authors systematically discuss what is now a familiar question:
What is in a text? Of course, a text rarely "stores" a specific meaning. Any significance or meaning attributed to a perceived sequence of signs is a cognitive
construct. Reading, like listening or observing, is in fact a process of meaning
construction. What changes with different media is the *degree of liberty* available to users when *they* construct what *they* take to be the meaning of a message
offered by a specific medium. With respect to a text, this freedom seems to be
very great. As a result, we find that, for example, in theology, jurisprudence, and
literary studies much time is devoted to teaching readers "how to read" a particular text. The common "solution" consists of creating an authoritarian institution, e.g., the Pope in Catholicism, or the Supreme Court in American jurisprudence. Wherever such a social solution fails, competing or even antagonistic
constructs of "true" meanings proliferate, often with anarchic social consequences but occasionally with a cultural transformation toward pluralism and
tolerance.

2. *Audio-visual media* seem to work somewhat differently from written text.
Here is just one example from television news broadcasting. Frey and his collaborators have analyzed the impact of evolved "old psychology." Following the
social intelligence hypothesis, we expect human observers to assess rapidly
women and men appearing in their near environment.[5] In a large experimental
study conducted in the United States, France, and Germany, the Frey group presented their research participants with short news clips showing politicians from
these three countries (Frey 2000, 99-129). The results were startling (and quite
disastrous for social constructivists in the nurture-only tradition): Within 25 mil-
liseconds study participants felt able to evaluate in detail the character and competence of the individuals presented. Increasing the length of exposure did *not*
lead to any significant modification of their judgments. Judgments were relatively independent of the participants' respective national backgrounds. Even
when they were able to identify the politicians presented, participants' assessments differed little from the assessments of those unaware of the identity of the
political figures presented. Finally, when Frey and his collaborators replaced the
clips with computer-generated models representing only the body postures of the
politicians, assessments remained unchanged!

Apparently, media activate cognitive mechanisms linked to communication
that are much older than contemporary "cultural" or "artificial" media. Whereas
Frey used film clips to present out-of-context political actors to research participants in order to elicit their assessments, mass communication outside the labo-
ratory seems to be much closer to how our ancestors exchanged news and talked

or listened to stories for entertainment. Hence, to explore evolved aspects of human sociality in more depth we have to answer the question: What is it that we find most interesting in entertainment and news?

As early as 1922, Walter Lippman discussed "news values" in his famous book *Public Opinion* (Lippmann 1997). His ideas led to a tradition of research on the impact of the media on public policy. This perspective was taken up during the mid-1960s in Europe, where peace researchers (e.g., Galtung and Ruge 1965) sought to evaluate the role journalists play in selecting events, thereby transforming occurrences into news. In the same context, Östgard (1965) related the functioning of news factors to general aspects of human perception. Research on "news values" or "news factors" continues to constitute a relatively large part of empirical media research (e.g., Kamps 1999; Ruhrmann, Woelke, Maier, and Diehlmann 2003). This research usually makes extensive use of content analysis and typically finds that only a limited number of factors is sufficient to account for variation in reported news. Until the advent of evolutionary theory, surprisingly little theoretical work had been developed capable of accounting on a general level for these phenomena. Indeed, evolutionists find that news values are just a special case of a broad theory of the role of entertainment in human life (e.g., Berghaus 1994; Schwender 2001; Shoemaker and Cohen 2006). If one asks media consumers or even media professionals what they consider to be entertaining and hence interesting, a frequent answer consists of a reference to "something new." A couple of years ago, I happened to analyze television programs and classified their content. Unexpectedly, I found that television programs in general cover only a few topics. At the same time, all surveys demonstrate that both the size of the television-viewing audience and the total amount of time spent viewing continue to expand (e.g., Nielsen Media Research 2006). This situation can best be described as "always the same program – but no boredom," a counterintuitive finding calling for further explanation.

Consequently, and as a complement to news factor studies, I initiated a research project on "social and anthropological factors of media use," focusing on entertainment. The working hypothesis, derived from the evolutionist's expectation that human cognition evolved to solve the recurring problems of our ancestors, was that we should expect only a *few topics to be of recurrent and hence universal interest, both in news and in entertainment.* Of course, not every evolutionarily relevant issue may be capable of being both news and entertainment, but we would expect a substantial degree of overlap. In addition, we would anticipate that many issues would be susceptible to treatment either as news *or* as entertainment, or *partly* as news and *partly* as entertainment.

After much internal and external discussion, our research group[6] began by developing a list of potentially universal topics or issues classified as "main," "necessary," and "other" issues with respect to their importance in various films. These issues were: "kinship," "mate selection," "friendship," "status," "group conflict," "resources" (cognitive, material, social), "physical danger," and "revenge." We then developed a questionnaire of more than 600 items for detailed content analyses of films from the world's two major film centers (in terms of the number of films produced per year), Hollywood and Bollywood. The analyses were conducted by four groups each consisting of three trained student experts. We selected the 100 highest-grossing films from Hollywood and the 50 highest-grossing films from Bollywood.[7] We chose economic success as an indicator of popular success in order to reduce culture-specific influence on sample choice. This procedure allowed us to look both for shared and for nonshared items of content. Table 16.1 provides some of our results.[8]

The first general prediction from evolutionary theory was that certain issues should appear in films of different cultures, hence in both Hollywood *and* in Bollywood productions. As Table 16.1 shows, this prediction was confirmed. Moreover, and much to our surprise, only three films had to be excluded from further analysis because our categories did not appear to be relevant to them.[9]

As the expression of universal interest structures is subject to historical and cultural influences, we assumed that cultural context should modify the importance and the ranking of issues. Thus, we were not surprised to find that, compared to Hollywood productions, Bollywood films focus more on mate selection as a central issue, often linked to danger, kinship, status, and revenge (both low, but more important than in the West). In contrast, Hollywood films focus more on danger followed by mate selection, and then by friendship or group conflict. Kinship has a much lower importance than on Bollywood screens. Without further comment we may note in addition that the film production of the richest and most powerful country of the world scores high on "danger," "resources," and "group conflict," whereas the major film production of India, a country with sixteen official languages, numerous ethnic groups, and persistent conflicts among certain groups and with some of its neighbors, scores low on the issue "group conflict."

Table 16.1 Ranking of Issues in Hollywood and Bollywood Films

(From Hejl, Kammer, and Uhl, "Media and Universals – Focus on Film and Print," Workshop at the University of Siegen, Germany, February 3-5, 2005.)

Order of Issues, Complete Sample (in %, *n* = 150)	Hollywood (in %, *n* = 100)	Bollywood (in %, *n* = 50)
78.0 danger	82.0 danger	88.0 mate selection
68.7 mate selection	59.0 mate selection	70.0 danger
54.7 resources	58.0 resources	62.0 kinship
46.0 friendship	51.0 friendship	48.0 resources
45.3 kinship	46.0 group conflict	36.0 friendship
38.0 group conflict	37.0 kinship	36.0 status
27.3 status	23.0 status	28.0 revenge
22.7 revenge	20.0 revenge	22.0 group conflict

CONCLUDING REMARKS

Any notion of human sociality assumes a number of characteristics to be part of human nature. In a strictly scientific context, such assumptions have to be based on evolutionary theory. Though the principles of evolutionary theory seem to be rather clear, their application to the social sciences encounters numerous difficulties. Not the smallest difficulty is that scientific research takes place within the science systems of our societies. Hence, it is part of social processes involving social, cultural, and economic resources, and where identities and norms are at stake. As a result, even when a finding is intended as an "application," it is often considered to be part of discussions "in support of X" or "against Y." The advantage evolutionary theory offers, in this context, is its potential to integrate theoretical considerations and empirical results from other disciplines, to look for ways to test propositions, and to accept – even enjoy – evidence or arguments that push us to modify our positions. By arguing theoretically and empirically for the importance of communication and media for our understanding of human sociality, I have tried to respond to this potential.

ACKNOWLEDGMENTS

I am pleased to thank Peter Meyer for comments on an earlier version of this paper and Jerome Barkow, not only for many suggestions on and discussions of the argument of this paper, but for our ongoing stimulating exchanges as well. I am also very grateful to Stephen Sanderson for his excellent editorial assistance.

NOTES

1. The mainstream conviction, especially in the humanities and social sciences, holding that there is no or only very limited accumulation of knowledge possible, is not shared here.

2. "Similarity" does not mean consent. Understanding intentions or expressions of emotions correctly may or may not coincide with shared interests.

3. It remains to be seen if and how concepts of coevolution will become more important as genetic research leads to new insights (cf. Wooding 2007).

4. In addition, all complex organisms are "individuals" in the sense that even "true twins" are "identical, but not the same" (Segal 1999).

5. In fact, audio-visual media, especially TV, not only mimic a social environment but also make it important by introducing it into the sphere where everything happening is important, our near environment or even our home. This effect of evolution leads, for example, to the phenomenon of "parasocial interactions" discussed in media studies, though this discussion largely ignores evolutionary psychology (cf. Bryant and Vorderer 2006, and, as an exception, Kanazawa 2002).

6. The core research team included P. M. Hejl, M. Kammer (until 2004), and M. Uhl. K. Kumar, Dept. of Communication and Journalism, Pune University, participated in the preparation of the project, the development of the questionnaire, and its testing. In addition, he conducted several focus groups in India and helped to evaluate the list

of Bollywood films used to select our sample. He was of course an indispensable help in the analysis of the Indian films. G. Chapman, University of Lancaster, contributed his expertise on Indian history and culture as well as his experience with media research in India. For numerous discussions, we have to thank Chr. Antweiler, Universität Trier; J. H. Barkow, Dalhousie University, Halifax; S. Frey, Universität Duisburg; and E. Voland, Universität Giessen. The research was part of the Centre of Cultural Research "Media Upheavals," Universität Siegen, funded by Deutsche Forschungsgemeinschaft.

7. The lists were for "all times." The earliest entry is from 1921. Entries are adjusted for inflation.

8. For more details, see Uhl (2007) and Hejl and Uhl (forthcoming).

9. *Fantasia*, 1940, W. Disney; *Close Encounters of the Third Kind*, 1977, S. Spielberg; *Back to the Future*, 1985, R. Zemeckis. We replaced them by the next films from our list.

Part IV

REFLECTIONS AND FINAL THOUGHTS

17

DARWINIAN CONFLICT THEORY AND EVOLUTIONARY SOCIOLOGY

A Reply to Critics and Fellow Travelers

Stephen K. Sanderson

Let me begin by thanking Tamás Meleghy, Peter Meyer, and Heinz-Jürgen Niedenzu for organizing the conference at Innsbruck in June 2006, during which the original versions of these papers were presented. It is certainly gratifying, to say the least, to know that there are scholars out there who think highly enough of one's work to devote most of an international academic conference to it. And I thank all of the critics for their contributions. They have forced me to go back and reexamine many of my arguments and, in some cases, to rethink them and to clarify them. It has also been a real pleasure to discover that there are European scholars of a Darwinian persuasion whose work I was unaware of. But without further ado, let me turn to the critics' comments.[1]

MICHAEL SCHMID

Michael Schmid's critique of Darwinian conflict theory (DCT) is perhaps the most incisive that anyone has ever written. His brief summary of it is so good that I could hardly have improved on it myself. I wish I had had him as a critic

---

[1] *Note:* This reply is a condensed version of a much longer reply, which is posted on my website: http://www.stephenksanderson.org

before the publication of *The Evolution of Human Sociality*, because he raises so many excellent questions that he certainly would have helped me refine DCT and make the book a better book. It is difficult to overstate how welcome it is to have someone who has an excellent and very nuanced grasp of what I have been trying to say. He realizes, for example, that DCT is much more subtle than a simple sociobiological reductionism; as he points out, in DCT biological needs and capacities are predispositions, not hard determinants, and these needs and capacities must be actualized by circumstances. What follows is basically a response to some of the many insightful questions and suggestions that Schmid raises.

It would be desirable if Sanderson would distinguish more clearly between "energizing" and "constraining" factors as causal mechanisms. Indeed. As Schmid notes, the so-called energizing factors in DCT are primarily the interests and needs of human organisms. These are what I have called the deep wellsprings of human action, and these wellsprings are grounded in the fundamental theoretical principle of sociobiology, the modified maximization principle. These are the things that individuals are struggling to do, some of them consciously and others more or less unconsciously. But what humans strive to do and what they are able to do are two different things. Thus, enter what Schmid is quite rightly calling the constraining factors. I have now taken to calling these, when taken collectively, the *socioecological context* of human action, by which I mean the entire range of external (especially ecomaterialist and polimaterialist) contingencies to which human action must adjust itself. As Schmid notes, in my scheme these do not really produce outcomes so much as *steer, restrict*, or *guide* them. For example, one of the fundamental wellsprings of human action for the male of the species is the desire to copulate with a large number of young and attractive females. In many societies at least some of the males, especially the higher-status and more resource-endowed males, are able to achieve this goal, or at least approximate it. Polygyny is found in 85 percent of the world's known societies, and in some of these societies a surprisingly large number of males are at some point in their lives polygynously married. But not all societies permit polygyny. A good many forbid it by law, and modern Western societies are among the best known of these. There are several competing theories of this so-called socially imposed monogamy, and it is not clear which of them is the correct one (or if any are). But one thing is clear: Socially imposed monogamy is the result of constraints on what it is natural for most males to do, which is why Laura Betzig can say with perfect accuracy that although not all men *marry* polygynously, in every society they seek to *mate* polygynously.

Now the question is, does one of these types of factors, energizing or constraining, have a privileged causal status? Schmid apparently thinks that the real causes in my theory are the energizing ones and that constraining factors are not genuine causal mechanisms. I am not sure I agree. What we regard as a causal mechanism depends on the question. If our question is, "Why is polygyny so common throughout the world?" then surely the causal mechanism is the typical heterosexual male sexual inclination. But if we change the question and ask,

"Why do some societies have socially prescribed monogamy?" then our causal mechanism is the constraints that male sexual inclinations are subject to. The starting point of analysis should always be the energizing factors, but they can do their work only within a socioecological context. Thus, the energizing factors cannot in the abstract be regarded as more genuine causes as the constraining factors, and vice versa. But I agree with Schmid that it is important to keep these separate, and in a later installment of DCT I will seek to do so more systematically.

Sanderson does not refer to the Darwinian notions of "variation," "selection," "retention," "descent," or "modification," and thus in what sense are his arguments truly evolutionary? The answer to this question depends on recognizing that there are at least three different ways in which the term "evolutionary" can be employed, and thus three different types of "evolutionary explanations." These can be distinguished as follows:

- *Type 1 Evolutionary Explanations*: Explanations that rely on sociobiological principles concerning the evolution of human nature to ground an explanation of any social phenomenon. *Example*: *The Evolution of Human Sociality* and all of the work of the sociobiologists and evolutionary psychologists.
- *Type 2 Evolutionary Explanations*: Explanations relying on any type of causal mechanism whose *explanandum* is social evolution. *Examples*: Sanderson's *Social Transformations* (1995, 1999a), but also Talcott Parsons's *Societies: Evolutionary and Comparative Perspectives* (1966) and Robert Bellah's "Religious Evolution" (1964). Probably we should stop calling these evolutionary *explanations*. They are not, because a theory can only be appropriately categorized or labeled in terms of its *explanans*, not its *explanandum*. These "explanations" are various and sundry attempts (materialist, idealist, eclectic, etc.) to account for *social evolution in the sense of directional sequences of social change*.
- *Type 3 Evolutionary Explanations*: Explanations of social phenomena and changes occurring therein that transfer classical natural selectionist concepts (variation, selection, retention, etc.) to the realm of human social life. In this case, evolution is the *explanans* rather than the *explanandum*. *Examples*: the very well known work of Donald T. Campbell (1965, 1975), which would have launched this tradition except that it was preceded by the (now largely forgotten) early work of Albert Galloway Keller, *Societal Evolution* (1931); Philippe van Parijs's *Evolutionary Explanation in the Social Sciences* (1981); Boyd and Richerson's *Culture and the Evolutionary Process* (1985); and W. G. Runciman's *A Treatise on Social Theory* (1989, 285-450).

I use the term *evolutionary* only in the first two senses and rarely in this third sense, so my explanations cannot be described as evolutionary in this last sense.

I have been reluctant to use natural selectionist reasoning to explain trajectories of social evolution because these kinds of evolutionary explanations are largely explanations by analogy and thus do not reveal to us any necessary or sufficient causes. They provide only a rough indication of how a process might be characterized, and even then the characterization can be misleading because of several important disanalogies between biological and social evolution (cf. Sanderson 2007c, 287-89).

Sanderson's attempt to ground evolutionary theory in a conflict theory has nothing to do with his materialist historical analyses. I am not completely sure what is intended here, but let me simply say that a conflict theory is not necessarily one in which individuals are in open conflict with each other and/or in which some are *dominating* or *exploiting* others. A conflict theory is a theory of interests, or at least that is how I use the term. Randall Collins is the preeminent conflict theorist in modern sociology, and he says that individuals are extraordinarily conflict prone. Indeed they are, if by this is meant that *they have competing interests* (e.g., bourgeoisie and proletariat in the classical Marxian sense) or that *they have the same interests but the resources available to satisfy them are insufficient for everyone to fully realize their interests.* My materialist historical analyses, best represented in my *Social Transformations*, are at the same time conflict analyses. Conflict and materialist analyses are simply two sides of the same coin. Schmid says in a related vein that I *have no systematic theory to explain historical development.* Well, I do. Actually, I have a general theoretical strategy, evolutionary materialism (see Antweiler, Chapter 5 this volume), and then several more specific evolutionary materialist theories devoted to explaining major social transitions (these are the *single causal explanations* – of the transition to agriculture, of the rise of the state, of the transition to modern capitalism – of which Schmid speaks). I think that Schmid must be combing my work looking for a *single general mechanism* that is a Type 3 evolutionary explanation that will account for all long-term social developmental dynamics, but he will not find one there. And I don't have one because I don't think there can be one. (However, if Schmid wants to regard, as seems to be the case, the *mechanism of conflict* as a *selection mechanism*, I have no objection, because social life, including social change, is all about people struggling to satisfy their interests. But I do not find this sufficiently interesting or specific to be intellectually satisfying as a single Type 3 evolutionary explanation.)

Sanderson's conflict theory does not take into account highly diverse forms of conflict (e.g., zero-sum games, "battles of the sexes," "mixed motive games") and thus is in need of further specification. This is a very good point and one that I shall try to address in later work.

Are the needs and dispositions with which Sanderson concerns himself only those that are genetically based? The short answer is no, although in truth I am more concerned with these kinds of needs and dispositions than with others. However, it is clearly essential to recognize that in the course of human affairs humans acquire new needs and dispositions. A simple example would be the "need for other-worldly salvation." I see no real evidence that religious behavior in most societies has this as a fundamental goal. It seems mainly to have arisen as a result of massive politico-military and economic changes occurring some 2,500 years ago. And even then many people had no such need and many have no such need even today. Relatedly, I see no strong evidence that, as Weber seemed to imply, humans have a deep need for a sense of cosmic meaning. This seems to be a need of only some individuals at certain times and places.

Sanderson at times speaks of "maximizing" and at other times of "satisficing," thus taking irreconcilable positions. Actually, my position is that humans are *not necessarily maximizers* and that much of the time (perhaps even most of the time) they are *satisficers*. It depends on what goals are being pursued and what constraints are being imposed. Capitalists really are maximizers rather than satisficers; great tennis players like Roger Federer or golfers like Tiger Woods are also maximizers in the sense that they want to win as many tournaments as they can and ultimately be proclaimed as the greatest of all time in their respective sport; and great womanizers like Bill Clinton or Jean-Paul Sartre may be maximizers of the number of women sexually conquered (in Sartre's case, it was also the number of *teenage virgin* women). But most of the time most people are satisficers because the constraints on maximizing are too great, and in any event the whole question is an empirical one.

Sanderson relies on a flawed method of testing hypotheses, which is the reliance on statistics and the amount of variance being explained. This means that his so-called explanations are necessarily false. This claim is quite surprising and I still do not understand it. I rely on a probabilistic model of causation, one that is widely accepted in the social sciences as the best we can do. Probabilistic causal models are not false; they are simply *incomplete*. If I perform a multiple regression analysis and find that I have explained, say, 60 percent of the variance in my *explanandum*, then I am going to be extremely happy since that is far more than most pieces of sociological research explain. Schmid also believes that I regard high correlations as sufficient to establish causal relationships. No, certainly not. I learned in my first year of graduate school forty years ago that more is required to establish causal relationships than this. If A and B are highly correlated, A could be causing B, B could be causing A, or the relationship could be the spurious result of some third variable, C, which is itself highly correlated with both A and B. I am usually quite careful when inferring causation to have a reasonable basis for doing so – which doesn't mean my inferences are always right, of course.

NICO WILTERDINK

Wilterdink questions my fourfold division of societies into biostructure, ecostructure, structure, and superstructure. He suggests that this division is arbitrary because it does not correspond very closely to social reality, grouping together things that belong apart and setting apart things that belong together. Wilterdink questions in particular the coherence of my notion of ecostructure because it involves both the natural environment and economic relations that are in fact social relations. But I would call Wilterdink's attention to the origin of the prefix "eco." It is the Greek word *oikos*, which means household. What is a household but, among other things, a unit of economic production, and how does economic production take place but in a particular kind of natural environment with all its enabling resources and specific constraints. The "eco" refers to people engaged in one of the two most fundamental activities that they must carry out, namely the production of a living. That is hardly incoherent.

Wilterdink goes on to claim that my model implies a distinction between "social structure" and "culture," but this is problematic he says because structure (social relations) always implies culture (norms, symbols, etc.). This is an un-demonstrated assumption that is part of the sociological heritage going back to Durkheim and coming up through Parsons, Alexander, and other "culturalists." I find it not only unpersuasive, but utterly wrong and highly detrimental. Wilterdink also contends that I provide no clear argument linking biostructure to ecostructure, ecostructure to structure, and structure to superstructure. I must refer Wilterdink to my proposition 3.4: "The components of societies are related as they are because such causal dynamics flow from the deep wellsprings of human action. *The biostructure and the ecostructure have a logical causal priority because they concern vital human needs and interests relating to production and reproduction.*" I have italicized the second sentence because it represents about as clear a statement of the linkages between the components as could possibly be made. But I suspect that Wilterdink does not really mean that my argument is not clear; probably he simply means that it is one that he does not agree with. Thus, we find the following (rather astonishing) statement from Wilterdink: "The biostructure, if it is defined as 'individuals themselves as biological organisms,' crucially depends on the social relations individuals have with one another (the social structure) as well as on the ways they have learned to cope with their environment (which is part of their culture): Human individuals 'as organisms' can only survive in groups that have patterned social relations and common social traits." Does Wilterdink really believe this?

To illustrate my conceptualization of the causal relations among my four components let me engage in a little *Gedankenexperiment*. Imagine that I have invented a machine that I point at a group of, say 50, people that *decultures* them, i.e., removes all of their learned traditions and leaves them as naked as jaybirds, although with a rudimentary language of approximately 500 words relating to the most basic things humans need to talk about in daily life. Imagine also that I have a jet plane in which I place these people, which then transports them to a deserted island in the middle of the Pacific Ocean. Now, let's watch what happens. Two things would happen first, and rather quickly. Everyone would first busy themselves trying to figure out what kinds of plants and animals were available on the island that they could eat and, once they had figured that out, they would busy themselves devising tools and methods with which to capture and process them for eating. Once they had done these things – actually, in all probability in conjunction with them – they would begin to pair off and mate, and offspring would ultimately be produced. Enter stage left the modes of production and reproduction in accordance with biologically given predispositions, or, in my terms, biostructure and ecostructure. These patterned activities would then give rise to other concerns, those involving structure (providing leadership, maintaining order, establishing family and kin structures) and superstructure (crystallizing out certain norms and values on the basis of the adaptive behavior patterns already established). Thus a social system emerges eventually in full bloom with "culture" coming in at the end (although "material culture" would be there early on if the 50 individuals are to survive). But once a patterned social system had begun to form and new generations born, these new generations would be constrained in their behavior by the patterns created in the past. These are the environmental contingencies or socioecological context that are a crucial part of DCT, which Wilterdink (and some of the other critics in this volume) thinks I am ignoring or underplaying.

Now I submit that this is a realistic appraisal of how things would work themselves out if we could actually do the experiment "on the ground." And imagine that we could do it not just once, but 1,000 times: 1,000 groups of 50 decultured people placed in 1,000 different ecosystems. What we would see would be the same biological predispositions at work creating slightly different ecostructures adapting to slightly different ecosystems; and then slightly different structures and superstructures coming into play once the fundamental problems of human adaptation and survival had been met; and then finally the constraining effects of the sociocultural patterns so created. This illustrates in a very sketchy and rudimentary way the kind of argument my DCT is making. And, after all, something like it did happen way back when humans did not yet have this thing called "culture," which then evolved along parallel, convergent, and divergent lines to produce what we see today in the basic findings of sociology, ethnography, archaeology, and history.

And note also that in my little *Gedankenexperiment* there is nothing at all static about my societal components? They are dynamic dimensions of humankind and its creations, constantly adapting themselves to ever-different and ever-changing conditions. Wilterdink's claim that the concepts are static is an attribution entirely unsupported by any argument or evidence.

I see two reasons why Wilterdink has gone wrong in his critique of DCT. First, he is a victim of his sociological education. As Pierre van den Berghe (1990) has commented, most sociological training is actually an occupational hazard for the understanding of human social life. Wilterdink is still in thrall to an old-fashioned sociology that looks amazingly like the kind of sociology established by Talcott Parsons. Wilterdink invokes again and again "culture," "symbolic communication," "social norms," and so on in the manner laid out by Parsons and his epigones. What we need instead is a complete reinvention of sociology that radically reconceptualizes "culture." As George Homans (1984) has famously said, culture does not explain anything *but itself has to be explained*. Wilterdink is, in Homans's nifty neologism, a "culture vulture." Note that in trying to explain the reduced fertility rates in modern societies, and the voluntary

childlessness of some couples, Wilterdink merely falls back on a very vague notion of "humans as cultural animals who make choices in accordance with meanings." This tired old refrain is the last thing sociology needs in the early third
millennium CE. Soon I hope to begin writing a book on the concept of culture,
tentatively entitled *Culture Vultures: Darwinian and Pre-Darwinian Theories of
Mind and Behavior*, in which I will suggest a complete reformulation of the culture concept in sociology and anthropology.

Wilterdink's other mistake is to implicitly reduce DCT to sociobiology and
represent sociobiology as some sort of simplistic biological determinism. But
DCT is a complex, multidimensional theory that gives a major role to a wide
range of socioecological contingencies in shaping human behavior and social
patterns. Wilterdink totally ignores my strongly stressed point about the *facultative* nature of nearly all human behavior: Humans have complex brains that allow them to assess their social environments and to respond to the contingencies
they find with behaviors that are adaptive *within the context of those particular
sets of contingencies*. That is why, for example, even though most societies have
been polygynous, some have been monogamous and a few polyandrous. And it
is why fertility levels in the modern socioecological context have been adjusted
downward.

As the title of his chapter indicates, Wilterdink thinks my materialism is a
metaphysical materialism in the sense that it is based on *a priori* assumptions
rather than empirical evidence. Wilterdink is partially right: My materialism is
metaphysically grounded. However, it is not metaphysically grounded in the pe-
jorative Comtean sense intended by Wilterdink, but rather in the classical philosophical sense of metaphysics as *a concern to establish first principles*. This is
something that very few sociologists and anthropologists, in their worshiping of
the notion of emergence, seem to understand. One must always have first principles, or grounding principles beyond which it is not necessary or even possible
to go in formulating explanations. One of our leading sociological theorists on
the world scene today, Randall Collins, would do better if his version of conflict
theory had some metaphysical grounding. Humans, Collins avers, are extraordinarily conflict-prone organisms. Indeed, he is quite right, but he *fails to explain
why humans are conflict prone, taking this as an unexplained given.* Collins has
given us an extremely useful conflict sociology, but it is a sociology with no
first principles, and thus is very incomplete and often inaccurate. In real science,
one does not try to be as *emergentist* as possible, but rather as *reductionist* as
possible. This point Durkheim got completely backwards. And so do most sociologists, Nico Wilterdink among them.

ROSEMARY HOPCROFT

I found reading Hopcroft's paper especially pleasurable for several important
reasons, not least of which is her contention that "as a set of macrosociological
orienting statements, it [DCT] is probably the best sociology has to offer." It is

seldom that one receives such praise, so I am going to bask in it for the short time that it is available. But Hopcroft's paper is also quite admirable because she is one of the few contemporary sociologists to have genuinely and fully embraced neo-Darwinian evolutionary theory, whether we call it sociobiology, evolutionary psychology, or Darwinian social science. Moreover, she knows what she is talking about. There are no mere caricatures or distortions here, but a real understanding of the key theoretical principles and how they can be put to use to understand many features of human social life, social and gender stratification and family relationships in particular. And Hopcroft has done something else well worth noting: She has taken a number of pieces of empirical sociological research that were never written from a Darwinian standpoint (or necessarily from any systematic theoretical standpoint at all) and shown how they are highly consistent with Darwinian principles: the importance of family and kin networks for personal physical and psychological well-being ("marriage is good for you"), the adverse psychological consequences of divorce for children, the greater parental solicitude of mothers compared to fathers because it is the human female that produces the rarer and more precious gamete, the greater likelihood of fathers compared to mothers disengaging from their children upon divorce, the different characteristics that men and women are looking for in their mates, the sexual double standard (in all likelihood a true cultural universal), the universal human drive for status and resources that results in sharp economic inequalities when socioecological conditions permit, and the virtual obsession that parents have with promoting the reproductive and productive careers of their children.

Hopcroft's list is long, but I am sure she would agree that were more space available to her it could have been much longer. There is also sociological research in other topical areas that is highly consistent with DCT. Hopcroft mentions Weeden's (2002) article on the role of occupational monopolies in producing higher incomes for professionals, and I quite agree. Indeed, the whole neo-Weberian tradition that emphasizes *social closure* is highly compatible with DCT (e.g., Parkin 1979; Murphy 1988), and to this I would even add theories like Edna Bonacich's (1972, 1979) split labor market theory of racial and ethnic antagonism, which was driven by a kind of neo-Marxism. (Strange bedfellows, don't you think, neo-Marxism and DCT? Quite interestingly, not always.)

Hopcroft says that my *Evolution of Human Sociality* is incomplete. Indeed, she is completely right, but then what book is not? Any book that covered its entire topic without any loose ends and nothing more of importance to be said would be either focused on an awfully trivial topic, or else written by someone of genius far exceeding the greatest scholarly geniuses the world has seen so far. So of course my book is incomplete. But Hopcroft has a solution: I should write another book in which I survey sociological knowledge of contemporary industrial societies and integrate this knowledge into my paradigm. Not only do I like this suggestion, but I fully intend to follow it. A few years from now I hope to begin writing a book tentatively entitled *Foundations of Darwinian Sociology: Steps to the Dream of a Final Theory*. This second book would do what Hopcroft is asking for, but it would go further: It would refine and expand DCT, update the discussions of existing topics, and apply the updated theory to phenomena not discussed in *The Evolution of Human Sociality* – especially religion and ethnicity, but possibly also conformity and deviance, organizations, law, art, music, literature, science, and even the microsociology of the self, norms, and roles. In this book I shall attempt the task of actually reinventing sociology. What unbelievable hubris! Can I be serious? Indeed, I am completely serious. Can it be done? Well, there can of course be no such thing as a truly final theory, but we can move toward one.

CHRISTOPH ANTWEILER

Antweiler's chapter is short but pithy and he raises a lot of useful points for discussion. I very much appreciate the fact that he notes that my DCT is a genuine explanatory theory. Indeed, that is precisely what it is intended to be. I follow the sociologist George Homans, who said that that is what theory is: Theory is explanation. Too often in sociology and the other social sciences we get concepts, typologies, and other conceptual schemes passed off as theories, but the identifying mark of a theory in science is that it explains (or offers an explanation).

Antweiler has a special interest in human universals, a topic that takes up much of his discussion. There is some inconsistency here. He starts by defining a human universal as a trait that is found in all societies, but then retreats from this by distinguishing between two kinds of universals, *diachronic* and *newly emergent* universals. I take it that so-called diachronic universals are "true" or "genuine" universals, that is, traits found in all known societies throughout prehistory and history. Newly emergent universals are traits, such as all-purpose money, that are universal to only one particular type of society, such as modern industrial society. I would caution against using the term universal in this way because it significantly weakens it. A universal is a trait that must be found in all known societies. This is a critical point, because if something is found in all places and times that is a fascinating fact which cries out for explanation. I think this explanation must be biological, or at least make reference to a biological predisposition. Antweiler, however, is not so sure, and in fact is critical of me for assuming that universals must always have biological explanations. But my response would be that, given the striking variations in human societies, the discovery of characteristics that every single society possesses strongly suggests to me the likelihood of a biological predisposition to create that characteristic. At the very least this provides us with a warrant to study the trait with this idea in mind.

Antweiler complains that my work almost completely ignores social institutions. This is not quite right. In *Social Transformations*, a book that Antweiler includes within the purview of his essay, I discuss several institutions, in particular economics and politics, but also education and science, and in *The Evolution of Human Sociality* there are ample discussions of economics, politics, and family and kinship. Antweiler is right to point out, though, that religion is completely neglected in these works, as are media. But I will be rectifying this situation in the years to come, as I am now engaged in a major project on the evolution of religion and eventually hope to take up the evolution of science, art, music, and literature.

KHALED HAKAMI

Hakami's chapter seems more like an academic version of a drive-by shooting than a closely reasoned critique. Mostly it is a series of blunders which show that its author is both an uninformed and a misinformed critic. I would summarize these blunders approximately as follows.

Blunder Number 1: Hakami thinks that the theoretical strategy I have called *evolutionary materialism* is a synthesis of two opposing strategies, cultural materialism and sociobiology. Certainly not. Evolutionary materialism is the strategy I developed over a dozen years ago to study long-term social evolution. It is not an opposing strategy to cultural materialism at all, but merely a modification of it along certain lines. The synthesis I created out of what are usually thought of as opposing strategies, cultural materialism and sociobiology, is *Darwinian conflict theory*, itself developed several years after evolutionary materialism and intended as a more general strategy that takes the principles of evolutionary materialism to a deeper level and grounds proximate explanations in ultimate explanations. Strangely, Hakami does not even use the name Darwinian conflict theory in his critique, and therefore does not really address it. He basically reduces me to "just one of those sociobiologists" and as a result distorts and grossly oversimplifies what is a much more nuanced and complex theoretical approach.

Blunder Number 2: Hakami uses the arguments of C. R. Hallpike to demolish the notion that Darwinian natural selectionist thinking can be applied directly to social evolution and criticizes me for failing to cite Hallpike. But, having done this, he then turns right around and *endorses* natural selectionist approaches to social evolution. This time he appeals to the authority of Robert Carneiro, quoting him to the effect that the concept of natural selection "is just as valid, fruitful, and essential in explaining cultural evolution as organic evolution" (Carneiro 1992, 117). Although this is bad enough, things get even worse. Hakami has quoted Carneiro completely out of context, because the article of Carneiro's that Hakami refers to *is mainly a critique of natural selectionist theories of social evolution*! We could hardly fault anyone for concluding that Hakami has made a total mess of this matter.

Blunder Number 3: Hakami contends that methodological individualism is wrong because no single Kwakiutl developed the potlatch, no single Kachin created a complex alliance system, and so on. Of course not, but such a preposterous claim has never been made or would ever be made by a methodological individualist.

Blunder Number 4 is Hakami's argument that hunter-gatherers are really gatherer-hunters. The most comprehensive survey of the proportions of meat and plant matter in the diets of foragers has been carried out by Carol Ember (1978) in an article of which Hakami appears ignorant. She shows that, although gathering may be more important than hunting in most *African* hunter-gatherers, *in the world as a whole* meat makes up a majority of the diet among foragers (cf. Sanderson 2001a, 260).

Blunder Number 5 is the claim that optimal foraging theory is based mainly on the study of nonhuman animals. Although optimal foraging theory is derived from evolutionary ecology and was originally based on studies of animal foraging patterns, it started to be applied to human foraging nearly thirty years ago and there is an extensive literature involving human applications, most of which supports the theory (cf. Sanderson 2001a, 260-64).

Blunder Number 6: Hakami contends that, although I was not a staunch sociobiologist at the time that I formulated evolutionary materialism, things have not changed. I thought the problem was that *things have changed*, and for the worse because now *I am* a staunch sociobiologist. Actually, this is really two blunders, because I have never been a staunch sociobiologist and am not one now. I am a Darwinian conflict theorist, which means that I make use of key sociobiological principles but go considerably beyond them. (I wonder, how many times do I have to repeat this point for some people?!)

In addition to these outright blunders, Hakami makes several other very dubious claims. For example, he argues that the members of hunter-gatherer societies are not more altruistic toward their offspring than towards other members of their bands. Not only is this untrue, but *in every known type of human society* humans are more altruistic toward kin than toward nonkin, and more altruistic toward close kin, especially offspring, than toward more distant kin. In addition, he attacks Marvin Harris by claiming that he was not a true evolutionist. He was a pseudoevolutionist who strung together a bunch of synchronic studies, calling the result a theory of social evolution, and he wrote only one book on social evolution, *Cannibals and Kings* (1977). This is a bit like saying that Darwin was not a real biological evolutionist because he made numerous observations in South America and the Galapagos Islands on present-day species, and, besides, he wrote only one important book on evolution, *On the Origin of Species*. Finally, Hakami avers that Harris and I are sitting in the same boat, which, if we put the biological baggage aside, is just cultural materialism. Actually, Marvin's boat was called the *Maddy Sue*, which he liked to sail off the coast of Maine, where he spent his summers. I knew Marvin only slightly, and certainly not well enough to be invited to sit beside him in his boat. Therefore, I have had to build my own boat, the name of which at least the other contributors to this volume know.

PETER MEYER

Meyer seems to be saying that I don't give enough emphasis to human cooperation as springing from a genuine feeling of sympathy, citing Adam Smith's famous discussion of natural human sympathy in his *The Theory of Moral Sentiments*. Even though I do not discuss Smith in *The Evolution of Human Sociality*,
I have no difficulty agreeing that the emotion of sympathy is an innate human
emotion, and that it is often extended beyond close kin or even distant kin; humans often feel sympathy for unrelated individuals, including those they have
never seen before. Let me try to clarify my position.

A careless mistake I made in formulating the theoretical propositions of
DCT was to have used the word "selfish" when what I meant was "self-
interested." This is an important distinction. I behave selfishly if, say, I have a
jar of black currant jam, my very favorite jam, which I dearly love, and I refuse
to share it with anyone. I either keep it out of sight or refuse to allow anyone to
have some of it upon request. All of us act selfishly from time to time, and some
of us act selfishly most of the time. But all of us all of the time act in accordance
with our self-interests. I have felt sympathy on many occasions for a number of
individuals, but in particular for my children. When they were still very young I
was deeply distressed when I saw that they were suffering in some way. Their
suffering was indeed my own suffering. My own mother many years ago explained that she had these same feelings; I understood her point at the time but
did not *feel* the force of it until I became a parent myself. So of course sympathy
is a primordial human emotion that drives much behavior, and of course people
cooperate with others because they want to and it gives them pleasure. Cooperation is not always the result of individuals making careful calculations of the
costs and benefits of cooperation and deciding accordingly. Natural selection
has built into us fundamental emotions of unselfish behavior, but these emotions
originally evolved because they benefited the individuals who felt them, at least
over the long run. Thus cooperation and altruism and grounded in individual
self-interest *at the ultimate level*.

Meyer also suggests that I am too much of a materialist, a criticism of me
made many times by many scholars, including Nico Wilterdink, as we just saw,
and Heinz-Jürgen Niedenzu, as we shall soon see. But I am completely unre-
pentant. Meyer suggests in particular that "mentalistic approaches" are fully
compatible with evolutionary theory and that I should be more open to them.
However, he does not explain what he means by "mentalistic." This can mean
two very distinct things. First, it can refer to those things that Marx and the
Marxian materialists (and Marvin Harris as well) place in the ideological superstructure: beliefs, values, philosophies, art, literature, religion, and so on. Or it
can be used very differently to refer to the basic mental architecture of the brain.
I believe that it is this second meaning that Meyer intends. If so, I fully agree
with him, but I would not use the term "mentalistic" in this case because the
brain is about as materialistic a structure as can be found. Just as the heart is a
material object or structure, so is the brain; both are parts of the body. Brain

functioning involves billions of neurons and their synapses and the transmission of neurochemical messages across those synapses. So if this is the meaning of mental, than I am all for mental, and of course this kind of mental is perfectly compatible with evolutionary theory. But this mental is material, and it evolved by natural selection because it benefited the organisms that contained it.

HEINZ-JÜRGEN NIEDENZU

Niedenzu alleges that the central problem with my DCT is that it does not give any systematic role to human constructivity and creativity; correlatively, it makes ecomaterialist and polimaterialist explanations dependent on biomaterialist explanations and, as such, derivative. Let me address each of these concerns.

Niedenzu acknowledges that I do not deny the reality of human constructivity, but he apparently feels that I underplay it. As I read and reread his chapter, I came to the conclusion that his central concern is to make human constructivity *autonomous* from human biology. This is an argument that has been made many times by social scientists ever since the beginnings of social science, and most humanists would make it even more strongly, denying the biological organism any role at all. I do not think that it works, however, and I doubt that there can be any such thing as *pure constructivity* or *pure creativity* entirely free from biological constraints, either in the case of individuals taken alone or in the case of groups of individuals taken as collectivities. In this regard I suppose I am a firm determinist.

Several major realms of human creativity are literature, art, and religion. Because space is short, let me limit myself to the last of these. At the moment I am working on the long-term evolution of religion, with a special focus on the evolution of the major world religions during the Axial Age (the last six centuries BCE). All of the new religions that developed during this time were very different in several crucial ways from the polytheistic state religions that preceded them, and yet they were very similar to each other, especially in their conception of *a transcendent reality*. It is remarkable that throughout much of the Old World very similar religions arose in a very concentrated period of time, even though it is not likely that these religions had much direct influence on each other (Bentley 1993). Where did the new religious ideas come from? As Max Weber has argued, such ideas spring from religious virtuosi, individuals who have special religious skills and insights. I accept this, but would add that such individuals are quite likely persons with a very unusual brain organization, probably combined with special social experiences. And then of course the ideas have to be accepted – have to resonate with and catch on among the masses. This suggests another kind of determinism, viz., the right kinds of socioecological conditions that would make such ideas attractive. Currently I am trying to identify what these conditions most likely would have been (Sanderson 2007d, 2008).

So I think it is doubtful that human constructivity and creativity are ever autonomous. They only appear autonomous because we have not yet been able to identify the conditions under which the various forms of constructivity and creativity emerge, both in the special brain organization of uniquely creative individuals and in the socioecological conditions that make entire groups or societies receptive to creative thoughts. This of course makes me appear to be a very hard-headed determinist, but I think such a view will be vindicated in the end, although how long it will be before we reach that end is very difficult to say. It also makes me a resolute antidualist, since I would contend that ideas can only reside in the brain, whether one brain, several, or many. (If they are not in the brain and derivative from it, *where on earth could they possibly be*?) And why do I myself take such stances? Are they purely creative constructions? This is doubtful. Ever since I was a small boy I always thought in very scientific, materialist ways and had little interest in those things that preoccupy the humanists. My brain is probably wired such that the left hemisphere is highly dominant over the right. Science is quite easy for me and extremely interesting to me, whereas art has always been mostly a complete mystery.

Let me conclude by addressing Niedenzu's point that DCT makes ecomaterialist and polimaterialist explanations derivative. This is true only in the most general sense that such explanations must refer back in some way to the human organism and its nature. Actually, in most of my work I have given ecomaterialist and polimaterialist explanations pride of place. In the first edition of my book *Social Transformations* (Sanderson 1995), which presents a general theory of social evolution, such explanations occupy the entire theoretical space. In the second edition of the same book (Sanderson 1999a), I added an Afterword in which I discussed the role of biological *constraints* on social evolution. Niedenzu is surely right when he says that social evolution cannot be reduced to and is in many ways quite different from biological evolution. I could not agree more (cf. Sanderson 2007c, 287-90). In 2005 I published two books, *World Societies: The Evolution of Human Social Life* (coauthored with Arthur Alderson) and *Revolutions: A Worldwide Introduction to Political and Social Change*. Neither of these books makes any reference whatsoever to humans as biological organisms. The explanations found in *World Societies* are mostly ecomaterialist in the broadest sense (ones that invoke demographic, ecological, economic, and technological conditions), and the explanations emphasized in *Revolutions* are largely polimaterialist.

In the end, whether our explanations are to be biomaterialist, ecomaterialist, or polimaterialist (or some combination of these) depends mostly on what it is we are trying to explain and on how fine-grained a level. Although all ecomaterialist and polimaterialist explanations have to be grounded in human biology, such explanations are often quite fundamental and much more than merely derivative.

TAMÁS MELEGHY

Meleghy wishes to advance Lévi-Strauss's structuralist theoretical agenda by adding to it the principle of inclusive fitness. I quite agree with Meleghy's argument that in matrilineal societies the greater investment of men in their sisters' offspring than in their own offspring makes sense in terms of higher levels of paternity uncertainty. In preliminary research I did a few years ago, and as yet unpublished, I used a cross-cultural sample of 60 preindustrial societies and cross-tabulated a measure of paternity certainty with a society's mode of descent. I found that 92 percent of matrilineal societies had low paternity certainty compared to 20 percent of bilateral societies and just 18 percent of patrilineal societies. I conclude that matrilineal descent should basically be conceptualized as a strategy of investment by men in their sisters' offspring whereas patrilineal descent should be conceptualized as a strategy of men's investment in their wives' offspring. And matrilineal descent is a lot less common than patrilineal descent because men have fairly high levels of paternity confidence in most societies.

To me this is a satisfying explanation, but Meleghy doesn't want to stop there. He wants to tack this onto Lévi-Strauss's basic explanation of exogamy rules, which he takes to be based on a fundamental law of reciprocal exchange. However, there are at least three problems with this recommendation. First, as Marvin Harris (1979) has pointed out, the empirical evidence strongly contradicts this so-called law. As he says, reciprocal exchange is "the basis of marriage systems only in egalitarian societies. To the degree that a society is stratified into politically and economically superordinate and subordinate groups, marriage systems function to prevent reciprocal exchange" (1979, 173). Exogamy rules have much more to do with whom one may *not* marry than with some sort of reciprocal relationship between groups. Of 752 societies in Murdock's *Ethnographic Atlas* known to practice exogamy, only 188 (or 25%) have any of the forms of preferential cross-cousin marriage discussed by Lévi-Strauss, and reciprocal exchange of marriage partners is not found in all of these.

Second, the paternity confidence explanation is itself probably a sufficient explanation of matrilineal descent, and therefore I recommend that we use Occam's Razor and discard all unnecessary concepts or hypotheses. Third, trying to mix the idea of reciprocal exchange with the idea of inclusive fitness produces, at least in this particular case, theoretical incoherence. Meleghy contends that reciprocal exchange is for Lévi-Strauss a fundamental principle of human thought that is genetically fixed. There does seem to be a universal human sense of reciprocity that is part of the basic human sense of fairness, but this is a notion that applies to the moral sense rather than to marriage practices. Meleghy imagines that Lévi-Strauss's "law of reciprocal exchange" is essentially a kind of biomaterialist principle that fits well within DCT. But what Lévi-Strauss is talking about is utterly alien to DCT and unsynthesizable with it.

JOHAN VAN DER DENNEN

The focus of van der Dennen's chapter is my Darwinian conflict analysis of war. Let me say at the outset that war is one of the phenomena discussed in *The Evolution of Human Sociality* that I have studied the least and concerning which I am least knowledgeable. I have much more to learn, and I hope to accomplish that in the years to come. However, I suspect that any changes in my viewpoint with be matters of detail and nuance rather than any fundamental change of perspective.

Van der Dennen says that I do not distinguish between genocidal wars, instrumental (coercive) wars, and ritualized wars, and that I also fail to distinguish between ambush-like or raiding warfare and disciplined, phalanx-like warfare. He is right, I do not, at least in those terms. I doubt that there is any such thing as ritualized war, despite the claims of some anthropologists. War is much too serious a business for that. I certainly recognize genocidal wars, but were I to discuss them and try to explain them I would do so under the heading of ethnic conflict. I am not sure what van der Dennen means by instrumental or coercive wars. As for ambush-like war versus combat-type warfare, I certainly recognize the distinction even if I do not use that specific language. My discussion of tribal warfare is basically a discussion of ambush-like war. Combat-type warfare is characteristic of chiefdoms and, especially, states, and I offer a very different explanation for it. This type of warfare is devoted primarily to political conquest of other societies, the main purpose of which is economic gain – of land, resources, tribute, slaves and other types of coerced workers, and so on. In this connection van der Dennen contends that I have fallen victim to the "great war figures hoax." It may well be true that numerous scholars have overestimated the number of war deaths in agrarian states and empires, but there can be no serious doubt that war is perhaps the single most important activity pursued by the rulers of these kinds of political systems (cf. Kautsky 1982; Snooks 1996, 1998).

What then of van der Dennen's own preferred explanations of war in all of its varieties? He is not easy to pin down. He seems to object to all types of materialist explanations (regarding them as "vulgar") and even criticizes Brian Ferguson for claiming that the desire for security or safety is a material desire. But what on earth could be more material than one's own physical safety? Is one's living body not a material object? Van der Dennen objects to single-factor explanations, regarding them as too simplistic. I read him as a type of eclectic who wishes to entertain a wide range of explanations.

However, in the concluding section of his paper he claims that the most important proximate cause of war is fear. People fight with neighboring bands and villages primarily because they are afraid of them and wish to protect themselves against their own extermination. The problem with this explanation is that it begs a crucial question: Why should people fear being exterminated by their neighbors? Is it because *they have good reason to fear the intentions of their neighbors* and, if so, is this because *their neighbors have acquired a reputation for belligerence*? We are thus right back where we started from: The fear of attack by neighbors does not explain anything so much as it must itself be explained. Societies at all levels of political complexity often fear their neighbors because they have something to fear.

C. R. HALLPIKE

I read Hallpike's chapter with great interest and enjoyed it in spite of the fact that he is not the least bit sympathetic to any of my ideas – or at least to what he presumes them to be. Hallpike is an antimaterialist and anti-Darwinian. He is supremely antagonistic to applying Darwinian thinking to social life, either in terms of sociobiological principles or as "variation-and-selective-retention" theories of social evolution. Hallpike is, nonetheless, an evolutionist, and he has written a whole book on the subject entitled *The Principles of Social Evolution* (1986). But he turns out to embrace a type of evolutionism that is of the cultural idealist variety. Unlike most social evolutionists, Hallpike rejects the concept of adaptation as useful, especially when applied to preliterate bands and tribes. Such societies, he contends, are under little or no pressure to produce social arrangements that are highly adaptive; just about anything is workable for people living at this "cognitively undemanding" level, and the "survival of the mediocre" rather than the survival of the fittest is the order of the day. It is societies at more advanced levels of sociopolitical organization that are under much greater pressure to produce adaptive solutions to the problems they face. I rather think that the evidence is overwhelmingly against Hallpike's notion that competitive pressures are mild in bands and tribes. Indeed, the evidence, much of it reviewed in *The Evolution of Human Sociality*, seems to point in exactly the opposite direction: Competitive pressures in terms of the struggle for survival and the competition for mates are actually *more intense* in these types of societies than in others.

So it is not difficult to see why Hallpike would strenuously object to both my evolutionary materialism and my DCT. In his contribution to this volume, he uses the example of the development of science, especially modern science, to refute me. I have written very little on science (cf. Sanderson 1988, 410-31, 1999a, 317-32), and, truth be told, this is one of the most difficult of all social phenomena to explain from a biomaterialist or an ecomaterialist perspective. The human brain is not exactly "wired for science" in the strict sense of devising hypotheses and submitting them to demanding empirical tests. Only a small number of people have either the necessary brainpower or the capacity for objective and dispassionate reasoning that science requires, and there are several biases of the human mind that seem to be a real hindrance to scientific understanding (e.g., the strong tendencies toward teleological and essentialist thinking, the tendency to attribute agency not only to individuals but also to other animals and even to inanimate objects or forces).

What then of ecomaterialist explanations of science? Hallpike contends that our biological needs do not exert a constant pressure for invention. He is indeed correct so long as we note the qualification "constant." I have never asserted otherwise. Throughout history and prehistory inventions have come in fits and starts, and there are long periods where little is happening. And of course I recognize that there was a tendency for technological invention to stagnate in the ancient world, and for the very reason that Hallpike gives: the dominance of parasitic aristocratic classes that valued brain work and devalued practical knowledge and that did not stand to benefit economically from technological advance. I also agree with Hallpike concerning many of the preconditions for the development of modern science and industrial technology, in particular the shift from a feudal to a capitalist economic system in which the dominant capitalist class, unlike ancient aristocratic landowners, could benefit enormously from the technological applications modern science made possible. These conditions came together in the seventeenth century, which is really the takeoff point for the development of modern science. And Hallpike is surely right to suggest that it took the buildup of many historical antecedents to provide a foundation for this takeoff point.

Hallpike seems to think that science is largely a matter of smart people thinking smart thoughts, and that both scientific advance and its corollary, technological advance, have little to do with biological or economic needs. But Hallpike's historical vision is remarkably compressed: He focuses almost exclusively on the last few centuries, which constitute a very unusual period. He either ignores earlier technological advances or sees them as having little or no practical significance. He contends that the development of metallurgy, for example, was stimulated by ornamental rather than practical needs. Perhaps, but the new metals were quickly put to use in the development of more sophisticated tools and weapons, first of bronze and then of iron. Hallpike makes no reference at all to the invention of the plow, which was first a wooden plow and then later came to be made of metals. This was an enormously practical invention, and was indeed developed for "materialistic" reasons (Pryor 1985), mainly the need for greater economic productivity to feed expanding populations. Nor does Hallpike make any reference to the great transition from hunting and gathering to early agriculture beginning about 10,000-11,000 years ago and occurring largely independently all over the world. Archaeologists used to think of this as the result of a smart person thinking a smart thought, whose smart idea then spread, but this theory has now been almost totally abandoned in favor of theories emphasizing the role of population pressure and ecological change. The transition to agriculture was a "materialistic" process if ever there were one.

Hallpike is surely right when he suggests that "nature does not merely impose itself on our senses," but must be interrogated. This volume alone is proof of that, since there is wide disagreement among many of the contributors on how to interpret a wide range of empirical data, and indeed on whether these data are "facts." But I have never suggested that scientists merely look at nature and then know how to explain it. When Hallpike quotes me as saying that "the empirical world acts as a powerful constraint on scientific beliefs" he fails to mention the context of that quotation. In making that statement I was arguing against the postmodernists, who claim that science is a largely social or political process in which empirical evidence plays no important role.

Hallpike concludes his chapter by saying that the origins of such modern inventions as steam power and electricity entirely contradict any ecomaterialist explanation. But they do not, since such inventions occurred within a new economic context, that of capitalism, and in fact in the second half of the seventeenth century more than half of the scientific investigations undertaken by members of the British Royal Society were directly or indirectly stimulated by economic concerns (Merton 1957). The ups and downs of scientific advance actually closely track the ups and downs of commercialism. Ancient Greek science arose within one of the world's first highly commercialized civilizations, and the bursts of scientific activity in the Arab world and in China between approximately the eighth and fourteenth centuries seem to have been closely tied to commercial expansion. Chinese science, in fact, was much less theoretical than either Arabic science or later Western science, having preponderantly practical and technological aims (Huff 1993).

It is important in this connection to distinguish two different dimensions of scientific activity and the motivations that underlie them. Many scientists themselves are often purely intellectual in their concerns; they are interested only in how the world works. But science requires patronage, else it cannot proceed very far, and patronage requires wealth and a belief on the part of the patrons that scientific findings will have important technological spinoffs. When I originally classified science as part of the superstructure, I was thinking only of this first dimension of science: the concepts and theories. But the rest of science might well be considered part of the ecostructure, since that part is technological knowledge. This is another emendation in DCT to be made in a future installment.

J. P. ROOS

Roos's extremely important article shows conclusively what I myself have been learning over the past couple of years, namely, that Edward Westermarck was a major classical sociologist whose thinking was both deep and broad and whose ideas are turning out to be much more empirically accurate than those of his leading rival, Émile Durkheim. I have known of Westermarck for years, but until recently I thought he was only important for his theory of incest avoidance, which is turning out to be extremely well supported by numerous lines of empirical evidence. But Westermarck did more than that – much more! As Roos points out, he had a well-developed theory of moral emotions rooted in Darwinian principles, and he contributed many insights regarding a wide range of marriage and family patterns. And methodologically Westermarck was vastly superior to Durkheim in that he drew on a far greater range of historical and ethnographic data.

The only reservation I have about Roos's chapter is his strong claim that on every important issue where Westermarck and Durkheim disagreed Westermarck got it right and Durkheim wrong. I suspect that this is largely true, but Roos does not present any real evidence to document his claim. With respect to incest avoidance, there is now a great deal of evidence to support Westermarck, whereas Durkheim's argument is completely speculative and, in fact, highly implausible. And concerning morality, there is now a rapidly growing literature on the evolution of the moral sense that is highly consistent with Westermarck (e.g., Arnhart 1998; de Waal 2006; Hauser 2006), and that even acknowledges his work on the moral emotions. But these are only two issues. What of all of the other issues that both thinkers investigated and theorized about? Even though I suspect that Westermarck will have gotten the better of Durkheim on most of these, all the evidence is not yet in. Durkheim didn't get everything wrong. His analysis of suicide was a meticulous piece of first-rate sociological research and there is little doubt that suicide rates and levels of social cohesion are related. And Westermarck didn't get everything right. For example, he was highly critical of Darwin on sexual selection, and yet this is turning out to be one of Darwin's most important ideas. So the jury is still out concerning whether Westermarck got the better of Durkheim on *all* major issues.

ANNA ROTKIRCH

Anna Rotkirch's chapter on baby fever is fascinating and brimming with insights. Prior to reading her paper I had never heard of the term "baby fever," but I immediately recognized the phenomenon she is discussing because I have observed a number of instances of it among friends and acquaintances. And consider the following much more public examples. Recently a book entitled *Baby Love* was published by the well-known writer Rebecca Walker (2007). Walker, a feminist, explains that in her 20s and early 30s she had a strong desire to have a child but put this urge aside in order to concentrate on her career. Finally, in her mid-30s, she gave in to her desire, became pregnant, and gave birth. About the same time, one of the actresses on the popular American television program *Desperate Housewives* gave birth to her first child in her mid-40s and described her new motherhood as the greatest experience of her life. And two or three years ago the long-running American news program *60 Minutes* featured a segment about four women who were apparently extremely talented and educated at some of the United States's finest universities only to abandon their professional careers completely in order to stay home full-time with their children. All four women told the interviewer, Lesley Stahl, that they fully intended to remain home with their children full-time and had no plans to resume their careers. (Predictably, they were then chastised for their "wrong" choice by a prominent feminist that Stahl later interviewed!)

A central concern of Rotkirch's paper is why people have children. Why do they? For a long time I endorsed the view of such scholars as Marvin Harris

(1989; Harris and Ross 1987) and Ester Boserup (1981) that people have them largely for their economic benefits. However, in research I did a number of years ago, I discovered that the economic value of children's labor seemed to make little if any difference in why people in some societies have many and in other societies have few (Sanderson and Dubrow 2000; Sanderson 2001d). Moreover, if the economic utility hypothesis were true people in modern affluent societies should not have so much as a single child since children are extremely costly in such societies and provide virtually no economic benefits at all to the vast majority of parents. And yet people continue to have children, and I suspect the reason is Darwinian: People have offspring because that is what they have been designed by nature to do. Of course, how many they have is very sensitive to environmental cues, especially the survival rate of infants and young children.

Rotkirch distinguishes four kinds or "levels" of explanation of childbearing and fertility, and she calls my explanation a population level explanation. Actually, it is more correctly labeled a household (or even individual) level explanation. It is individuals, usually within households, who make decisions about childbearing, and what happens at the population level is simply the aggregate effect of individual choices. So this is part of the answer to Rotkirch's question as to whether my explanation applies to the other levels. Yes – to all of them. Rotkirch also refers to the so-called fertility opportunity hypothesis, suggesting that it contradicts other explanations, which predict that increased wealth leads to declining fertility. But I don't think there is necessarily any contradiction, because it depends on how much wealth and on the circumstances under which wealth may be increasing. In Western industrial societies after World War II, in the United States in particular, there ensued a period of great and rapidly growing economic affluence, and this was associated with the famous "baby boom." Working-class and middle-class people were able to increase their fertility because of a rather sudden and unexpected affluence, and the baby boom only lasted about ten years before fertility leveled off and began to decline. The fertility opportunity hypothesis may be simply a special case of a more general phenomenon. (The fact that people previously of limited means may have more children during a period of sudden affluence means that the economic argument is not totally without merit. But again, this is a special case, not a general phenomenon.)

In her concluding section Rotkirch says that human fertility decisions are highly sensitive to environmental cues, especially levels of infant and child mortality and the availability of economic resources. She is exactly right, and Sarah Blaffer Hrdy's wonderful book *Mother Nature* (1999), which Rotkirch discusses, exemplifies this beautifully. Human males and females are primed for reproduction and parenthood, but they seem to be exquisitely sensitive, often in unconscious ways, to a broad range of environmental contingencies that make producing (or not producing) children a good (or bad) bet, and that help to determine the number of children it is optimal to have. Hrdy's book is highly compatible with DCT and in fact can actually be regarded as a type of Darwinian conflict analysis. This shows once again what I said earlier in my replies to Wilterdink and Niedenzu: DCT presents no simplistic biological determinism, but on the contrary takes full account of a host of socioecological conditions that interact with the evolved psychology of the brain to generate specific patterns of behavior at various times and places. I find that one cannot emphasize this too much, and I am extremely pleased to see that Rotkirch is someone who is already fully aware of it.

FRANK SALTER

Frank Salter's contribution is especially welcome for a variety of reasons, but mainly because he dares to violate what Charles Murray (2005) calls "the inequality taboo": the injunction against assuming that individuals are anything but the same in their propensities and abilities. As such, Salter provides a very useful counterpoint to the standard sociological wisdom that individual achievement and social mobility have no genetic basis. But Salter is no genetic determinist: Although rejecting pure environmentalist theories as inadequate because they are one-sided and contradicted by much evidence, he opts for a genetic-environmental interactionism that, I think, is what the evidence tells us is happening. Salter identifies his theory as a Darwinian conflict theory, and I accept this without reservation. DCT is a broad theoretical and research strategy that permits numerous theories of stratification and individual outcomes in industrial societies. I also accept Salter's contention that I myself have not really developed a Darwinian conflict analysis of modern industrial stratification systems. This is indeed true, and I have always considered this a lacuna that has needed to be filled. I am very grateful to Salter for starting the ball rolling, and perhaps at some future point I can extend what he has started.

I was pleased to see Salter refer to François Nielsen's (2006) important behavior genetic study showing a very large genetic effect on several measures of individual achievement, a moderate effect for unshared environment, and a quite small (sometimes vanishingly small) effect for shared environment. I also think Salter should be congratulated for actually using his own understanding of DCT to provide a set of recommendations – a sort of "user's manual" – regarding the mate choice strategies most likely to produce high levels of success down through the generations. One of his recommendations is: "Parents should encourage children to choose spouses with genealogical evidence of distinction in activities related to resource acquisition." Indeed, the evidence shows that many parents do this already.

W. G. RUNCIMAN

It is instructive to compare Runciman with Hallpike because they have radically opposing perspectives and have recently engaged in some heated disputations

(Hallpike 1999, 2000; Runciman 1999, 2001). Hallpike, of course, rejects entirely the very project in which Runciman has been engaged for over twenty
years, that of a "variation-and-selective-retention" model of social evolution. He
contends that "such basic Darwinian concepts as the unit of selection, fitness,
adaptation, competition, and mutation are irrelevant to social evolution." I agree
with some of this. Hallpike is right that in social evolution there is no unit of social reproduction that is equivalent to the gene, and also that in evolutionary biology the concept of fitness is a statistical concept that has no close parallel in
social life. There is also a disanalogy regarding the source of variation, which in
evolutionary biology is random genetic mutation but in social life is much more
likely to be purposive invention. Hallpike is quite critical of the concept of
memes as well (a concept endorsed by Runciman), seeing it as a nebulous concept that adds little or nothing to our understanding. It is, he says, a search for
the elementary building blocks of culture that is ultimately futile, a contention
with which I completely agree. Of course, as already noted, I part company with
Hallpike regarding the usefulness of the concepts of competition and adaptation
since these are critical elements of DCT. Here I am very much on Runciman's
side.

In fact, despite the critical remarks above, I have long been an admirer of
several features of Runciman's treatment of social evolution in the second volume of his *Treatise on Social Theory* (Runciman 1989, 285-450). In addition to
being an adaptationist, he brings to the table an excellent command of historical
and comparative materials, especially on the ancient world, and he gives us a
theory of social evolution that is explicitly a kind of conflict theory in its focus
on the selection of social practices that will be advantageous to dominant social
groups. Elsewhere (Sanderson 2007c) I have discussed what I feel is the main
difficulty with Runciman's approach to social evolution, viz., its tendency to offer explanations that, although in many instances likely to be correct, remain
empirically underdetermined and dangerously close to being "just-so stories."

Now what of Runciman's essay in the present volume? This essay seems to
set forth two main arguments. The first is his contention that there was a second
major transition in human sociality that followed the transition from nature to
culture, which is *the transition from culture to society*. This second transition,
allegedly occurring around 10,000 to 12,000 years ago, involved the emergence
of a new form of human sociality involving roles and institutions. Prior to this
time, Runicman contends, humans were cultural animals and lived in societies,
but these societies had no "positions in a multidimensional social space whose
incumbents are required to act consistently and predictably in consequence of
the rule-governed practices which define them"; in other words, they had no
roles, and thus no institutions as complexes of roles. But how could Runciman
possibly know that there were no roles or institutions when everyone was still
living by hunting and gathering? It would be exceedingly difficult to infer the
absence of roles and institutions from archaeological materials alone. In any
event, I very strongly doubt this because the period between 10,000 and 12,000

years ago marked the beginnings of the first transition to agricultural (horticul-tural) societies, and these early cultivating societies were only slightly more dif-ferentiated than their hunter-gatherer predecessors, a fact that provides little warrant for assuming some qualitatively new form of sociality. Besides, ethno-graphies of surviving hunter-gatherers reveal that they have roles and institu-tions, and thus there is a strong presumptive case that earlier hunter-gatherers would have had them too.

The other major idea in Runciman's chapter is the notion of *evolutionary dead-ends*. The example he gives is the Archaic Greek *polis*, an example that he discussed at greater length in his *Treatise on Social Theory*. There are indeed dead-ends in social evolution just as there are in biological evolution, but what Runciman is calling a dead-end seems to me more like a preparatory stage or even a "preadaptation." The Greek *polis* was not a dead-end but a way-station on the path to a more developed state. Runciman has also referred to Melanesian "big man" societies as dead-ends, but they were not dead-ends at all. They did not lead to an evolutionary cul-de-sac, which is what a dead-end would be, but rather to further social evolution, in this case the chiefdom. A much better ex-ample of an evolutionary dead-end would be twentieth-century Communism, an utter ruin that has had to be completely dismantled (although only partially so in the cases of China and Vietnam) before any further social evolution could pro-ceed. This was perhaps the greatest evolutionary dead-end in all of human his-tory.

PETER HEJL

Hejl's chapter reveals that he is by and large a sympathetic critic. His most im-portant criticism is that my DCT omits human communication and is therefore missing a vital element. He is certainly correct that I simply assume human communication rather than explicitly consider it. I must plead guilty. How seri-ous an omission this is I am uncertain, but when I get around to reworking and updating my DCT in that second book that Rosemary Hopcroft wants me to write, I will seek to look into some of the important literature and see what I can come up with.

In his discussion of the media of communication Hejl distinguishes three types, which he calls *primary, secondary,* and *tertiary* media. I take him to mean by primary media of communication the use of language in face-to-face interac-tion, as well as the use of nonlinguistic modes of communication: visual, olfac-tory, gustatory, tactile, and acoustical. By secondary media he means "the repre-sentation of knowledge by objects outside human memory," in particular writing. Here Hejl refers to the work of the anthropologist Jack Goody, which shows that dramatic social consequences followed the invention of writing. The general point is undoubtedly correct. Indeed, in recent research that I have undertaken on the long-term evolution of religion (Roberts and Sanderson 2005), my collaborator and I found that writing was a critical prerequisite to the development of ecclesiastical religions of the monotheistic variety.

Tertiary media for Hejl include such modern inventions as the telegraph, telephone, phonograph, film, radio, and television. He seems to be making the point that these new media produced dramatic consequences, and who could seriously disagree with that. But let me add an example of my own of a less obvious consequence. Many years ago I happened to read a book entitled *Teaching as a Conserving Activity*, written by Neil Postman (1979). One of the things I learned, much to my surprise and delight, was that there was a field called *media ecology*, and that Postman was apparently one of this field's leading practitioners. Postman defined media ecology as "the study of information environments," and went on to say that the field "is concerned to understand how technologies and techniques of communication control the form, quantity, speed, distribution, and direction of information; and how, in turn, such information configurations or biases affect people's perceptions, values, and attitudes." Postman was highly critical of certain pedagogic practices that had begun to enter higher education, especially the use of television videos and films in the classroom. He argued that modern television, film, and electronic media had already had dramatically negative effects on students' abilities to read the printed word and that the last thing university professors should be doing was allying themselves with these modern media. As an example, he mentioned the National Education Association's giving an award to the originator of the children's television program *Sesame Street*, noting that what it teaches is the same thing that Burger King commercials teach!

Postman was writing these things nearly thirty years ago, but the situation is far worse today. People wonder why today's college students cannot read or think at appropriate levels, but it has never been much of a mystery to me. From an early age they are inundated by tertiary media that have come to replace the secondary medium of the printed word. Reading and writing are hard work that do not come naturally to humans because writing is only 5,000 years old at best; in the ancestral environment it did not exist, and therefore there would have been no selective pressures exerted on people's ability to read or write. But television and film watching, highly passive activities, are much less cognitively demanding, and so young people quickly gravitate to them and after considerable exposure learn to dislike reading and writing. Most undergraduate students today cannot read anything of any degree of sophistication at all, cannot dissect or make intelligent arguments, and cannot write coherent sentences let alone entire paragraphs or essays. All of this is mostly the effect of the new tertiary media that dominate our communicative world. I believe that this is a good example of one of the major arguments that Hejl is making. The question is, with the massive technological changes that are now occurring, what is waiting for us several decades down the road? Actually, I don't think I want to know.

CONCLUSION

In conclusion, let me simply reiterate what I said at the beginning of this reply: I am delighted to have had this opportunity to engage a number of Western sociologists on key issues of mutual concern. Evolutionary sociology is still in its infancy, but I hope this volume will go some way toward launching it into its early childhood. We are still a long way from evolutionary sociology's adolescence and adulthood, but at least we are starting to take the necessary steps to get there.

REFERENCES

Abernethy, Virginia D. (1999). "A Darwinian Account of the Fertility Opportunity Hypothesis." *Population and Environment* 21:119-48.

Adams, Richard Niebold (1988). *The Eighth Day: Social Evolution as the Self-Organization of Energy.* Austin: University of Texas Press.

Aiello, Leslie C., and Robin I. M. Dunbar (1993). "Neocortex Size, Group Size, and the Evolution of Language." *Current Anthropology* 34:184-93.

Ala-Risku, Päivi (2005). "Nicole Kidman haluaa miehen ja vauvan." *Anna* 20.10:54-56.

Albert, Hans (1999). "Die Soziologie und das Problem der Einheit der Wissenschaften." *Zeitschrift fur Soziologie und Sozialpsychologie* 51:215-32.

Alexander Richard D. (1986). "Ostracism and Indirect Reciprocity: The Reproductive Significance of Humor." Pp. 105-22 in *Ostracism: A Social and Biological Phenomenon,* ed. Margaret Gruter and Roger D. Masters. New York: Elsevier.

Amato, Paul R., and Jacob Cheadle (2005). "The Long Reach of Divorce: Divorce and Child Well-being across Three Generations." *Journal of Marriage and the Family* 67:191-206.

Antweiler, Christoph (1985). "Das Einzige und die vielen Gesichter kultureller Evolution." *Anthropos* 80:483-506.

―――― (1988). *Kulturevolution als transgenerationaler Wandel. Zur neueren angloamerikanischen Diskussion um sogenannte "kulturelle Selektion."* Berlin: Dietrich Reimer.

―――― (2005). "Social Evolution Revisited." *Anthropos* 100:233-40.

―――― (2007). *Was ist den Menschen gemeinsam? Über Kultur und Kulturen.* Darmstadt: Wissenschaftliche Buchgesellschaft.

Antweiler, Christoph, and Richard Niebold Adams, eds. (1991). *Social Reproduction, Cultural Selection, and the Evolution of Social Evolution.* Leiden: E. J. Brill. (Special issue of *Cultural Dynamics,* vol. 4, no. 2.)

Arnhart, Larry (1998). *Darwinian Natural Right: The Biological Ethics of Human Nature.* Albany: State University of New York Press.

Aschke, Manfred (2002). *Kommunikation, Koordination und soziales System. Theoretische Grundlagen für die Erklärung der Evolution von Kultur und Gesellschaft.* Stuttgart: Lucius & Lucius.

Avital, Eytan, and Eva Jablonka (2000). *Animal Traditions: Behavioural Inheritance in Evolution.* Cambridge, UK: Cambridge University Press.

Axelrod, Robert (1984). *The Evolution of Cooperation.* New York: Basic Books.

Badcock, Christopher (1991). *Evolution and Individual Behavior.* Oxford: Blackwell.

Baldus, Bernd (2002). "Darwin und die Soziologie. Kontingenz, Aktion, und Struktur im menschlichen Sozialverhalten." *Zeitschrift für Soziologie* 31:316-31.

Barkow, Jerome H., and N. Burley (1980). "Human Fertility, Evolutionary Biology, and the Demographic Transition." *Ethology and Sociobiology* 1:163-80.

Barkow, Jerome H. (1992). "Beneath New Culture Is Old Psychology: Gossip and Social Stratification." Pp. 627-37 in *The Adapted Mind,* ed. Jerome H. Barkow, Leda Cosmides, and John Tooby. New York: Oxford University Press.

Barkow Jerome H., Leda Cosmides, and John Tooby, eds. (1992). *The Adapted Mind: Evolutionary Psychology and the Generation of Culture*. New York: Oxford University Press.

Barner-Barry, Carol (1986). "Ethological Methods in the Study of Basic Types of Political Behavior." Pp. 133-47 in *Ostracism: A Social and Biological Phenomenon*, ed. Margaret Gruter and Roger D. Masters. New York: Elsevier.

Barrett, Louise, Robin I. M. Dunbar, and John Lycett (2002). *Human Evolutionary Psychology*. London: Palgrave.

Beauchamp, Guy (1994). "The Functional Analysis of Human Fertility Decisions." *Ethology and Sociobiology* 15:31-53.

Becker, Gary S. (1981). *A Treatise on the Family*. Cambridge, MA: Harvard University Press.

Bellah, Robert (1964). "Religious Evolution." *American Sociological Review* 29:358-74.

Belsky, Jay, Laurence Steinberg, and Patricia Draper (1991). "Childhood Experience, Interpersonal Development, and Reproductive Strategy: An Evolutionary Theory of Socialization." *Child Development* 62:647-70.

Bentley, Jerry (1993). *Old World Encounters: Cross-Cultural Contacts and Exchanges in Pre-Modern Times*. New York: Oxford University Press.

Bergesen, Albert J. (2004). "Durkheim's Theory of Mental Categories: A Review of Evidence." *Annual Review of Sociology* 30:395-408.

Berghaus, Margot (1994). "Wohlgefallen am Fernsehen." *Publizistik* 39:141-60.

Betzig, Laura (1986). *Despotism and Differential Reproduction: A Darwinian View of History*. New York: Aldine.

_____ (1989). "Causes of Marital Dissolution: A Cross-Cultural Study." *Current Anthropology* 30:654-76.

_____ (1993). "Where are the Bastards' Daddies"? *Behavioral and Brain Sciences* 16:284.

_____ (1995). "Medieval Monogamy." *Journal of Family History* 20:181-216.

Betzig, Laura, and Samantha Weber (1995). "Polygyny in American Politics." *Politics and the Life Sciences* 14:61-64.

Biblarz, Timothy J., and Adrian E. Raftery (1999). "Family Structure, Educational Attainment, and Socioeconomic Success: Rethinking the 'Pathology of Matriarchy.'" *American Journal of Sociology* 105:321-65.

Biblarz, Timothy J., Adrian E. Raftery, and Alexander Bucur (1997). "Family Structure and Social Mobility." *Social Forces* 75:1319-41.

The Biological Clock. 60 minutes on Julia Hewlett's book *Creating a Life*. CBS, Aug. 17, 2003.

Bierstedt, Alexander (1997). *Darwins Erben und die Vielfalt der Kultur. Zur Kausalität kulturellen Wandels aus darwinistischer Sicht*. Frankfurt: Peter Lang. (Europäische Hochschulschriften, Reihe XIX, Abt. B. Ethnologie, 48.)

Bischof, Norbert (1985). *Das Rätsel Ödipus*. München: Piper.

Blumstein, Phillip, and Pepper Schwartz (1983). *American Couples: Money, Work, Sex*. New York: William Morrow.

Bock, John (1999). "Evolutionary Approaches to Population: Implications for Research and Policy." *Population and Environment* 21:193-222.

Boehm, Christopher (1989). "Ambivalence and Compromise in Human Nature." *American Anthropologist* 91:921-39.

Bogucki, Peter (1999). *The Origins of Human Society*. Oxford: Blackwell.

_____ (2004). "Human Universals, Human Nature, and Human Culture." *Daedalus* 133:47-54.

Bonacich, Edna (1972). "A Theory of Ethnic Antagonism: The Split Labor Market." *American Sociological Review* 37:547-59.

_____ (1979). "The Past, Present, and Future of Split Labor Market Theory." In *Research in Race and Ethnic Relations*, vol. 1, ed. Cora B. Marrett and Cheryl Leggon. Greenwich, CT: JAI Press.

Bond, Rod, and Peter Saunders (1999). "Routes of Success: Influences on the Occupational Attainment of Young British Males." *British Journal of Sociology* 50:217-49.

Borgerhoff Mulder, Monique (1998). "The Demographic Transition: Are We Any Closer to an Evolutionary Explanation?" *Trends in Ecology and Evolution* 13:266-70.

Boserup, Ester (1981). *Population and Technological Change: A Study of Long-Term Trends*. Chicago: University of Chicago Press.

Bouchard, Thomas J. (1997). "The Genetics of Personality." Pp. 273-96 in *Handbook of Psychoneurogenetics*, ed. K. Blum and E. P. Noble. Boca Raton, FL: CRC Press.

Boyd, Robert, and Peter J. Richerson (1985). *Culture and the Evolutionary Process*. Chicago: University of Chicago Press.

_____ (1996). "Why Culture Is Common, but Cultural Evolution Is Rare." *Proceedings of the British Academy* 88:77-93.

Boyd, Robert, Herbert Gintis, Samuel Bowles, and Peter J. Richerson (2003). "The Evolution of Altruistic Punishment." *Proceedings of the National Academy of Sciences* 100:3531-35.

Boyd, Robert, and Joan B. Silk (2003). *How Humans Evolved*. New York: Norton.

Boyer, Pascal (2005). "Ten Problems for Integrated Behavioural Science: How to Make the Social Sciences Relevant." Global Fellow Seminar Paper No. 7, University of California, Los Angeles. URL http://repositories.cdlib.org/globalfellows/2005/7.

Bratter, Jennifer, and Kelly R. Raley (2004). "Not Even If You Were the Last Person on Earth! How Marital Search Constraints Affect the Likelihood of Marriage." *Journal of Family Issues* 25:2167-81.

Breen, Richard, and Jan O. Jonsson (2005). "Inequality of Opportunity in Comparative Perspective: Recent Research on Educational Attainment and Social Mobility." *Annual Review of Sociology* 31:223-43.

Brown, Donald E. (1991). *Human Universals*. New York: McGraw-Hill.

Bryant, Jennings, and Peter Vorderer, eds. (2006). *Psychology of Entertainment*. Mahwah, NJ: Erlbaum.

Buller, David J. (2006). *Adapting Minds: Evolutionary Psychology and the Persistent Quest for Human Nature*. Cambridge, MA: MIT Press.

Burch, Rebecca L., and Gordon G. Gallup (2000). "Perceptions of Paternal Resemblance Predict Family Violence." *Evolution and Human Behavior* 21:429-35.

Burke, J. A., and Hamer, R. L., eds. (1999). *Works of Edmund Burke*. Vol. 2. New York: Harper & Row.

Burt, Cyril (1961). "Intelligence and Social Mobility." *British Journal of Statistical Psychology* 14:3-24.

Buss, David M. (1985). "Human Mate Selection." *American Scientist* 73:47-51.

_____ (1989). "Sex Differences in Human Mate Preferences: Evolutionary Hypotheses Tested in 37 Cultures." *Behavioral and Brain Sciences* 12:1-49.

_____ (1994). *The Evolution of Desire: Strategies of Human Mating*. New York: Basic Books.

_____ (1999). *Evolutionary Psychology: The New Science of the Mind*. Boston: Allyn & Bacon.

Buss, David M., Max Abbott, Alois Angleitner, Armen Asherian, and Angela Biaggio (1990). "International Preferences in Selecting Mates: A Study of 37 Cultures." *Journal of Cross-Cultural Psychology* 21:5-47.

Buunk, Bram, Pieternel Dijkstra, Detlef Fetchenhauer, and Douglas T. Kenrick (2002). "Age and Gender Differences in Mate Selection Criteria for Various Involvement Levels." *Personal Relationships* 9:217-78.

Byrne, Richard W., and Andrew Whiten, eds. (1988). *Machiavellian Intelligence*. Oxford: Oxford University Press (Clarendon Press).

Campbell, Anne (2003). *A Mind of Her Own: The Evolutionary Psychology of Women*. Oxford: Oxford University Press.

Campbell, Donald T. (1965). "Variation and Selective Retention in Socio-Cultural Evolution." Pp. 19-49 in *Social Change in Developing Areas: A Reinterpretation of Evolutionary Theory*, ed. Herbert R. Barringer, George I. Blanksten, and Raymond W. Mack. Cambridge, MA: Schenkman.

_____ 1975. "On the Conflicts Between Biological and Social Evolution and Between Psychology and Moral Tradition." *American Psychologist* 30:1103-26.

_____ (1983). "The Two Distinct Routes Beyond Kin Selection to Ultrasociality: Implications for the Humanities and Social Sciences." Pp. 11-41 in *The Nature of Prosocial Development*, ed. Diane L. Bridgeman. New York: Academic Press.

Carlson, Marcia J. (2006). "Family Structure, Father Involvement, and Adolescent Behavioral Outcomes." *Journal of Marriage and the Family* 68:137-54.

Carlson, Marcia J., Sara McLanahan, and Paula England (2004). "Union Formation in Fragile Families." *Demography* 2:237-61.

Carneiro, Robert L. (1970). "A Theory of the Origin of the State." *Science* 169:733-38.

_____ (2000). *The Muse of History and the Science of Culture*. New York: Kluwer Academic.

_____ (1981). "Herbert Spencer as an Anthropologist." *Journal of Libertarian Studies* 5:153-210.

_____ (1992). "The Role of Natural Selection in the Evolution of Culture." *Cultural Dynamics* 5:113-40.

_____ (2000) "The Transition from Quantity to Quality: A Neglected Causal Mechanism in Accounting for Social Evolution." *Proceedings of the National Academy of Sciences* 97(23):12926-31.

_____ (2003). *Evolutionism in Cultural Anthropology: A Critical History*. Boulder, CO: Westview Press.

Case, Ann, I-Fen Lin, and Sara McLanahan (2001). "Educational Attainment of Siblings in Stepfamilies." *Evolution and Human Behavior* 22:269-89.

Cashdan, Elizabeth (1993). "Attracting Mates: Effects of Paternal Investment on Mate Attraction Strategies." *Ethology and Sociobiology* 14:1-24.

Cashman, Greg (1993). *What Causes War? An Introduction to Theories of International Conflict*. Lexington, MA: Lexington Books.

Catalano, Ralph A. (2003). "Sex Ratios in the Two Germanies: A Test of the Economic Stress Hypothesis." *Human Reproduction* 18:1972-75.

Caton, Hiram P. (1983). "Descriptive Political Ethology." Manuscript, Griffith University, Brisbane, Australia.

Cavalli-Sforza, Luigi L., and Walter F. Bodmer (1971). *The Genetics of Human Populations*. Mineola, NY: Dover.

Chagnon, Napoleon A. (1996). "Chronic Problems in Understanding Tribal Violence and Warfare." Pp. 202-36 in *Genetics of Criminal and Antisocial Behavior*, ed. G. R. Bock and J. A. Goode. New York: Wiley.

Chacon-Puignau, Grace Cristina, and Klaus Jaffe (1996). "Sex Ratio at Birth Deviations in Modern Venezuela: The Trivers-Willard Effect." *Social Biology* 43:257-70.

Cherlin, Andrew J., and Frank F. Furstenberg (1994). "Stepfamilies in the United States: A Reconsideration." *Annual Review of Sociology* 20:359-81.

Cherlin, Andrew J. (2000). "Toward a New Home Economics of Union Formation." Pp. 126-46 in *The Ties that Bind: Perspectives on Marriage and Cohabitation*, ed. Linda J. Waite, Christine Bachrach, Michelle Hindin, Elizabeth Thomson, and Arland Thornton. New York: Aldine.

Chesnais, Jean-Claude (1992). *The Demographic Transition.* Oxford: Oxford University Press (Clarendon Press).

Christian, David (2005). *Maps of Time: An Introduction to Big History.* Berkeley: University of California Press.

Claessen, Henri J. M. (2000). *Structural Change. Evolution and Evolutionism in Cultural Anthropology.* Leiden: Onderzoekschool voor Aziatische, Afrikaanse, en Amerindische Studies (Research School CNWS), Universiteit Leiden.

Cohen, Lawrence E., and Richard Machalek (1988). "A General Theory of Expropriative Crime: An Evolutionary Ecological Approach." *American Journal of Sociology* 94:465-501.

Cohen, Philip N., and Miruna Petrescu-Prahova (2006). "Gendered Living Arrangements among Children with Disabilities." *Journal of Marriage and the Family* 68:630-38.

Collins, Randall (1981). "Micro-translation as a Theory-building Strategy." Pp. 81-108 in *Advances in Social Theory and Methodology: Toward an Integration of Micro- and Macro-sociologies*, ed. Karin D. Knorr-Cetina and Aaron Cicourel. Boston: Routledge.

Corning, Peter A. (1982). "Durkheim and Spencer." *British Journal of Sociology* 33:359-82.

_____ (1983). *The Synergism Hypothesis: A Theory of Progressive Evolution.* New York: McGraw-Hill.

_____ (1998). "Holistic Darwinism: Synergy and the New Evolutionary Paradigm." Pp. 17-43 in *Research in Biopolitics*, Vol. 6, ed. Vincent Falger, Meyer Peter, and Johan M. G. van der Dennen. Stamford, CT: JAI Press.

_____ (2003). *Nature's Magic: Synergy in Evolution and the Fate of Humankind.* New York: Cambridge University Press.

_____ (2005). *Holistic Darwinism: Synergy, Cybernetics, and the Bioeconomics of Evolution.* Chicago: University of Chicago Press.

Cosmides, Leda, and John Tooby (1989). "Evolutionary Psychology and the Generation of Culture, Part II. Case Study: A Computational Theory of Social Exchange." *Ethology and Sociobiology* 10:51-97.

Crippen, Timothy (1994). "Toward a Neo-Darwinian Sociology: Its Nomological Principles and Some Illustrative Applications." *Sociological Perspectives* 37:309-35.

Daly, Martin, and Margo Wilson (1978). *Sex, Evolution, and Behavior.* North Scituate, MA: Duxbury Press.

_____ (1983). *Sex, Evolution, and Behavior.* 2nd ed. Belmont, CA: Wadsworth.

_____ (1988). *Homicide.* New York: Aldine de Gruyter.

Davie, Maurice R. (1929). *The Evolution of War: A Study of Its Role in Early Societies.* New Haven, CT: Yale University Press

Davis, Shannon N., and Theodore N. Greenstein (2004). "Cross-National Variations in the Division of Household Labor." *Journal of Marriage and the Family* 66:1260-71.

Dawkins, Richard (1976). *The Selfish Gene.* Oxford: Oxford University Press.

_____ (1986). *The Blind Watchmaker.* New York: Norton.

Degler, Carl N. (1991). *In Search of Human Nature: The Decline and Revival of Darwinism in American Social Thought*. New York: Oxford University Press.

Dempster, W. J. (1983). *Patrick Matthew and Natural Selection*. Edinburgh: Harris.

Dennett, Daniel (1995). *Darwin's Dangerous Idea: Evolution and the Meanings of Life*. New York: Simon & Schuster.

Dentan, Robert K. (1992). "The Rise, Maintenance, and Destruction of Peaceable Polity: A Preliminary Essay in Political Ecology." Pp. 214-70 in *Aggression and Peacefulness in Humans and Other Primates*, ed. J. Silverberg, and J. P. Gray. Oxford: Oxford University Press.

de Waal, Frans (1996). *Good Natured: The Origins of Right and Wrong in Humans and Other Animals*. Cambridge, MA: Harvard University Press.

_____ (2006). *Primates and Philosophers: How Morality Evolved*. Princeton, NJ: Princeton University Press.

Diamond, Jared (1997). *Why Sex Is Fun: The Evolution of Human Sexuality*. London: Weidenfeld & Nicholson.

Dickemann, Mildred (1979). "Female Infanticide, Reproductive Strategies, and Social Stratification: A Preliminary Model." Pp. 321-67 in *Evolutionary Biology and Human Social Behavior*, ed. Napoleon A. Chagnon and William Irons. North Scituate, MA: Duxbury Press.

Divale, William Tulio, and Marvin Harris (1978). "The Male Supremacist Complex: Discovery of a Cultural Invention." *American Anthropologist* 80:668-71.

Dougherty, J. E., and R. L. Pfaltzgraff (2001). *Contending Theories of International Relations*. 5th ed. New York: Longman.

Duby, Georges (1994). *Love and Marriage in the Middle Ages*. Chicago: University of Chicago Press.

Dunbar, Robin I. M. (1996). *Grooming, Gossip, and the Evolution of Language*. London: Faber & Faber.

Durham, William H. (1991). *Coevolution: Genes, Culture, and Human Diversity*. Stanford. CA: Stanford University Press.

Durkheim, Émile (1895a). "Origine du mariage dans l'éspèce humaine d'après Westermarck." *Revue philosophique* 40:606-23.

_____ (1895b). *Les règles de la methode sociologique*. Paris: Flammarion.

_____ (1896). "La prohibition de l'inceste et ses origines." *L'Année sociologique* 1:1-70.

_____ (1907). "Sur l'évolution générale des idées morales (Revue de Westermarck, *The Origin and Development of the Moral Ideas*, Vol. I)." *L'Année sociologique* 10:383-95.

_____ (1912). *Les formes élémentaires de la vie religieuse*. Paris: Editions de minuit.

Duvander, Ann-Sofie, and Gunnar Andersson (2003). *När har vi råd att skaffa fler barn? En studie om hur inkomst påverkar fortsatt barnafödande*. Stockholm: Riksförsäkringsverket.

Dux, Günter (2000). *Historisch-genetische Theorie der Kultur. Instabile Welten – Zur prozessualen Logik im kulturellen Wandel*. Weilerswist: Velbrück.

Eagly, Alice H., and Wendy Wood. (1999). "The Origins of Sex Differences in Human Behavior: Evolved Dispositions versus Social Roles." *American Psychologist* 54:408-23.

Earle, Timothy, ed. (1991). *Chiefdoms: Power, Economy, and Ideology*. New York: Cambridge University Press.

Eco, Umberto (1979). *A Theory of Semiotics*. Bloomington: Indiana University Press.

Edelman, Gerald M., and Giulio Tononi (1997). "Neuronaler Darwinismus. Eine selektionistische Betrachtungsweise des Gehirns." Pp. 187-234 in *Der Mensch und sein Gehirn*, ed. Heinrich Meier and Detlev Ploog. München: Piper.

Eibl-Eibesfeldt, Irenäus (1970). *Liebe und Hass. Zur Naturgeschichte elementarer Verhaltensweisen*. München: Piper.

_____ (1982). "Warfare, Man's Indoctrinability, and Group Selection." *Ethology (Zeitschrift für Tierpsychologie)* 60:177-98.

_____ (1989). *Human Ethology*. New York: Aldine de Gruyter.

Eibl-Eibesfeldt, Irenäus, and Frank K. Salter, eds. (1998). *Indoctrinability, Ideology, and Warfare*. Oxford: Berghahn.

Eigen, Manfred, and Ruthild Winkler (1981). *Das Spiel. Naturgesetze steuern den Zufall*. München: Piper.

Elias, Norbert (1971). "Sociology of Knowledge: New Perspectives."*Sociology* 5:355-70.

_____ (1978). *What Is Sociology?* London: Hutchinson.

_____ (1987). *Engagement und Distanzierung*. Frankfurt am Main: Suhrkamp.

Ellis, Lee (1977). "The Decline and Fall of Sociology, 1975-2000." *American Sociologist* 12:56-66.

_____ (1995). "Dominance and Reproductive Success among Nonhuman Animals: A Cross-Species Comparison." *Ethology and Sociobiology* 16:257-333.

_____ (1996). "A Discipline in Peril: Sociology's Future Hinges on Curing Its Biophobia." *American Sociologist* 27:21-41.

Ellis, Lee, ed. (1993). *Social Stratification and Socioeconomic Inequality*. New York: Praeger.

Ellis, Lee, and M. Ashley Ames (1987). "Neurohormonal Functioning and Sexual Orientation: A Theory of Homosexuality-Heterosexuality." *Psychological Bulletin* 101:233-58.

Ellis, Lee, and Steven Bonin (2002). "Social Status and the Secondary Sex Ratio: New Evidence on a Lingering Controversy." *Social Biology* 49:35-43.

Ellis, Lee, and Harry Hoffman, eds. (1990). *Crime in Biological, Social, and Moral Contexts*. New York: Praeger.

Elwell, Frank E. (1991). *The Evolution of the Future*. New York: Praeger.

Ember, Carol R. (1978). "Myths about Hunter-Gatherers." *Ethnology* 17:439-48.

Engels, Eve-Marie (2000). "Darwins Popularität im Deutschland des 19. Jahrhunderts: Die Herausbildung der Biologie als Leitwissenschaft." Pp. 91-145 in *Menschenbilder. Zur Pluralisierung der Vorstellung von der menschlichen Natur (1850-1914)*, ed. Achim Barsch and Peter M. Hejl. Frankfurt am Main: Suhrkamp.

England, Paula (2004). "More Mercenary Mate Selection? Comment on Sweeney and Cancian." *Journal of Marriage and the Family* 66:1034-37.

Essock-Vitale, Susan M. (1984). "The Reproductive Success of Wealthy Americans." *Ethology and Sociobiology* 5:45-49.

Entwistle, Doris R., Karl L. Alexander, and Linda Steffel Olson (2005). "First Grade and Educational Attainment by Age 22: A New Story." *American Journal of Sociology* 110:1458-1502.

Erikson, Robert, and John H. Goldthorpe (1993). *The Constant Flux: A Study of Class Mobility in Industrial Societies*. New York : Oxford University Press.

Euler, Harald, and Barbara Weitzel (1996). "Discriminative Grandparental Solicitude as Reproductive Strategy." *Human Nature* 7:39-59.

European Foundation for the Improvement of Living and Working Conditions (2004). *Fertility and Family Issues in an Enlarged Europe*. URL http://www.eurofound. eu.int

Faulstich, Werner (1996-2004). *Die Geschichte der Medien.* 5 vols. Göttingen: Vandenhoeck & Ruprecht.

Fehr, Ernst, Urs Fischbacher, and Simon Gächter (2002). "Strong Reciprocity, Human Cooperation, and the Enforcement of Social Norms." *Human Nature* 13:1-25.

Feinman, Gary M., and Linda Manzanilla, eds. (2000). *Cultural Evolution: Contemporary Viewpoints.* New York: Kluwer Academic.

Ferguson, R. Brian (1984). "Introduction: Studying War." Pp. 1-81 in *Warfare, Culture, and Environment,* ed. R. Brian Ferguson. New York: Academic Press.

_____ (1990). "Explaining War." Pp. 26-55 in *The Anthropology of War,* ed. Jonathan Haas. New York: Cambridge University Press.

_____ (1995). "Infrastructural Determinism." Pp. 21-38 in *Science, Materialism, and the Study of Culture,* ed. Martin F. Murphy and Maxine L. Margolis. Gainesville: University Press of Florida.

Figueredo, Aurelio J., Geneva Vasquez, Barbara H. Brumbach, Stephanie Schneider, Jon A. Sefcek, Ilanit Tal, Dawn Hill, Christopher J. Wenner, and Jake W. Jacobs (2006). "Consilience and Life History Theory: From Genes to Brain to Reproductive Strategy." *Developmental Review* 26:243-75.

Finley, M. I. (1956). *The World of Odysseus.* London: Chatto & Windus.

_____ (1973). *The Ancient Economy.* London: Chatto & Windus.

Flinn, Mark V. (1989). "Household Composition and Female Strategies in a Trinidadian Village." Pp. 206-33 in *The Sociobiology of Sexual and Reproductive Strategies,* ed. Anna E. Rasa, Christian Vogel, and Eckart Voland. New York: Chapman & Hall.

Forbes, R. J. (1971). *Studies in Ancient Technology.* Vol. VIII. 2nd ed. Leiden: Brill.

Francis, Emerich K. (1981). "Darwins Evolutionstheorie und der Sozialdarwinismus." *Kölner Zeitschrift für Soziologie und Sozialpsychologie* 33:209-28.

Freese, Jeremy, Jui-Chung Allen Li, and Lisa D. Wade (2003). "The Potential Relevances of Biology to Social Inquiry." *Annual Review of Sociology* 29:233-56.

Freese, Jeremy, and Brian Powell (1999). "Sociobiology, Status, and Parental Investment in Sons and Daughters: Testing the Trivers-Willard Hypothesis." *American Journal of Sociology* 104:1704-43.

Frey, Siegfried (2000). *Die Macht des Bildes.* Bern: Huber.

Fuller, Steve (2000). "Science Studies through the Looking Glass: An Intellectual Itinerary." Pp. 185-217 in *Beyond the Science Wars: The Missing Discourse about Science and Society,* ed. Ullica Segerstråle. Albany: State University of New York Press.

Furstenberg, Frank F., Saul D. Hoffman, and Laura Shrestha (1995). "The Effect of Divorce on Intergenerational Transfers: New Evidence." *Demography* 32:319-33.

Gillette, Aaron (2007). *Eugenics and the Nature-Nurture Debate in the Twentieth Century.* New York: Palgrave Macmillan.

Galtung, Johan, and Mari H. Ruge (1965). "The Structure of Foreign News." *Journal of Peace Research* 2:64-91.

Gat, Azar (2000a). "The Human Motivational Complex: Evolutionary Theory and the Causes of Hunter-Gatherer Fighting. Part 1: Primary Somatic and Reproductive Causes." *Anthropological Quarterly* 73:20-34.

_____ (2000b). "The Human Motivational Complex: Evolutionary Theory and the Causes of Hunter-Gatherer Fighting. Part 2: Proximate, Subordinate, and Derivative Causes." 73:74-88.

Gehlen, Arnold (1963). *Studien zur Anthropologie und Soziologie.* Neuwied: Luchterhand.

_____ (1993). *Der Mensch. Seine Natur und seine Stellung in der Welt.* (Arnold Gehlen complete edition, vol. 3.1/3.2, ed. Karl-Siegbert Rehberg.) Frankfurt am Main: Klostermann. (First edition 1940.)

Ghiglieri Michael P. (1999) *The Dark Side of Man: Tracing the Origins of Male Violence.* Reading, MA: Perseus Books.

Gibson, Mhairi, and Ruth Mace (2003). "Strong Mothers Bear More Sons in Rural Ethiopia." *Biology Letters (Proceedings of the Royal Society Supplement Online),* May 20, 2003.

Goffman, Erving (1959). *The Presentation of Self in Everyday Life.* New York: Doubleday (Anchor Books).

Gottfredson, Linda S. (1997). "Why *g* Matters: The Complexity of Everyday Life." *Intelligence* 24:79-132.

Goldberg, Steven (1973). *The Inevitability of Patriarchy.* New York: William Morrow.

_____ (1993). *Why Men Rule.* Chicago: Open Court.

Goldscheider, Frances, and Sharon Sassler (2004). "Revisiting Jane Austen's Theory of Marriage Timing: Changes in Union Formation among American Men in the Late 20th Century." *Journal of Family Issues* 25:139-66.

Goody, Jack (1986). *The Logic of Writing and the Organization of Society.* Cambridge, UK: Cambridge University Press.

Goody, Jack, and Ian P. Watt (1963). "The Consequences of Literacy." *Comparative Studies in Society and History* 5:304-45.

Goudsblom, Johan (2002). "Introductory Overview: The Expanding Anthroposphere." Pp. 21-46 in *Mappae Mundi: Humans and their Habitats in a Long-Term Socio-Ecological Perspective,* ed. Bert de Vries and Johan Goudsblom. Amsterdam: Amsterdam University Press.

Goudsblom, Johan, and Nico Wilterdink, eds. (2000). *Sociaal evolutie. Het evolutieperspektief in de sociologie.* Groningen: Wolters-Noordhoff. (Special issue of *Amsterdams Sociologisch Tijdschrift,* vol. 27, nos. 1-2.)

Gould, Stephen Jay (2000). "More Things in Heaven and Earth." Pp. 101-26 in *Alas, Poor Darwin: Arguments Against Evolutionary Psychology,* ed. Hilary Rose and Steven Rose. New York: Harmony Books.

Gould, Stephen J., and Richard C. Lewontin (1997). "The Spandrels of San Marcos and the Panglossian Paradigm." Pp. 126-39 in *Evolution,* ed. Mark Ridley. New York: Oxford University Press.

Green, Penny Anthon (1991). "A Biocultural Analysis of Revolution." *Journal of Social and Biological Structures* 14:435-54.

_____ (1995). "Evolutionary Insights into Problems of Sexism, Classism, and Racism, Including Prospects for Their Elimination." *Race, Gender, and Class* 2:65-83.

Gruter, Margaret, and Roger D. Masters (1986). *Ostracism: A Social and Biological Phenomenon.* New York: Elsevier.

Guzmán, Ricardo Andrés, Carlos Rodríguez-Sickert, and Robert Rowthorn (2007). "When in Rome, Do as the Romans Do: The Coevolution of Altruistic Punishment, Conformist Learning, and Cooperation." *Evolution and Human Behavior* 28:112-17.

Haaga, John G. (2001). "Comment: The Pace of Fertility Decline and the Utility of Evolutionary Approaches." *Population and Development Review* 27:53-59.

Hacker, Andrew (1997). *Money: Who Has How Much and Why.* New York: Scribner's.

Haldane, John Burdon Sanderson (1955). *Population Genetics.* New York: Penguin.

Hallpike, C. R. (1979). *The Foundations of Primitive Thought.* Oxford: Oxford University Press (Clarendon Press).

_____ (1986). *The Principles of Social Evolution.* New York: Oxford University Press.

_____ (1999). "Greek Hoplites." *Journal of the Royal Anthropological Institute (n.s.)* 5:627-29.

_____ (2000). "Greek Hoplites." *Journal of the Royal Anthropological Institute (n.s.)* 6:526.

_____ (2001). "Further Response to Runciman." *Journal of the Royal Anthropological Institute (n.s.)* 7:573-74.

Hällsten, Annika (2005). "Babyfeber på vita duken." *Hufvudstadsbladet* 29.1:26-27.

Hamilton, William D. (1964). "The Genetical Evolution of Social Behaviour." *Journal of Theoretical Biology* 7:1-52.

_____ (1975). "Innate Social Aptitudes of Man: An Approach from Evolutionary Genetics." Pp. 133-55 in *Biosocial Anthropology*, ed. Robin Fox. London: Malaby Press.

Hammond, Michael (1999). "Arouser Depreciation and the Expansion of Social Inequality." *Social Perspectives on Emotion* 5:339-58.

_____ (2003). "The Enhancement Imperative: The Evolutionary Neurophysiology of Durkheimian Solidarity." *Sociological Theory* 21:359-74.

Harpending, Henry (2002). "Kinship and Population Subdivision." *Population and Environment* 24:141-47.

Harris, Marvin (1977). *Cannibals and Kings: The Origins of Cultures*. New York: Random House.

_____ (1979). *Cultural Materialism: The Struggle for a Science of Culture*. New York: Random House.

_____ (1983). *Cultural Anthropology*. New York: Harper & Row.

_____ (1984). "A Cultural Materialist Theory of Band and Village Warfare: The Yanomamö Test." Pp. 111-40 in *Warfare, Culture, and Environment*, ed. R. Brian Ferguson. New York: Academic Press.

_____ (1989). *Our Kind*. New York: Harper & Row.

_____ (1993). *Culture, People, Nature: An Introduction to General Anthropology*. 6th ed. New York: HarperCollins.

_____ (1997). "Comment on O'Meara." *Current Anthropology* 38:410-15.

Hauser, Marc D. (2006). *Moral Minds: How Nature Designed Our Universal Sense of Right and Wrong*. New York: HarperCollins.

Haydon, Barry (1962). *The Great Statistics of War Hoax*. Santa Monica, CA: RAND Corporation.

Hejl, Peter M. (2000). "Biologische Metaphern in der deutschsprachigen Soziologie der zweiten Hälfte des 19. Jahrhunderts." Pp. 167-214 in *Menschenbilder. Zur Pluralisierung der Vorstellung von der menschlichen Natur (1850-1914)*, ed. Achim Barsch and Peter M. Hejl. Frankfurt am Main: Suhrkamp.

_____ (2001). "Konstruktivismus und Universalien – eine Verbindung contre nature?" Pp. 7-67 in *Universalien und Konstruktivismus*, ed. Peter M. Hejl. Frankfurt am Main: Suhrkamp.

Hejl, Peter M., and Matthias Uhl (forthcoming). "The Really Interesting Stories Are the Old Ones." To appear in *You Can't Turn It Off: Media, Mind, and Evolution*, ed. Jerome H. Barkow and Peter M. Hejl. New York: Oxford University Press.

Henrich, Joseph, Robert Boyd, Samuel Bowles, Colin Camerer, Herbert Gintis, Richard McElreath, and Ernst Fehr (2001). "In Search of Homo Economicus: Behavioral Experiments in 15 Small-Scale Societies." *American Economic Review* 91:73-78.

Hermans, Cor (2003). *De dwaalwegen van het sociaal-darwinisme*. Amsterdam: Uitgeverij Nieuwezijds.

Herrnstein, Richard J., and Charles Murray (1994). *The Bell Curve: Intelligence and Class Structure in American Life*. New York, Free Press.

Hill, Sarah E., and H. Kern Reeve (2005). "Low Fertility in Humans as the Evolutionary Outcome of Snowballing Resource Games." *Behavioral Ecology* 16:398-402.

Hilton, Susanne F. (1990). "Haihais, Bella Bella, and Owekeeno." Pp. 312-22 in *Handbook of North American Indians. Vol. 7: Northwest Coast*, ed. W. C. Sturtevant and W. Suttles. Washington DC: United States Government Printing Office.

Hobbes, Thomas (1909). *Hobbes's Leviathan.* Reprinted from the edition of 1651. Oxford: Oxford University Press (Clarendon Press).

Hockett, Charles Francis (1973). *Man's Place in Nature.* New York: McGraw-Hill.

Homans, George C. (1964). "Bringing Men Back In." *American Sociological Review* 29:809-18.

_____ (1972). *Grundfragen soziologischer Theorie.* Opladen: Westdeutscher Verlag. [George C. Homans, "The Sociological Relevance of Behaviorism." Pp. 1-24 in *Behavioral Sociology: The Experimental Analysis of Social Process*, ed. R. L. Burgess and D. Bushell. New York: Columbia University Press, 1969.]

_____ (1984). *Coming to My Senses: The Autobiography of a Sociologist.* New Brunswick, NJ: Transaction.

Hopcroft, Rosemary L. (2002). "The Evolution of Sex Discrimination." *Psychology, Evolution, and Gender* 41:43-67.

_____ (2005). "Parental Status and Differential Investment in Sons and Daughters: Trivers-Willard Revisited." *Social Forces* 8:169-93.

_____ (2006a). "Sex, Status, and Reproductive Success in the Contemporary United States." *Evolution and Human Behavior* 27:104-20.

_____ (2006b). "Status Characteristics among Older Individuals: The Diminished Significance of Gender." *Sociological Quarterly* 47:361-74

Horne, Christine (2004). "Values and Evolutionary Psychology." *Sociological Theory* 22:477-503.

Hrdy, Sarah Blaffer (1997). "Raising Darwin's Consciousness: Female Sexuality and the Prehominoid Origins of Patriarchy." *Human Nature* 8:1-49.

_____ (1999). *Mother Nature: A History of Mothers, Infants, and Natural Selection.* New York: Pantheon.

_____ (2000). *Mutter Natur.* Berlin: Berlin Verlag. [German translation of *Mother Nature.*]

Huber, Peter B. (1975). "Defending the Cosmos: Violence and Social Order Among the Anggor of New Guinea. Pp. 483-514 in *War, Its Causes and Correlates*, ed. M. A. Nettleship, R. D. Givens, and A. Nettleship. The Hague: Mouton.

Huff, Toby E. (1993). *The Rise of Early Modern Science: Islam, China, and the West.* New York: Cambridge University Press.

Hume, David (1817). *A Treatise on Human Nature.* London: Thomas & Joseph Allman.

_____ (1902). *Enquiries Concerning the Human Understanding and Concerning the Principles of Morals.* Oxford: Oxford University Press (Clarendon Press).

Hur, Yoon-Mi, and Thomas J. Bouchard (1995). "Genetic Influences on Perceptions of Childhood Family Environment: A Reared Apart Twin Study." *Child Development* 66:330-45.

Ingold, Tim (1986). *Evolution and Social Life.* Cambridge, UK: Cambridge University Press.

Ingold, Tim, ed. (1991). *Evolutionary Models in the Social Sciences.* Leiden: Brill. (Special issue of *Cultural Dynamics*, vol. 4, no. 3.)

Jencks, Christopher (1972). *Inequality: A Reassessment of the Effect of Family and Schooling in America.* New York: Basic Books.

Jensen, Arthur R. (1998). *The g Factor: The Science of Mental Ability* Westport, CT: Praeger.

Johnson, Allen W., and Timothy Earle (2000). *The Evolution of Human Societies: From Foraging Group to Agrarian State*. 2nd ed. Stanford, CA: Stanford University Press.

Johnson, W., Matt McGue, Robert F. Krueger, and Thomas J. Bouchard (2004). "Marriage and Personality: A Genetic Analysis." *Personality Processes and Individual Differences* 86:285-94.

Jongman, Berto, and Johan M. G. van der Dennen (1988). "The Great 'War Figures' Hoax: An Investigation in Polemomythology." *Bulletin of Peace Proposals* 19:197-204.

Kalmijn, Matthijs (1998). "Marriage and Homogamy: Causes, Patterns, Trends." *Annual Review of Sociology* 24:395-421.

Kamps, Klaus (1999). *Politik in Fernsehnachrichten*. Baden-Baden: Nomos.

Kanazawa, Satoshi (2002). "Bowling with Our Imaginary Friends." *Evolution and Human Behavior* 23:167-71.

_____ (2005). "An Empirical Test of a Possible Solution to 'The Central Theoretical Problem of Human Sociobiology.'" *Journal of Cultural and Evolutionary Psychology* 3:249-60.

Kanazawa, Satoshi, and Jody L. Kovar (2004). "Why Beautiful People are More Intelligent." *Intelligence* 32:227-43.

Kanazawa, Satoshi, and Mary C. Still (1999). "Why Monogamy?" *Social Forces* 78:25-50.

_____ (2000). "Why Men Commit Crimes (and Why They Desist)." *Sociological Theory* 18:434-47.

Kaplan, Hillard S., and Jane B. Lancaster (2003). "An Evolutionary and Ecological Analysis of Human Fertility, Mating Patterns, and Parental Investment." Pp. 170-223 in *Offspring: Fertility Behavior in Biodemographic Perspective*, ed. Kenneth W. Wachter and Rodolfo A. Bulatao. Washington, DC: National Academies Press.

Kautsky, John (1982). *The Politics of Aristocratic Empires*. Chapel Hill: University of North Carolina Press.

Keller, Albert Galloway (1931). *Societal Evolution: A Study of the Evolutionary Basis of the Science of Society*. Rev. ed. New Haven, CT: Yale University Press. (1st ed. 1915.)

Kelsen, Hans (1946). *Society and Nature*. Chicago: University of Chicago Press. (Reprinted edition 1974.)

Klein, Richard G. (2000). "Archaeology and the Evolution of Human Behavior." *Evolutionary Anthropology* 9:17-36.

Kohler, Hans-Peter, Joseph L. Rodgers, and Kaare Christensen (1999). "Is Fertility Behavior in Our Genes? Findings From a Danish Twin Study." *Population and Development Review* 25:253-88.

Kroeber, Alfred (1917). "The Superorganic." *American Anthropologist* 17:283-89.

Küppers, Bernd-Olaf (1986). *Der Ursprung biologischer Information*. München: Piper.

Lang, Hartmut (1998). "Kultur und Evolutionstheorie." *Zeitschrift für Ethnologie* 123:5-20.

Lagerborg, Rolf (1942). *I egna ögon – och andras. En bok om att känna sig själv*. Helsingfors: Söderström & Co.

_____ (1951). *Edvard Westermarck och verken från hans verkstad under hans sista tolv år 1927-39*. Helsingfors: Holger Schildts Förlag.

_____ (1953). "The Essence of Morals: Fifty Years (1895-1945) of Rivalry between French and English Sociology." *Transactions of the Westermarck Society II*:9-26. Copenhagen: Ejnar Munksgaard.

La Mettrie, Julien Offray de (1974). *Textes choisies. Préface, commentaires, et notes explicatives par M. Bottigelli-Tisserand*. Paris: Editions Sociales.

Lareau, Annette (2002). "Invisible Inequality: Social Class and Childrearing in Black Families and White Families." *American Sociological Review* 67:747-76.

Lenski, Gerhard E. (1966). *Power and Privilege: A Theory of Social Stratification*. New York: McGraw-Hill.

_____ (1970). *Human Societies: A Macro-Level Introduction to Sociology*. New York: McGraw-Hill.

_____ (2005). *Ecological-Evolutionary Theory: Principles and Applications*. Boulder, CO: Paradigm Publishers.

Lenski, Gerhard, Patrick Nolan, and Jean Lenski (1995). *Human Societies: An Introduction to Macrosociology*. 7th ed. New York: McGraw-Hill.

Lett, James (1997). *Science, Reason, and Anthropology*. Lanham, MD: Rowman & Littlefield.

Lévi-Strauss, Claude (1964-71). *Mythologiques*. 4 vols. Paris: Plon.

_____ (1967). *Strukturale Anthropologie*. Vol. 1. Frankfurt am Main: Suhrkamp. [Claude Lévi-Strauss, *Structural Anthropology*, Vol. 1. New York: Basic Books, 1963.]

_____ (1968). *Das wilde Denken*. Frankfurt am Main: Suhrkamp. [Claude Lévi-Strauss, *The Savage Mind*. London: Weidenfeld & Nicolson, 1966.]

_____ (1969). *The Elementary Structures of Kinship*. Trans. James Harle Bell, John Richard von Sturmer, and Rodney Needham. Boston: Beacon Press.

_____ (1985). *Der Blick aus der Ferne*. München: Fink. [Claude Lévi-Strauss, *The View from Afar*. New York: Basic Books, 1985.]

Lewontin, Richard, Steven Rose, and Leon Kamin (1984). *Not in Our Genes: Biology, Ideology, and Human Nature*. New York: Pantheon.

Lieberman, Debra, John Tooby, and Leda Cosmides (2007). "The Architecture of Human Kin Detection." *Nature* 445:13-14.

Lippmann, Walter (1997). *Public Opinion*. New York: Free Press. (Originally published 1922.)

Lopreato, Joseph (1984). *Human Nature and Biocultural Evolution*. Winchester, MA: Allen & Unwin.

Lopreato, Joseph, and Timothy Crippen (1999). *Crisis in Sociology: The Need for Darwin*. New Brunswick, NJ: Transaction.

Lord, Jane T., and Stephen K. Sanderson (1999). "Current Theoretical and Political Perspectives of Western Sociological Theorists." *American Sociologist* 30:37-61.

Lorenz, Konrad (1977). *Behind the Mirror: A Search for a Natural History of Human Knowledge*. London: Methuen.

_____ (1981). *The Foundations of Ethology*. New York: Springer.

Low, Bobbi S. (1991). "Reproductive Life in Nineteenth-Century Sweden: An Evolutionary Perspective on Demographic Phenomena." *Ethology and Sociobiology* 12:411-48.

_____ (2000). "Sex, Wealth, and Fertility: Old Rules, New Environments." Pp. 323-44 in *Adaptation and Human Behavior: An Anthropological Perspective*, ed. Lee Cronk, Napoleon Chagnon, and William Irons. New York: Aldine de Gruyter.

Low, Bobbi S., Carl P. Simon, and Kermyt Anderson (2002). "An Evolutionary Ecological Perspective on Demographic Transitions: Modeling Multiple Currencies." *American Journal of Human Biology* 14:149-67.

Luhmann, Niklas (1995). *Social Systems*. Stanford, CA: Stanford University Press.

_____ (1997). *Die Gesellschaft der Gesellschaft*. 2 vols. Frankfurt am Main: Suhrkamp.

Lukes, Steven (1972). *Émile Durkheim, His Life and Work: A Historical and Critical Study*. New York: Harper & Row.

Lynn, Richard (1990). "The Role of Nutrition in Secular Increases in Intelligence." *Personality and Individual Differences* 11:273-85.

———— (1994). "Some Reinterpretations of the Minnesota Transracial Adoption Study." *Intelligence* 19:21-28.

———— (1996). *Dysgenics: Genetic Deterioration in Modern Populations*. Westport, CT: Praeger.

MacDonald, Kevin B. (1983). "Production, Social Controls, and Ideology: Toward a Sociobiology of the Phenotype." *Journal of Social and Biological Structures* 6:297-317.

———— (1992). "Warmth as a Developmental Construct – An Evolutionary Analysis." *Child Development* 63:753-73.

———— (1995). "The Establishment and Maintenance of Socially Imposed Monogamy in Western Europe." *Politics and the Life Sciences* 14:3-46.

———— (1999). "An Evolutionary Perspective on Human Fertility." *Population and Environment* 21:223-46.

Mace, Ruth (1998). "The Coevolution of Human Fertility and Wealth Inheritance Strategies." *Philosophical Transactions of the Royal Society of London B* 353(1367):389-97.

Machalek, Richard (1992). "The Evolution of Macrosociety: Why Are Large Societies Rare?" *Advances in Human Ecology* 1:33-64.

———— (1995). "Basic Dimensions and Forms of Social Exploitation: A Comparative Analysis." *Advances in Human Ecology* 4:35-68.

———— (1996). "The Evolution of Social Exploitation." *Advances in Human Ecology* 5:1-32.

Machalek, Richard, and Michael W. Martin (2004). "Sociology and the Second Darwinian Revolution: A Metatheoretical Analysis." *Sociological Theory* 22:455-76.

MacLean, Paul D. (1994). "Human Nature: Duality or Triality?" *Politics and the Life Sciences* 13:107-12.

Malinowski, Bronislaw (1929). *The Sexual Life of Savages in North-Western Melanesia*. London: George Routledge & Sons.

Mann, Michael (1986). *The Sources of Social Power. Vol. 1: From the Beginning to AD 1760*. New York: Cambridge University Press.

Manning, Wendy D. (2004). "Children and the Stability of Cohabiting Couples." *Journal of Marriage and the Family* 66:674-89.

Maryanski, Alexandra, and Jonathan H. Turner (1992). *The Social Cage: Human Nature and The Evolution of Society*. Stanford, CA: Stanford University Press.

Mason, Karen O., and A. M. Taj (1987). "Differences Between Men's and Women's Reproductive Goals in Developing Countries." *Population and Development Review* 13:611-38.

Massey, Douglas S. (2002). "A Brief History of Human Society: The Origin and Role of Emotion in Social Life." *American Sociological Review* 67:1-29.

Maynard Smith, John, and Eörs Szathmáry (1995). *The Major Transitions in Evolution*. Oxford: Freeman.

Mazumder, Bhash (2002). "Analyzing Income Mobility Over Generations." *Chicago Fed Letter* 181:4.

McCabe, Justine (1983). "FBD Marriage: Further Support for the Westermarck Hypothesis of the Incest Taboo?" *American Anthropologist* 85:50-69.

McGarry, Kathleen, and Robert F. Schoeni (1995). "Transfer Behavior in the Health and Retirement Study." *Journal of Human Resources* 30:S184-225.

Mealey, Linda, and Wade Mackey (1990). "Variation in Offspring Sex Ratio in Women of Differing Social Status." *Ethology and Sociobiology* 11:83-95.

Meleghy, Tamás (2001a). "Verhaltenstheoretische Soziologie: George Caspar Homans." Pp. 30-51 in *Soziologische Theorie*, 7th ed., ed. Julius Morel, Eva Bauer, Tamás Meleghy, Heinz-Jürgen Niedenzu, Max Preglau, and Helmut Staubmann. München: Oldenbourg.

_____ (2001b). "Der Strukturalismus: Claude Lévi-Strauss." Pp. 116-46 in *Soziologische Theorie*, 7th ed., ed. Julius Morel, Eva Bauer, Tamás Meleghy, Heinz-Jürgen Niedenzu, Max Preglau, and Helmut Staubmann. München: Oldenbourg.

_____ (2003a). "Die 'Versozialwissenschaftlichung' der Soziologie. Zur Transformation einer Disziplin." Pp. 3-28 in *Soziale Evolution. Die Evolutionstheorie und die Sozialwissenschaften*, ed. Tamás Meleghy and Heinz-Jürgen Niedenzu. Wiesbaden: Westdeutscher Verlag. (*Österreichische Zeitschrift für Soziologie*, spezial edition, vol. 7.).

_____ (2003b). "Methodologische Grundlagen einer evolutionären Soziologie." Pp. 114-46 in *Soziale Evolution. Die Evolutionstheorie und die Sozialwissenschaften*, ed. Tamás Meleghy and Heinz-Jürgen Niedenzu. Wiesbaden: Westdeutscher Verlag. (*Österreichische Zeitschrift für Soziologie*, spezial edition, vol. 7.).

Meleghy, Tamás, and Heinz-Jürgen Niedenzu, eds. (2001). *Soziale Evolution. Die Evolutionstheorie und die Sozialwissenschaften*. Wiesbaden: Westdeutscher Verlag.

Merton, Robert K. (1957). *Social Theory and Social Structure*. New York: Free Press.

Meyer, Peter (1977). *Kriegs- und Militärsoziologie*. München: Goldmann.

_____ (1981). *Evolution und Gewalt: Ansätze zu einer bio-soziologischen Synthese*. Hamburg: Parey Verlag.

_____ (1990a). "Human Nature and the Function of War in Social Evolution: A Critical Review of a Recent Form of the Naturalistic Fallacy." Pp. 227-40 in *Sociobiology and Conflict: Evolutionary Perspectives on Competition, Cooperation, Violence, and War*, ed. Johan M. G. van der Dennen and Vincent Falger. London: Chapman & Hall.

_____ (1990b). "Universale Muster sozialen Verhaltens: Wie entstehen aus genetischer Variabilität strukturell ähnliche Lösungen?" *Homo: Journal of Comparative Biology* 38:133-44.

_____ (1999). "The Sociobiology of Human Cooperation: The Interplay of Ultimate and Proximate Causes." Pp. 49-67 in *The Darwinian Heritage and Sociobiology*, ed. Johan M. G. van der Dennen, David Smillie, and Daniel R. Wilson. Westport, CT: Praeger.

_____ (2002). "Ethnic Solidarity As Risk Avoidance: An Evolutionary View." Pp. 219-43 in *Risky Transactions: Trust, Kinship, and Ethnicity*, ed. Frank K. Salter. Oxford: Berghahn Books.

Milgram, Stanley (1974). *Obedience to Authority: An Experimental View*. New York: Harper & Row.

Miller, Warren B. (1986). "Proception – An Important Fertility Behavior." *Demography* 23:579-94.

_____ (1992). "Personality Traits and Fertility Expectations as Antecedents of Childbearing Motivations." *Demography* 29:265-85.

Morgan, S. Philip, and S. B. King (2001). "Why Have Children in the 21st Century? Biological Predisposition, Social Coercion, Rational Choice." *European Journal of Population* 17:3-20.

Mueller, Ulrich. 1993. "Social Status and Sex." *Nature* 363:490.

Mühlmann, Wilhelm E. (1940). *Krieg und Frieden: Ein Leitfaden der politischen Ethnologie*. Heidelberg: C. Winters Universitätsbuchhandlung.

Müller, Hans-Peter, and Michael Schmid, eds. (1995). *Sozialer Wandel. Modellbildung und theoretische Ansätze*. Frankfurt am Main: Suhrkamp.

Murdock, George P. (1932). "The Science of Culture." *American Anthropologist* 34:200-15.

———— (1945). "The Common Denominator of Cultures." Pp. 123-40 in *The Science of Man in the World Crisis*, ed. Ralph Linton. New York: Columbia University Press.

Murphy, Raymond (1988). *Social Closure: The Theory of Monopolization and Exclusion*. Oxford: Oxford University Press (Clarendon Press).

Murray, Charles (1997). "IQ and Economic Success." *The Public Interest* 128(Summer):21-35.

———— (2005). "The Inequality Taboo." *Commentary* 120(2):13-22.

Nettle, Daniel (2003). "Intelligence and Class Mobility in the British Population." *British Journal of Psychology* 94:551-61.

Nettle, Daniel, and Robin I. M. Dunbar (1997). "Social Markers and the Evolution of Reciprocal Exchange." *Current Anthropology* 38:93-99.

Nicolson, Paula (1997). "Motherhood and Mothers' Lives." Pp. 375-99 in *Introducing Women's Studies: Feminist Theory and Practice*, ed. Victoria Robinson and Diane Richardson. London: Macmillan.

Niedenzu, Heinz-Jürgen (2003). "Die 'Große Evolution' und die Humangeschichte. Überlegungen zur Verknüpfung von Evolutions- und Entwicklungstheorie bei Norbert Elias." Pp. 277-301 in *Subjekte und Gesellschaft. Zur Konstitution von Sozialität*, ed. Ulrich Wenzel, Bettina Bretzinger, and Klaus Holz. Weilerswist, Germany: Velbrück.

Nielsen, François (1994). "Sociobiology and Sociology." *Annual Review of Sociology* 20:267-303.

———— (2006). "Achievement and Ascription in Educational Attainment: Genetic and Environmental Influences on Adolescent Schooling." *Social Forces* 85:193-216.

Nielsen Media Research (2006). *Nielsen Media Research Reports Television's Popularity Is Still Growing*. URL http://www.nielsenmedia.com/nc/portal/site/Public/menuitem

Nomaguchi, Kei M., Melissa A. Milkie, and Suzanne M. Bianchi (2005). "Time Strains and Psychological Well-Being: Do Dual-Earner Mothers and Fathers Differ?" *Journal of Family Issues* 26:756-92.

Ofek, Haim (2001). *The Second Nature: Economic Origins of Human Evolution*. Cambridge, UK: Cambridge University Press.

O'Meara, Tim (1997). "Causation and the Struggle for a Science of Culture." *Current Anthropology* 38:399-410.

Oppenheimer, Valerie Kincade (2000). "The Continuing Importance of Men's Economic Position in Marriage Formation." Pp. 283-301 in *The Ties that Bind: Perspectives on Marriage and Cohabitation*, ed. Linda J. Waite, Christine Bachrach, Michelle Hindin, Elizabeth Thomson, and Arland Thornton. New York: Aldine de Gruyter.

Östgaard, Einar (1965). "Factors Influencing the Flow of News." *Journal of Peace Research* 2:39-63.

Otterbein, Keith F. (2004). *How War Began*. College Station: Texas A & M University Press.

Parkin, Frank (1979). *Marxism and Class Theory: A Bourgeois Critique*. New York: Columbia University Press.

Parsons, Talcott (1951). *The Social System*. Glencoe, IL: Free Press.

_____ (1966). *Societies: Evolutionary and Comparative Perspectives.* Englewood Cliffs, NJ: Prentice-Hall.

Peritore, Patrick N. (1998). "Complexity vs. Hierarchy in Biological Explanation." Pp. 65-88 in *Sociobiology and Politics*, ed. Vincent Falger, Peter Meyer, and Johan M. G. van der Dennen. Stamford, CT: JAI Press.

Pérusse, Daniel (1993). "Cultural and Reproductive Success in Industrial Societies: Testing the Relationship at the Proximate and Ultimate Levels." *Behavioral and Brain Sciences* 16:267-322.

Piaget, Jean (1952). "The Child and Moral Realism." Pp. 417-35 in *Moral Principles of Action*, ed. Ruth Nanda Anshen. New York: Harper.

Pinker, Steven (1995). *The Language Instinct: The New Science of Language and Mind.* London: Penguin.

_____ (1997). *How the Mind Works.* New York: Norton.

_____ 2003). *Das unbeschriebene Blatt. Die moderne Leugnung der menschlichen Natur.* Berlin: Berlin Verlag (German translation of original English edition, *The Blank Slate: The Modern Denial of Human Nature.* New York: Viking, 2002.)

Pluciennik, Mark (2005). *Social Evolution.* London: Duckworth.

_____ (2006). "Deep Commonalities Between Life and Mind." Pp. 130-41 in *Richard Dawkins: How a Scientist Changes the Way We Think*, ed. Alan Grafen and Mark Ridley. Oxford: Oxford University Press.

Pohlmann, Friedrich (2004). "Review of *Soziale Evolution. Die Evolutionstheorie und die Sozialwissenschaften.*" *Österreichische Zeitschrift für Soziologie* 29:78-80.

Popper, Karl (1972). *Objective Knowledge: An Evolutionary Approach.* Oxford: Oxford University Press (Clarendon Press).

Postman, Neil (1979). *Teaching as a Conserving Activity.* New York: Delacorte Press.

Pryor, Frederic L. (1985). "The Invention of the Plow." *Comparative Studies in Society and History* 27:727-43.

Pyysiäinen, Ilkka (2005). "Yhteisö ja agenttius Durkheimin uskontoteorioissa." *Sosiologia* 4:298-308.

Radcliffe-Brown, Alfred R. (1924). "The Mother's Brother in South Africa." *South African Journal of Science* 21:542-55.

Radkau, Joachim (2005). *Max Weber. Die Leidenschaft des Denkens.* München: Hanser.

Rambo, A. Terry, and Kathleen Gillogly, eds. (1991). *Profiles in Cultural Evolution: Papers from a Conference in Honor of Elman R. Service.* Ann Arbor: University of Michigan Press.

Raphael, David D. (1991). *Adam Smith.* Frankfurt am Main: Suhrkamp.

Raley, Sara B., Marybeth J. Mattingly, and Suzanne M. Bianchi (2006). "How Dual are Dual-Income Couples? Documenting Change from 1970 to 2001." *Journal of Marriage and the Family* 68:11-28.

Reichholf, Josef H. (1994). *Der schöpferische Impuls.* München: Dt. Taschenbuch-Verlag.

Reynolds, Vernon (1973). "Ethology of Social Change." Pp. 467-78 in *The Explanation of Cultural Change: Models in Prehistory*, ed. Colin Renfrew. London: Duckworth.

Richerson, Peter J. (1997). "Culture and Human Nature." *Politics and the Life Sciences* 16:40-41.

Richerson, Peter J., and Robert Boyd (1992). "Punishment Allows the Evolution of Cooperation (or Anything Else) in Sizable Groups." *Ethology and Sociobiology* 13:171-95.

_____ (1998). "The Evolution of Human Ultrasociality." Pp. 71-95 in *Indoctrinability, Ideology, and Warfare: Evolutionary Perspectives*, ed. Frank K. Salter and Irenäus Eibl-Eibesfeldt. Oxford: Berghahn Books.

_____ (2005). *Not by Genes Alone: How Culture Transformed Human Evolution.* Chicago: University of Chicago Press.

Richerson, Peter J., Robert Boyd, and Joseph Henrich (2002). "Cultural Evolution of Human Cooperation." Pp. 373-404 in *Genetic and Cultural Evolution of Cooperation*, ed. Peter Hammerstein. Cambridge, MA: MIT Press.

Richter, Dirk (2005). "Das Scheitern der Biologisierung der Soziologie. Zum Stand der Diskussion um die Soziobiologie und anderer evolutionstheoretischer Ansätze." *Kölner Zeitschrift für Soziologie und Sozialpsychologie* 57:523-42.

Robarchek, Clayton A. (1990) "Motivations and Material Causes: On the Explanation of Conflict and War." Pp. 56-76 in *The Anthropology of War*, ed. Jonathan Haas. New York: Cambridge University Press.

Roberts, Wesley W., and Stephen K. Sanderson (2005). "Social Evolution and Religious Evolution: A Cross-Cultural, Quantitative Analysis." Paper presented at the annual meetings of the American Sociological Association, Philadelphia.

Rodgers, Joseph Lee, Kimberly Hughes, Hans-Peter Kohler, Kaare Christensen, Debby Doughty, David C. Rowe, and Warren B. Miller (2001). "Genetic Influence Helps Explain Variation in Human Fertility: Evidence from Recent Behavioral and Molecular Genetic Studies." *Current Directions in Psychological Science* 10:184-88.

Roediger, David R. (1999). *The Wages of Whiteness: Race and the Making of the American Working Class*. New York: Verso.

Rogers, Alan R. (1995). "For Love or Money: The Evolution of Reproductive and Material Motivations." Pp. 76-85 in *Human Reproductive Decisions: Biological and Social Perspectives*, ed. Robin I. M. Dunbar. Basingstoke, UK: Macmillan Press.

Rogers, Everett M. (2003). *Diffusion of Innovations*. New York: Simon & Schuster.

Ross, E. A. (1896). "Social Control." *American Journal of Sociology* 1:513-35.

Rossi, Alice S. (1984). "Gender and Parenthood." *American Sociological Review* 49:1-19.

_____ (1987). "Parenthood in Transition: From Lineage to Child to Self-Orientation." Pp. 31-81 in *Parenting across the Life Span*, ed. Jane B. Lancaster, Lonnie Sherrod, and Alice S. Rossi. New York: Aldine de Gruyter.

Ruhrmann, Georg, Jens Woelke, Michaela Maier, and Nicole Diehlmann (2003). *Der Wert von Nachrichten im deutschen Fernsehen*. Opladen: Leske & Budrich.

Runciman, W. G. (1989). *A Treatise on Social Theory. Volume II: Substantive Social Theory*. Cambridge, UK: Cambridge University Press.

_____ (1990). "Doomed to Extinction: The *Polis* as an Evolutionary Dead-end." Pp. 347-67 in *The Greek City from Homer to Alexander*, ed. Oswyn Murray and Simon Price. Oxford: Oxford University Press (Clarendon Press).

_____ (1999). "Reply to Hallpike." *Journal of the Royal Anthropological Institute (n.s.)* 5:629.

_____ (2001). "Greek Hoplites: Rejoinder to Hallpike." *Journal of the Royal Anthropological Institute (n.s.)* 7:573.

_____ (2005). "Rejoinder to Fracchia and Lewontin." *History and Theory* 44:30-41.

Rushton, J. Phillipe (2004). "Genetic and Environmental Contributions to Pro-social Attitudes: A Twin Study of Social Responsibility." *Proceedings of the Royal Society of London B* 271:2583-85.

Sahlins, Marshall (1976). *The Use and Abuse of Biology: An Anthropological Critique of Sociobiology*. Ann Arbor: University of Michigan Press.

Salter, Frank K. (1995). *Emotions in Command*. Oxford: Oxford University Press.

_____ (1996). "'Drawn by Light': Visual Recording Methods in Biopolitics." Pp. 23-59 in *Research in Biopolitics*, Vol. IV, ed. Albert Somit and Steven A. Peterson. Greenwich: CT: JAI Press.

_____ (2002). "Estimating Ethnic Genetic Interests: Is it Adaptive to Resist Replacement Migration?" *Population and Environment* 24:111-40.

_____ (2006). *On Genetic Interests*. New Brunswick, NJ: Transaction.

Sanderson, Stephen K. (1988). *Macrosociology: An Introduction to Human Societies*. New York: Harper & Row.

_____ (1990). *Social Evolutionism: A Critical History*. Oxford: Blackwell.

_____ (1995). *Social Transformations: A General Theory of Historical Development*. Oxford: Blackwell.

_____ (1999a). *Social Transformations. A General Theory of Historical Development*. Updated ed. Lanham, MD: Rowman & Littlefield.

_____ (1999b). *Macrosociology: An Introduction to Human Societies*. 4th ed. Boston: Allyn & Bacon Longman.

_____ (1997). "Evolutionism and Its Critics." *Journal of World Systems Research* 3:94-114.

_____ (2001a). *The Evolution of Human Sociality: A Darwinian Conflict Perspective*. Lanham, MD: Rowman & Littlefield.

_____ (2001b). "Social Evolution: Overview." Pp. 14279-86 in *International Encyclopedia of the Social and Behavioural Sciences*, ed. Neil J. Smelser and Paul B. Baltes. New York: Elsevier.

_____ (2001c). "Explaining Monogamy and Polygyny in Human Societies: Comment on Kanazawa and Still." *Social Forces* 80:329-35.

_____ (2001d). "An Evolutionary Theory of Fertility Decline: New Evidence." *Population and Environment* 22:555-63.

_____ (2005). "The Incest Taboo: Biological Evolution, Cultural Evolution, or Coevolution?" (Review Essay on Jonathan H. Turner and Alexandra Maryanski, *Incest: Origins of the Taboo*. Boulder, CO: Paradigm Publishers, 2005.) *Evolution and Sociology Newsletter* 2(1):6-10.

_____ (2007a). "Edward Westermarck: The Invisible Master." Paper presented at the annual meetings of the American Sociological Association, New York City.

_____ (2007b). "Marvin Harris, Meet Charles Darwin: A Critical Evaluation and Theoretical Extension of Cultural Materialism." Pp. 194-228 in *Studying Societies and Cultures: Marvin Harris's Cultural Materialism and Its Legacy*, ed. Lawrence A. Kuznar and Stephen K. Sanderson. Boulder, CO: Paradigm Publishers.

_____ (2007c). *Evolutionism and Its Critics: Deconstructing and Reconstructing an Evolutionary Interpretation of Human Society*. Boulder, CO: Paradigm Publishers.

_____ (2007d). "Neo-Darwinian Theories of Religion and the Social Ecology of Religious Evolution." Paper presented at the annual meetings of the American Sociological Association, New York City.

_____ (2008). "Religious Attachment Theory and the Biosocial Evolution of the Major World Religions." Pp. 67-72 in *The Evolution of Religion: Studies, Theories, and Critiques*, ed. Joseph Bulbulia, Richard Sosis, Erica Harris, Russell Genet, Cheryl Genet, and Karen Wyman. Santa Margarita, CA: Collins Foundation Press.

Sanderson, Stephen K., and Joshua Dubrow (2000). "Fertility Decline in the Modern World and in the Original Demographic Transition: Testing Three Theories with Cross-cultural Data." *Population and Environment* 21:511-37.

Sanderson, Stephen K., and Lee Ellis (1992). "Theoretical and Political Perspectives of American Sociologists in the 1990s." *American Sociologist* 23:26-42.

Sanderson, Stephen K., D. Alex Heckert, and Joshua Dubrow (2005). "Militarist, Marxian, and Non-Marxian Materialist Theories of Gender Inequality: A Cross-Cultural Test." *Social Forces* 83:1425-42.

Saunders, Peter (1997). "Social Mobility in Britain: An Empirical Evaluation of Two Competing Explanations." *Sociology* 31:261-88.

_____ (2002). "Reflections on the Meritocracy Debate in Britain: A Response to Richard Breen and John Goldthorpe." *British Journal of Sociology* 53:559-74.

Savage, Mike, and Muriel Egerton (1997). "Social Mobility, Individual Ability, and the Inheritance of Class Inequality." *Sociology* 31:645-72.

Sayer, Liana C., and Suzanne M. Bianchi (2000). "Women's Economic Independence and the Probability of Divorce." *Journal of Family Issues* 21:906-43.

Sayer, Liana C., Suzanne M. Bianchi, and John P. Robinson (2004). "Are Parents Investing Less in Children? Trends in Mothers' and Fathers' Time With Children." *American Journal of Sociology* 110:1-43.

Schelkle, Waltraud, Wolf-Hagen Krauth, Martin Kohli, and Georg Elwert, eds. (2000). *Paradigms of Social Change: Modernization, Development, Transformation, Evolution.* Frankfurt: Campus Verlag.

Schiff, Michael, and Richard C. Lewontin (1986). *Education and Class: The Irrelevance of IQ Genetic Studies.* Oxford: Oxford University Press (Clarendon Press).

Schmandt-Besserat, Denise (1978). "The Earliest Precursor of Writing." *Scientific American* 128:38-47.

Schoen, Robert, and Yen-hsin Alice Cheng (2006). "Partner Choice and the Differential Retreat from Marriage." *Journal of Marriage and the Family* 681:1-10.

Schwender, Clemens (2001). *Medien und Emotionen.* Wiesbaden: Deutscher Universitätsverlag.

Scott, Colin (1988). "Property, Practice, and Aboriginal Rights among Quebec Cree Hunters." Pp. 35-51 in *Hunters and Gatherers*, Vol. 2, ed. Tim Ingold, David Riches, and James Woodburn. Oxford: Berg.

Segal, Nancy L. (1999). *Entwined Lives: Twins and What They Tell Us About Human Behavior.* New York: Dutton.

Segerstråle, Ullica (2000). *Defenders of the Truth: The Battle for Science in the Sociobiology Debate and Beyond.* New York: Oxford University Press.

Seltzer, Judith (1994). "Consequences of Marital Dissolution for Children." *Annual Review of Sociology* 20:235-66.

Sevón, Eija (2005). "Timing Motherhood: Experiencing and Narrating the Choice to Become a Mother." *Feminism and Psychology* 15:461-82.

Shankman, Paul (1969). "Le Rôti et le Bouilli: Lévi-Strauss's Theory of Cannibalism." *American Anthropologist* 71:54–69.

Shaw, R. Paul, and Yuwa Wong (1989). *Genetic Seeds of Warfare: Evolution, Nationalism, and Patriotism.* London: Unwin & Hyman.

Shepher, Joseph (1972). "Mate Selection Among Second-Generation Kibbutz Adolescents and Adults: Incest Avoidance and Negative Imprinting." *Archives of Sexual Behavior* 1:293-307.

_____ (1983). *Incest: A Biosocial View.* New York: Academic Press.

Shoemaker, Pamela J., and Akiba A. Cohen (2006). *News Around the World.* New York: Routledge.

Skinner, William G. (2004). "Grandparental Effects on Reproductive Strategizing: Nôbi Villagers in Early Modern Japan." *Demographic Research,* September 11, 2004. URL http://www.demographic-research.org.

Simon, Herbert A. (1990). "Invariants of Human Behavior." *Annual Review of Psychology* 41:1-19.

Singer, J. David, and Melvin Small (1972). *The Wages of War, 1816-1965: A Statistical Handbook.* New York: Wiley.

Smith, Thomas S., and Gregory T. Stevens (2002). "Hyperstructures and the Biology of Interpersonal Dependence: Rethinking Reciprocity and Altruism." *Sociological Theory* 20:106-30.

Smuts, Barbara (1995). "The Evolutionary Origins of Patriarchy." *Human Nature* 61:1-32.

Snooks, Graeme Donald (1996). *The Dynamic Society: Exploring the Sources of Global Change.* London: Routledge.

_____ (1997). *The Ephemeral Civilization: Exploding the Myth of Social Evolution.* London: Routledge.

_____ (1998). *The Laws of History.* London: Routledge.

Sorokin, Pitirim A. (1937). *Social and Cultural Dynamics. Vol. III: Fluctuations of Social Relationships, War, and Revolutions.* New York: American Books.

Sperber, Dan (1991). "The Epidemiology of Beliefs." Pp. 25-43 in *The Social Psychological Study of Widespread Beliefs,* ed. Colin Fraser and George Gaskell. Oxford: Oxford University Press.

Speier, Hans (1941). "The Social Types of War." *American Journal of Sociology* 46:445-54.

Spier, Fred (1996). *The Structure of Big History.* Amsterdam: Amsterdam University Press.

Spilerman, Seymour (2000). "Wealth and Stratification Processes." *Annual Review of Sociology* 26:497-524.

Staubmann, Helmut (2001). "Handlungstheoretische Systemtheorie. Talcott Parsons." Pp. 147-70 in *Soziologische Theorie,* 7th ed., ed. Julius Morel, Eva Bauer, Tamás Meleghy, Heinz-Jürgen Niedenzu, Max Preglau, and Helmut Staubmann. München: Oldenbourg.

Sweeney, Megan M. (2002). "Two Decades of Family Change: The Shifting Economic Foundations of Marriage." *American Sociological Review* 67:132-47.

Sweeney, Megan M., and Maria Cancian (2004). "The Changing Importance of White Women's Economic Prospects for Assortative Mating." *Journal of Marriage and the Family* 66:1015-28.

Taylor, Alan J. P. (1979) *How Wars Begin.* London: Hamish Hamilton.

Tiger, Lionel, and Robin Fox (1971). *The Imperial Animal.* New York: Holt, Rinehart and Winston.

Tomkin, Richard (2006). "Sweet Child of Mine." *London Financial Times,* June 24-25:W1-2.

Tooby, John, and Leda Cosmides (1989). "Evolutionary Psychology and the Generation of Culture, Part I: Theoretical Considerations." *Ethology and Sociobiology* 10:29-49.

Tooby, John, and Leda Cosmides (1992). "The Psychological Foundations of Culture." Pp. 19-136 in *The Adapted Mind: Evolutionary Psychology and the Generation of Culture,* ed. Jerome H. Barkow, Leda Cosmides, and John Tooby. New York: Oxford University Press.

Trigger, Bruce G. (1998). *Sociocultural Evolution.* Oxford: Blackwell.

Trivers, Robert L. (1971). "The Evolution of Reciprocal Altruism." *Quarterly Review of Biology* 46:35-57.

Trivers, Robert L., and Dan E. Willard (1973). "Natural Selection of Parental Ability to Vary the Sex Ratio of Offspring." *Science* 179 (Jan.):90-92.

Turke, Paul W. (1989). "Evolution and the Demand for Children." *Population and Development Review* 15:61-90.

Turner, Jonathan H. (2000). *On the Origin of Human Emotions: A Sociological Inquiry into the Evolution of Human Affect.* Stanford, CA: Stanford University Press.

_____ (2003). *Human Institutions: A Theory of Societal Evolution.* Boulder, CO: Rowman & Littlefield.

Turner, Jonathan H., and Alexandra Maryanski (2005). *Incest: Origins of the Taboo.* Boulder, CO: Paradigm Publishers.

Turney-High, H. H. (1949). *Primitive War: Its Practice and Concepts.* Columbia: University of South Carolina Press.

Udry, J. Richard (1996). "Biosocial Models of Low-fertility Societies." *Population and Development Review* 22 (*Supplement: Fertility in the US*):325-36.

_____ (2000). "Biological Limits of Gender Construction." *American Sociological Review* 65:443-57.

Uhl, Matthias (2007). "Alte Anlagen – neue Medien – evolutionäre Medienanthropologie." In *Im Rücken der Kulturen*, ed. Karl Eibl, Katja Mellmann, and Rüdiger Zymner. Paderborn: Mentis.

van den Berghe, Pierre L. (1975). *Man in Society: A Biosocial View.* New York: Elsevier.

_____ (1979). *Human Family Systems.* New York: Elsevier.

_____ (1981). *The Ethnic Phenomenon.* New York: Elsevier.

_____ (1990). "Why Most Sociologists Don't (and Won't) Think Evolutionarily." *Sociological Forum* 5:173-83.

_____ (1997). "Review of Steven Goldberg, *Why Men Rule.*" *European Sociobiological Society Newsletter* 44:2-3.

van den Berghe, Pierre L., and Joseph Whitmeyer (1990). "Social Class and Reproductive Success." *International Journal of Contemporary Sociology* 27:29-48.

van der Dennen, Johan M. G. (1995). *The Origin of War: The Evolution of a Male-Coalitional Reproductive Strategy.* 2 vols. Groningen, Netherlands: Origin Press.

van Parijs, Phillipe (1981). *Evolutionary Explanation in the Social Sciences: An Emerging Paradigm.* Totowa, NJ: Rowman & Littlefield.

Vining, Daniel R. (1986). "Social versus Reproductive Success: The Central Theoretical Problem of Human Sociobiology." *Behavioral and Brain Sciences* 9:167-87.

Voland, Eckhart (2002). *Grundriss der Soziobiologie.* Heidelberg: Spektrum.

Vowinckel, Gerhard (1995). *Verwandtschaft, Freundschaft, und die Gesellschaft der Fremden.* Darmstadt: Wissenschaftliche Buchgesellschaft.

_____ (2001). "Biotische, psychische, und soziokulturelle Konstruktionen der Wirklichkeit und wie sie zusammenhängen." Pp. 257-78 in *Universalien und Konstruktivismus*, ed. Peter M. Hejl. Frankfurt am Main: Suhrkamp.

_____ (2003). "Biotische und kulturelle Evolution: Eigengesetzlichkeit und Interdependenz." Pp. 147-62 in *Soziale Evolution. Die Evolutionstheorie und die Sozialwissenschaften*, ed. Tamás Meleghy and Heinz-Jürgen Niedenzu. (*Österreichische Zeitschrift für Soziologie*, spezial edition vol. 7.) Wiesbaden: Westdeutscher Verlag.

Waite, Linda J., ed. (2000). *The Ties that Bind: Perspectives on Marriage and Cohabitation.* New York: Aldine de Gruyter.

Waldman, Irwin D., Richard A. Weinberg, and Sandra Scarr (1994). "Racial-group Differences in IQ in the Minnesota Transracial Adoption Study: A Reply to Levin and Lynn." *Intelligence* 19:29-44.

Walker, Rebecca (2007). *Baby Love*. New York: Penguin (Riverhead Books).

Wallerstein, Immanuel (1974a). "The Rise and Future Demise of the World Capitalist System: Concepts for Comparative Analysis. " *Comparative Studies in Society and History* 16:387-415.

_____ (1974b). *The Modern World-System: Capitalist Agriculture and the Origins of the European World-Economy in the Sixteenth Century*. New York: Academic Press.

_____ (1980). *The Modern World-System II: Mercantilism and the Consolidation of the European World-Economy, 1600-1750*. New York: Academic Press.

_____ (1989). *The Modern World-System III: The Second Era of Great Expansion of the Capitalist World-Economy, 1730-1840s*. San Diego: Academic Press.

Wang, Xaio T. (1996). "Evolutionary Hypotheses of Risk-Sensitive Choice: Age Differences and Perspective Change." *Ethology and Sociobiology* 17:1-15.

Weber, Max (1958). *The Protestant Ethic and the Spirit of Capitalism*. Trans. Talcott Parsons. New York: Scribner's. (Originally published 1904-05.)

Weeden, Kim (2002). "Why Do Some Occupations Pay More than Others? Social Closure and Earnings Inequality in the United States." *American Journal of Sociology* 108:55-101.

Weingart, Peter (2000). "Biologie als Gesellschaftstheorie." Pp. 146-66 in *Menschenbilder. Zur Pluralisierung der Vorstellung von der menschlichen Natur (1850-1914)*, ed. Achim Barsch and Peter M. Hejl. Frankfurt am Main: Suhrkamp.

Weingart, Peter, Sandra Mitchell, Peter J. Richerson, and Sabine Maasen, eds. (1997). *Human by Nature: Between Biology and the Social Sciences*. Mahwah, NJ: Lawrence Erlbaum.

Westermarck, Edward (1891). *The History of Human Marriage*. 3 vols. London: Macmillan.

_____ (1894). *The History of Human Marriage*. 3 vols. 2nd ed. London: Macmillan.

_____ (1906). *The Origin and Development of the Moral Ideas*. Vol. 1. London: Macmillan.

_____ (1908). *The Origin and Development of the Moral Ideas*. Vol. 2. London: Macmillan.

_____ (1922a). *The History of Human Marriage*. Vol. 1. 5th ed. New York: Allerton.

_____ (1922b). *The History of Human Marriage*. Vol. 2. 5th ed. New York: Allerton.

_____ (1922c). *The History of Human Marriage*. Vol. 3. 5th ed. New York: Allerton.

_____ (1927). *Minnen ur mitt liv*. Helsingfors: Holger Schildts. (English version *Memories of My Life*, trans. Anna Barwell. New York: Macaulay, 1929.)

_____ (1932). *Ethical Relativity*. New York: Harcourt, Brace.

_____ (1934). *Freuds teori om Oedipus-komplexen*. Stockholm: Albert Bonniers Förlag.

Whiffen, Theo W. (1915) *The North-West Amazons: Notes on Some Months Spent among Cannibal Tribes*. New York: Scribner's.

White, Leslie A. (1949). *The Science of Culture: A Study of Man and Civilization*. New York: Grove Press.

_____ (1959). *The Evolution of Culture: The Development of Civilization to the Fall of Rome*. New York: McGraw-Hill.

Wiessner, Polly (1982). "Risk, Reciprocity, and Social Influences on !Kung San Economics." Pp. 61-84 in *Politics and History in Band Societies*, ed. Evan Peacock and Richard B. Lee. New York: Cambridge University Press.

Wilson, David Sloan, and Elliott Sober (1994). "Reintroducing Group Selection to The Human Behavioral Sciences." *Behavioral and Brain Sciences* 17:585-654.

Wilson, Edward O. (1971). "Competitive and Aggressive Behavior." Pp. 183-217 in *Man and Beast: Comparative Social Behavior*, ed. J. F. Eisenberg and W. S. Dillon. Washington, DC: Smithsonian Institution Press.

_____ (1975). *Sociobiology: The New Synthesis.* Cambridge, MA: Harvard University Press.

_____ (1978). *On Human Nature.* Cambridge, MA: Harvard University Press.

_____ (1998). *Consilience: The Unity of Knowledge.* New York: Random House (Vintage).

Wilterdink, Nico (2003). "The Concept of Social Evolution: Its Meanings and Uses." Pp. 53-73 in *Soziale Evolution. Die Evolutionstheorie und die Sozialwissenschaften*, ed. Tamás Meleghy and Heinz-Jürgen Niedenzu. (*Österreichische Zeitschrift für Soziologie*, spezial edition vol. 7.) Wiesbaden: Westdeutscher Verlag.

Wimmer, Hannes (1996). *Evolution der Politik. Von der Stammesgesellschaft zur modernen Demokratie.* Wien: WUV-Universitätsverlag.

Wissler, Clark (1965). *Man and Culture.* New York: Johnson. (Originally published 1923.)

Wolf, Arthur P. (1995). *Sexual Attraction and Childhood Association: A Chinese Brief for Edward Westermarck.* Stanford, CA: Stanford University Press.

Wolf, Arthur P., and William H. Durham, eds. (2004). *Inbreeding, Incest, and the Incest Taboo: The State of Knowledge at the Turn of the Century.* Stanford, CA: Stanford University Press.

Wolfe, John R. (1982). "The Impact of Family Resources on Childhood IQ." *Journal of Human Resources* 17:213-35.

Wooding, Stephen P. (2007). "Following the Herd." *Nature Genetics* 39:7-8.

Wouters, Cas (2004). *Sex and Manners: Female Emancipation in the West 1890-2000.* London: Sage.

Wrangham, Richard W. (1999). "Evolution of Coalitional Killing." *Yearbook of Physical Anthropology* 42:1-30.

INDEX

Abernethy, Virginia, 150
action, theory of, Schmid on, 29–30
air pump, 127
Albert, Hans, 81
Alexander, R. D., 85
altruism: Hakami on, 70; Hopcroft on, 54; kin selected, 4. *See also* reciprocal altruism
ambush-type warfare. *See* raiding-type warfare
American Sociological Association, 24
Ames, Ashley, 12
Anlagen, 10
anthropocentrism, and reception of sociobiology, 23
anthropology: and biology, 24; Westermarck and, 136
Antweiler, Christoph, 62–66; Sanderson on, 206–7
Aristotle, 123–24, 126
audio-visual media, 190–92

baboons, and war, 121
baby fever, 147–58; adaptations for, 151–58; antidote to, 151; definition of, 149; versus pregnancy and child care, 156
Badcock, Christopher, 17
Banks, Joseph, 131
Barot, Odysse, 118
Becker, Gary, 162–63
Betzig, Laura, 198
binary oppositions: Lévi-Strauss on, 102–3; Meleghy on, 109
biogrammar, 10
biological clock: definition of, 147–48, 157n1; Rotkirch on, 147–57
biological dispositions, and individual actions and social processes, 46

biology: Meyer on, 81; sociology and, 3–6, 90–91
biomaterialism, 22, 212–14; Lévi-Strauss on, 107–9; Niedenzu on, 95–97; Schmid on, 31; Wilterdink on, 43
biopsychic univerals, Antweiler on, 64
biopsychological needs, Hakami on, 69–70
biostructure, 20; Hallpike on, 122; Sanderson on, 203; Schmid on, 30; Wilterdink on, 43
biotic level, 98–99
Black, Joseph, 128
Bodmer, Walter, 164
Bollywood, topics in, 192, 192t
Boulton, Matthew, 128
Bourdieu, Pierre, 4
brain: function of, 94; and science, Sanderson on, 214–15
Brown, Donald E., 64
Burke, Edmund, 79
Burt, Cyril, 164–65

Campbell, Anne, 154
Campbell, Donald T., 176
cannibalism, Lévi-Strauss on, 102–3
Carlisle, Anthony, 131
carnage, wars of, 112
Carneiro, Robert, 63, 74, 76–77, 207
causal flow: Hallpike on, 122–23, 131–32; Sanderson on, 21, 201–2; Schmid on, 31, 36–37; Wilterdink on, 43–45
Cavalli-Sforza, Luigi, 164
Chagnon, N. A., 112–13
chimpanzees: and culture, 173; and war, 113–14, 114f, 121
clan, definition of, 140
class, social stratification by, 60–61

248

CONTRIBUTORS

Christoph Antweiler is currently professor of cultural anthropology at the University of Trier, Germany. He obtained his Ph.D. in 1987 in Cologne on the subject of models of long-term social change. His main regional research interest is Southeast Asia, especially Indonesia and South Asia. He has done research on cognition, cities, interethnic issues, practicing anthropology, and local knowledge. Among his latest books is an annotated bibliography of cultural anthropology, *Ethnologie lesen. Ein Führer durch den Bücherdschungel* (*Reading Anthropology. A Guide Through the Book Jungle*) (Lit Verlag, 4th ed. 2003). Recently he coedited (with Franz Wuketits) the *Handbook of Evolution. Volume 1: The Evolution of Cultures and Societies* (Wiley-VCH, 2004). A book-length anthropological study on transcultural universals, *Was ist den Menschen gemeinsam?* (Wissenschaftliche Buchgesellschaft, 2007), has just been published. Currently he is working on human universals and on cognition and ethnicity in Indonesia.

Khaled Hakami is an anthropologist and a lecturer in the Department of Social and Cultural Anthropology at the University of Vienna. He has done fieldwork in two hunter-gatherer societies, the Semang of Thailand and the Kubu of Sumatra. Besides his interest in this type of society, his major research interests include social evolution and the anthropology of war. Within his cultural materialist framework he recently published an article in German on the evolution of ancient societies and the function of war in tribal societies. His current research focuses on the structure and development of evolutionary theory in the social sciences, with a special emphasis on the role of Herbert Spencer. As a convinced exponent of the epistemological foundations of modern science he stands in strict opposition to postmodernist or humanistic approaches in anthropology.

C. R. Hallpike is emeritus professor of anthropology, McMaster University, Hamilton, Ontario, Canada. His major research interests are East Africa, Papua New Guinea, primitive warfare, social and cultural evolution, developmental psychology and modes of thought, and the history of science. His most important publications are *The Foundations of Primitive Thought* (Oxford University Press, 1979), *The Principles of Social Evolution* (Oxford University Press, 1986), and *The Evolution of Moral Understanding* (Prometheus Research Group, 2004). He has just completed the manuscript for *The Human Revolution: From Bows and Arrows to the Space Age in Only 10,000 Years*, which is an anti-Darwinian account of social and cultural evolution.

Peter M. Hejl holds a diploma in political science from Freie Universität Berlin and a Ph.D. in sociology from Bielefeld University, where he received his Habilitation (Priv. Dozent). Hejl teaches sociology, especially sociology of the media, in the Institute of Media Research (Vice-director) of the University of Siegen (Germany) and in Bielefeld (Faculty of Sociology). He is a guest professor at the University of Innsbruck (Austria). His theoretical and empirical research interests focus on a vertical integration of human perception, communication, and macrosocial phenomena from an evolutionary perspective. He has published widely on (cognitive) constructivism, systems theory, the history of sociology, and communication and media with applications to media analysis and management theory. In a recent empirical study supported by the Deutsche Forschungsgemeinschaft (DFG) he analyzed universal aspects of Hollywood and Bollywood films from an evolutionary perspective.

Rosemary L. Hopcroft is currently associate professor in the Department of Sociology at the University of North Carolina at Charlotte. Her major research interest and the focus of her current research is the application of evolutionary theory to sociological issues, and more generally the intersection between sociological and biological processes. Recent publications include "Parental Status and Differential Investment in Sons and Daughters: Trivers-Willard Revisited" (*Social Forces*, 2005), "Status Characteristics Among Older Individuals: The Diminished Significance of Gender" (*Sociological Quarterly*, 2006), "Sex, Status, and Reproductive Success in the Contemporary U.S." (*Evolution and Human Behavior*, 2006), and "The Sex Difference in Depression Across 29 Countries" (*Social Forces*, 2007) (with Dana Burr Bradley).

Tamás Meleghy was born in Budapest and studied economics and sociology at the Universities of Hamburg (Germany) and Innsbruck (Austria). He is a professor emeritus of sociology at the University of Innsbruck. His main research interests are sociological theory and the methodology of the social sciences. Some of his most recent books are *Soziologie als Sozial-, Moral- und Kulturwissenschaft* (Duncker & Humblot, 2001) and *Soziale Evolution* (Westdeutscher Verlag, 2003), coedited with Heinz-Jürgen Niedenzu.

Peter Meyer, now retired, was a professor of sociology at the University of Augsburg, Germany. His major research interests include transcultural studies of collective violence and the contribution of evolutionary science to sociology. Some of his publications are *Evolution und Gewalt* (*Evolution and Collective Violence*) (Parey, 1981); *Soziobiologie und Soziologie* (*Sociobiology and Sociology*) (Luchterhand, 1982); and "Social Evolution," in *Handbook of Evolution. Volume 1: The Evolution of Human Societies and Cultures*, ed. Franz M. Wuketits and Christoph Antweiler (Wiley-VCH, 2004).

Heinz-Jürgen Niedenzu, was born in Düsseldorf, Germany, and studied sociology, political science, and social anthropology at the Universities of Freiburg

(Germany) and Uppsala (Sweden). He is an associate professor of sociology at the University of Innsbruck (Austria). His main research interests are theories of sociocultural evolution, the long-term development of societal structures, and the anthropological foundations of social theory. Recently he coedited (with Tamás Meleghy) *Soziale Evolution* (Westdeutscher Verlag, 2003). He has also written numerous articles in German on Norbert Elias's process theory and on topics in the field of social evolution.

J. P. Roos is a professor of social policy, University of Helsinki. His major research interests are life stories, generations, and child welfare, all highly relevant to evolutionary sociology. His current research is about generational interactions between the baby boom generation in Finland and its parents and children. The survey is partly comparable to that of the SHARE project, which makes possible extensive European comparisons. His books include *Finnish Life: A Study of Ordinary Finns' Life Stories* (SKS Publishers, 1987), *Life Politics* (Gaudeamus, 1998), and *Bourdieu and Me* (Vastapaino, 2006).

Anna Rotkirch is a senior researcher and head of Family Studies at the Finnish Institute of Population Research, Family Federation, Finland. She is also docent of Social Policy and Women's Studies at the University of Helsinki. Rotkirch has specialized in comparative research on families, gender, and sexuality. Her publications include *Women's Voices in Russia Today* (coeditor) (Dartmouth, 1996), *The Man Question: Loves and Lives in Late-Twentieth-Century Russia* (University of Helsinki Press, 2000), *Sexual Lifestyles in the Twentieth Century* (coauthor) (Palgrave, 2002), and *On Living Through the Soviet System* (coeditor) (Routledge, 2003). Her current research interests include fertility behavior, later parenthood, and generational transfers.

W. G. Runciman is a fellow of Trinity College, Cambridge, and of the British Academy, of which he was president from 2001 to 2004. His major publications include his three-volume *Treatise on Social Theory* (Volume I, 1983; Volume II, 1989; Volume III, 1997). His principal research interest is the application of neo-Darwinian evolutionary theory to comparative and historical sociology.

Frank Salter is a researcher at the Max Planck Research Group for Human Ethology in Andechs, Germany. His research applies behavioral biological methods and theory to the study of sociological, political, and anthropological themes, including hierarchy, riots, mate choice, indoctrination, ethnicity, nationalism, and political theory. His book *On Genetic Interests* was reissued by Transaction Publishers in 2006, and his first monograph, *Emotions in Command,* is soon to be reissued by the same publisher. He is presently researching elite ethnic power in the United States and the rhetorical devices used by ethnic activists.

Stephen K. Sanderson, now retired from full-time teaching, is a visiting scholar at the University of California, Riverside. His main areas of specialization are comparative-historical sociology, sociological theory, the biological foundations of human societies, and long-term social evolution. He is the author or editor of ten books, including *Social Evolutionism: A Critical History* (Blackwell, 1990); *Social Transformations: A General Theory of Historical Development* (Blackwell, 1995, updated edition. Rowman & Littlefield, 1999); *The Evolution of Human Sociality: A Darwinian Conflict Perspective* (Rowman & Littlefield, 2001); *World Societies: The Evolution of Human Social Life* (Allyn & Bacon, 2005) (coauthored with Arthur S. Alderson); *Revolutions: A Worldwide Introduction to Political and Social Change* (Paradigm, 2005); *Evolutionism and Its Critics: Deconstructing and Reconstructing An Evolutionary Interpretation of Human Society* (Paradigm, 2007); and *Studying Societies and Cultures: Marvin Harris's Cultural Materialism and Its Legacy* (Paradigm, 2007) (coedited with Lawrence A. Kuznar). He has also written numerous articles for journals and edited collections on such topics as the origins of apartheid in South Africa, the transition to capitalism in Japan, historical European household structures, long-term world commercialization, fertility decline in the modern world, monogamy and polygyny in human societies, ethnic heterogeneity and welfare spending, cultural materialism and sociobiology, eclecticism in sociological theory, world-systems analysis, and reforming theoretical work in sociology. Currently he is working on books on Darwinian theories of culture and the long-term evolution of religion. He is also writing articles on religious evolution, world democratization, the empirical testing of sociological theories, and comparative family systems.

Michael Schmid is professor of general sociology at the University of the Armed Forces in Munich, Germany. His principal research interests include sociological theory, philosophy of the social sciences, interdisciplinary institutional theories, and problems of scientific explanation in sociology. Some of his most important publications are *Rationalität und Theoriebildung: Studien zu Karl R. Poppers Philosophie der Sozialwissenschaften, Schriftenreihe zur Philosophie Karl R. Poppers und des Kritischen Rationalismus, herausgegeben von Kurt Salamun* (Rodopi Verlag, 1996); *Soziales Handeln und strukturelle Selektion. Beiträge zur Theorie sozialer Systeme* (Westdeutscher, 1998); *Rationales Handeln und soziale Prozesse. Beiträge zur soziologischen Theoriebildung* (VS Verlag für Sozialwissenschaften, 2004); and *Die Logik mechanismischer Erklärungen* (VS Verlag für Sozialwissenschaften, 2006).

Johan M.G. van der Dennen, was born in Eindhoven, the Netherlands, studied behavioral sciences (psychology, ethology, psychobiology, sociobiology, and evolutionary ecology) at the University of Groningen, the Netherlands, and is at present a senior researcher in the Section on Political Science of the Department of Legal Theory in the University of Groningen. He has published extensively on all aspects of human and animal aggression, sexual violence, neuro- and psychopathology of human violence, political violence, criminal violence, theories of war causation, macro-quantitative research on contemporary wars, ethnocentrism, and the politics of peace and war in preindustrial societies. In 1995 he published his dissertation *The Origin of War: The Evolution of A Male-Coalitional Reproductive Strategy*, an evolutionary analysis of the origin of intergroup violence in humans and animals. Some of his other books are *Sociobiology and Conflict: Evolutionary Perspectives on Competition, Cooperation, Violence, and Warfare* (Chapman & Hall, 1990) (coedited with Vincent Falger); *Sociobiology and Politics* (JAI Press, 1998) (coedited with Peter Meyer and Vincent Falger); and *The Darwinian Heritage and Sociobiology* (Greenwood Press, 1999) (coedited with D. Smillie and D. R. Wilson). He is continuing his research on the politics of peace and war in preindustrial societies, violent intergroup competition in social animals, genocide and war atrocities in contemporary human societies, sexual violence in animals and man, combat motivation, and the origin of war in hominid phylogeny. He is currently president of the International Society for Human Ethology (ISHE) and an officer of the Association for Politics and the Life Sciences (APLS).

Nico Wilterdink is professor of sociology at the University of Amsterdam. He has done research and published on a variety of topics, including long-term trends in socioeconomic inequality, globalization processes, national identities in Western Europe, postmodernism as a cultural complex, and evolutionary theory. His book publications include *Vermogensverhoudingen in Nederland* (*Property Relations and Wealth Distribution in the Netherlands*, 1984), *The Ends of Globalization* (2000) (coedited with D. Kalb et al.), and the sociological textbook *Samenlevingen* (*Societies*; 6s edition 2007) (coauthored with B. van Heerikhuizen). At present he is focusing on a revision of the theory of the civilizing process in connection to evolutionary theory.